KU-692-823

AQA English Literature A

A LEVEL AND AS

Luke McBratney
Nicola Onyett
Andrew Ward

SERIES EDITOR:
Adrian Beard

OXFORD
UNIVERSITY PRESS

OXFORD
UNIVERSITY PRESS

Great Clarendon Street, Oxford, OX2 6DP, United Kingdom

Oxford University Press is a department of the University of Oxford. It furthers the University's objective of excellence in research, scholarship, and education by publishing worldwide. Oxford is a registered trade mark of Oxford University Press in the UK and in certain other countries

© Luke McBratney, Nicola Onyett, Andrew Ward 2015

The moral rights of the authors have been asserted

First published in 2015

All rights reserved. No part of this publication may be reproduced, stored in a retrieval system, or transmitted, in any form or by any means, without the prior permission in writing of Oxford University Press, or as expressly permitted by law, by licence or under terms agreed with the appropriate reprographics rights organization. Enquiries concerning reproduction outside the scope of the above should be sent to the Rights Department, Oxford University Press, at the address above.

You must not circulate this work in any other form and you must impose this same condition on any acquirer

British Library Cataloguing in Publication Data

Data available

ISBN 978-019-833600-6
Kindle edition ISBN 978-019-837459-6

10 9 8 7 6 5 4 3

Printed by CPI Group (UK) Ltd, Croydon CR0 4YY

Acknowledgements

The authors and publisher are grateful for permission to reprint extracts from the following copyright material:

Margaret Atwood: *The Handmaid's Tale* (Vintage, 2011), copyright © Margaret Atwood 1986, reprinted by permission of The Random House Group Ltd.

Carol Ann Duffy: 'Work' from *Feminine Gospels* (Picador 2002), copyright © Carol Ann Duffy 2002, reprinted by permission of the publishers, Pan Macmillan.

Terry Eagleton: *Literary Theory: An Introduction* (Blackwell, 1996), copyright © Terry Eagleton 1996, reprinted by permission of Wiley.

Gavin Ewart: 'They flee from me that sometime did me seek' from *Collected Poems 1980-1990* (Hutchinson, 1991), reprinted by permission of Mrs M A Ewart.

Sebastian Faulks: *Birdsong* (Vintage, 1994), copyright © Sebastian Faulks 2004, reprinted by permission of the Random House Group Ltd.

Brian Friel: *Translations* (Faber, 1981), copyright © Brian Friel 1981, reprinted by permission of Faber & Faber Ltd; from 'Words' in *Theatre by Brian Friel*, copyright © Brian Friel, reprinted by permission of The Agency (London) Ltd. All rights reserved and enquiries to The Agency (London) Ltd, 24 Pottery Lane, London W11 4LZ, info@theagency.co.uk.

Robert Graves: 'Two Fusiliers' first published in *Fairies and Fusiliers* (1917) and 'A Dead Boche' first published in *Goliath and David* (1938) from *The Complete Poems in One Volume* (Carcanet, 2000); and *Goodbye to All That and Other Great War Writings* (Carcanet, 2007), reprinted by permission of Carcanet Press Ltd.

Germaine Greer: *The Female Eunuch* (Flamingo, 1993), copyright © Germaine Greer 1979, reprinted by permission of HarperCollins Publishers Ltd.

David Haig: *My Boy Jack* (Nick Hern, 1997), copyright © David Haig 1997, reprinted by permission of the publishers, Nick Hern Books, www.nickhernbooks.co.uk.

Tony Harrison: 'Timer' from *Selected Poems* (Penguin, 1987), reprinted by permission of the author.

Ernest Hemingway: 'A Very Short Story' first published in *In Our Time* (Charles Scribner, 1930), from *The First Forty Nine Stories*, (Arrow, 2004), reprinted by permission of The Random House Group Ltd.

Ken Kesey: *One Flew Over the Cuckoo's Nest* (Penguin Classics, 2003), copyright © Ken Kesey 1962, copyright © renewed 1990, copyright © The Estate of Ken Kesey 2002, reprinted by permission of Penguin Books Ltd.

Philip Larkin: 'Talking in Bed', copyright © Philip Larkin 1964, from *The Complete Poems of Philip Larkin* (Faber, 2012), reprinted by permission of Faber & Faber Ltd.

C Day Lewis: 'Song' from *The Complete Poems* (Sinclair-Stevenson, 1992), reprinted by permission of The Random House Group Ltd and of Peters Fraser and Dunlop (www.petersfraserdunlop.com) on behalf of the Estate of C Day Lewis.

Joan Littlewood: *Oh! What a Lovely War* (Methuen, 1965, 2014), copyright © 1965 Joan Littlewood Productions Ltd, reprinted by permission of the Estate of Joan Littlewood and The Sayle Literary Agency.

Sylvia Plath: *The Bell Jar* (Faber, 1977), copyright © Sylvia Plath 1963, 'Lady Lazarus' and from an introduction to a reading of the poem on the BBC, from *Sylvia Plath: Collected Poems* edited by Ted Hughes (Faber, 1981), reprinted by permission of Faber & Faber Ltd.

Ezra Pound: 'In a Station of the Metro' first published in *Poetry* (April, 1913), from *Personae: Collected Shorter Poems* (Faber 1952, 1961/New Directions, 1976, 1990), copyright © Ezra Pound 1926, reprinted by permission of the publishers, New Directions Publishing Corp and Faber & Faber Ltd.

Erich Maria Remarque translated by Brian Murdoch: *All Quiet on the Western Front* (Vintage, 1996) translation copyright © 1994, reprinted by permission of the Random House Group Ltd.

Siegfried Sassoon: 'Finished with War: A Soldier's Declaration' (July, 1917), copyright © Siegfried Sassoon, reprinted by permission of the Estate of George Sassoon, c/o Barbara Levy Literary Agency.

Kathryn Stockett: A Conversation with Kathryn Stockett from 'Penguin Readers' Group Guide to *The Help*' on the Penguin website, copyright © Kathryn Stockett 2009, by permission of Amy Einhorn Books, an imprint of G P Putnam's Sons, a division of Penguin Group (USA) LLC, and from the author's notes to *The Help* (Fig Tree, 2009), copyright © Kathryn Stockett 2009, by permission of Penguin Books Ltd.

Graham Swift: *Waterland* (Picador, 1992), copyright © Graham Swift 1985, by permission of the publishers, Pan Macmillan.

Helen Thomas: *As It Was and World Without End* (Faber, 1972), reprinted by permission of Mrs R Vellender for the Estate of Helen Thomas.

Alice Walker: *The Color Purple* (Women's Press, 1983/Orion, 2009), copyright © Alice Walker 1982, reprinted by permission of David Higham Associates.

Rebecca West: *The Return of the Soldier* (Virago, 2010), reprinted by permission of Peters Fraser & Dunlop (www.petersfraserdunlop.com) on behalf of the Estate of Rebecca West.

Tennessee Williams: *Memoirs* (Penguin Modern Classics, 2007), copyright © The University of the South 1972, 1975, reprinted by permission of Penguin Books Ltd, and Georges Borchardt, Inc, for the Estate of Tennessee Williams. All rights reserved.

and to the following for their permission to reprint extracts from copyright material:

BOMB Magazine for interview 'Graham Swift by Patrick McGrath' commissioned by and first published in BOMB Magazine, from *BOMB 15*, Spring 1986, copyright © Bomb Magazine, New Art Publications, and its contributors. All rights reserved. The BOMB digital archive can be viewed at www.bombmagazine.org

The Geographical Association for Owen Sheers: 'Poetry and Place: Some personal reflections', Geography Vol 93: 3, Autumn 2008.

Guardian News & Media Ltd for 'A Life in Writing: Free Spirit: Alice Walker' by Aida Edemariam, 23 June 2007, copyright © Guardian News & Media Ltd 2007.

Independent Print Ltd for 'I shall never forget the silence that descended on my native town' by Don Mullan, *The Independent*, 15 June 2010, copyright © The Independent 2010.

Publishers Weekly, PWxyz LLC for book review of *The God of Small Things* by Arundhati Roy, 4 Jan 1997, copyright © Publishers Weekly 1997.

Telegraph Media Group Ltd (TMG) for Tony Clements: book review of *The Help* by Kathryn Stockett, *Daily Telegraph*, 24 July 2009, copyright © TMG 2009; Hermione Hoby: interview with Margaret Atwood, *Daily Telegraph*, 18 Aug 2013, copyright © TMG 2013; Andrew Hough: 'Carol Ann Duffy: Texting and Twitter "help students perfect poetry"', *Daily Telegraph*, 6 Sept 2011, copyright © TMG 2011; and Eliat Negev: interview with Ted Hughes, *Daily Telegraph*, 31 Oct 1998, copyright © TMG 1998.

Image acknowledgements:

Cover: Banauke/Shutterstock: **p20:** Morocco: Abd el-Ouahed ben Messaoud ben Mohammed Anoun, Moorish Ambassador to Queen Elizabeth I (1600)/Pictures From History/Bridgeman Images; **p27:** Scold's Bridle', c.1649 (engraving), English School, (17th century)/Private Collection/Bridgeman Images; **p32:** Angus McBean © Royal Shakespeare Company; **p52:** Shepherd and Shepherdess Reposing, 1761 (oil on canvas), Boucher, Francois (1703-70)/© Wallace Collection, London, UK/Bridgeman Images; **p99:** (518) Paths of Glory, 1917 (oil on canvas), Nevinson, Christopher Richard Wynne (1889-1946)/Imperial War Museum, London, UK/Bridgeman Images; **p120:** (l) Source: Modernist Journals Project, Estate of John David Roberts. By permission of the William Roberts Society, (r) Source: The William Roberts Society, Estate of John David Roberts. By permission of the William Roberts Society; **p123:** (2242) The Menin Road, 1919 (oil on canvas), Nash, Paul (1889-1946)/Imperial War Museum, London, UK/Bridgeman Images; **p127:** (tr) © Moreno, J./Corbis, (bl) Detail from the Royal Artillery Memorial 1914-18, 1925 (Portland stone) (photo), Jagger, Charles Sergeant (1885-1934)/Hyde Park Corner, London, UK/Bridgeman Images, (br) © Michael Jenner/Alamy; **p156:** Mary Evans/Everett Collection; **p164:** Mary Evans/Epic/Tallandier; **p172:** (l) Mary Evans Picture Library/Imagno, (r) Las Meninas No.31, 1957 (oil on canvas), Picasso, Pablo (1881-1973)/Museu Picasso, Barcelona, Spain/Bridgeman Images; **p175:** Veniamin Kraskov/Shutterstock; **p176:** With kind permission from www.simonspicer.com, background © Ladybird Books Ltd, 1965. Reproduced with permission by Ladybird Books Ltd.

Page layout by Phoenix Photosetting.

Although we have made every effort to trace and contact all copyright holders before publication this has not been possible in all cases. If notified, the publisher will rectify any errors or omissions at the earliest opportunity.

Contents

How to use this book

A strong principle behind this book, and indeed the specification which it supports, is that A Level English Literature, at both AS and A level, involves more than simply the study of a named collection of set texts. For this reason, it is important that you read this book carefully. Even though one part of it will cover an option that you (and/or your teachers) will not have chosen to study, even here there may still be some points to learn more generally. This is because a choice has to be made at A level about whether to study Option 2A 'World War I and Its aftermath' or Option 2B 'Modern times: Literature from 1945 to the present day' in Component 2 'Texts in shared contexts'.

This book's sequence of chapters is based on the numbered components in the AQA English Literature A specification, but you will not necessarily follow the course in this strict order – especially if you are working with more than one teacher, and/or studying A level only.

Chapter 1 provides an introduction to the specification (at both AS and A level). This introductory chapter should be read by all students early on in the course.

Chapters 2–4 look at different aspects of Component 1 'Love through the ages', which is the required component for both AS level and A level. These chapters loosely follow sections of the exam paper in their sequence.

Chapters 5–8, and 9–12 are for A Level students only (although AS students might like to look at what the full A Level has to offer). They cover Component 2 'Texts in shared contexts' and offer two options: Option 2A 'World War I and its aftermath' (Chapters 5-8), and Option 2B 'Modern times: Literature from 1945 to the present day' (Chapters 9–12). Both of these options are covered in much the same way: the subject is introduced via a review of the set text options, before the contextual possibilities are looked at more extensively; the final chapter covers working with unseen extracts and comparative approaches.

Chapter 13 covers Component 3 of the specification 'Independent critical study: Texts across time', and considers the non-exam assessment (coursework) part of the A level. You will need to use this chapter when preparing for and writing your independent submission.

The label 'Key term', used within this book, indicates that each term listed is important. The first time that each key term is used in the book, it has been emboldened in the main text and defined briefly in the margin. Many subsequent appearances of each key term throughout the rest of the book have also been emboldened, to emphasize that they are key terms. In addition, all of the separate key term definitions have been gathered together and repeated alphabetically on pages 209–211, as a glossary, for easy reference.

When it comes to revision for your exams, you should re-use this book sensibly – focusing on specific aspects that you are revising at the time. At this point, the glossary will also be of importance, by helping you to develop a critical vocabulary specific to this course.

Weblinks are included throughout this book. Please note that Oxford University Press is not responsible for third-party content and although all links were correct at the time of publication, the content and location of this material may change over time.

A note on spelling

Certain words, for example 'specialized' and 'organized' have been spelt with 'ize' throughout this book. It is equally acceptable to spell these words and others with 'ise'.

An introduction to AQA English Literature Specification A

Overarching principles and philosophy

This book supports the AQA English Literature A specification, the main approach of which is based upon connecting and comparing texts within a shared context. Working from the belief that no text exists in isolation, you will be encouraged to explore the relationships between texts and the contexts within which they were written, received and understood.

Of course, many of the skills that you associate with the study of literature – and which you have developed throughout your school career – will still be used. You will continue to read texts closely, and some of the exam questions that you will answer will be focused on a single text. But the specification also encourages you to adopt more advanced strategies and to develop both as an independent reader and an independent learner. You will, for example, be given plenty of opportunities to formulate your own views by considering those of other readers and critics, as well as by thinking about how your texts relate to other texts. For example, your independent critical study, while guided by your teacher, will be generated by your own interests and enthusiasms. When you compare two texts, you will be likely to evaluate or apply critical viewpoints, or to develop an interpretation that is informed by a critical approach, such as psychoanalysis, Marxism or feminism. In short, the approach taken towards literature by this specification will make for a dynamic and exciting course of study.

Considering the course as a whole, and its approach to literature, you might say that it draws inspiration from a range of fields within English literature, but that in its examined components it offers a broadly **historicist** approach. More specifically, in Component 1 'Love through the ages', the historical approach is **diachronic** – you will read texts from different time periods that explore the same theme; in Component 2, either 'World War 1 and its aftermath' or 'Modern times: Literature from 1945 to the present day', the historical approach is **synchronic** – you will read texts within a narrower and more clearly defined time period.

Rather than having a single list of set texts, you will be given choices regarding your route through the course. Component 2 offers a choice of two historical periods, each of which has a choice of six core set texts. Choice is also offered in Component 1, because you will select one of four Shakespeare plays, pick from a range of pre- and post-1900 novels, and choose either a pre- or post-1900 selection of verse. For the independent critical study, your focus will be very much on autonomous reading. The choice could hardly be wider: you will compare two texts, one of which must have been written before 1900, but the choice of texts and the topic of comparison can be – subject to an AQA adviser's guidance – whatever you want. Taken as a whole, this course offers a wealth of opportunities for independent study and for pursuing your own interests in the subject. It will not only equip you with the knowledge and skills needed for examination and coursework success, but also open up a rich, challenging and coherent approach to the study of English literature.

This introduction will:
- offer an overview of the course and its contents
- enable you to understand the principles and philosophy of the course
- develop your understanding of concepts related to the course, such as context and genre.

Key terms

Historicist / Historicism. Styles of criticism that highlight the importance of historical contexts in shaping the meaning of texts. For example, historicism recognizes how texts engage with historical events and ideas as well as with other texts; it also acknowledges that readers often interpret texts in ways that confirm their own experiences and ideas.

Diachronic study. A study that considers texts through a wide time period.

Synchronic study. A study that considers texts within a narrowly defined time period.

Did you know?

The terms 'diachronic' and 'synchronic' are easy to understand when you think about their Greek origins. *Chronos* means 'time'; *dia* means 'through'; so, a diachronic study is one that studies texts *through* time. *Syn* means 'with'; so a synchronic study is one that studies texts *within* a defined period.

Course contents

Let's look at how the course works in practice:

- Component 1 'Love through the ages' takes a diachronic approach; the texts are from a wide range of historical periods, but are unified by their exploration of the same theme: love.

  - In the first section of both the AS level and A level examinations you are invited to write about a play by Shakespeare in which love is a major theme. The question centres on a passage of around 400 words from the play; you write about the passage and broaden your discussion to consider relevant aspects of the play as a whole.

  - The next section invites you to compare two unprepared poems, which are each from a different historical period and are printed in the question paper. (This task applies to the A level only; the AS level requirements are outlined briefly on the next page, and in more detail in the relevant chapters.) To help you practise the skills for this task, you are likely to read – and write about – different types of love poetry from throughout the ages. This should build your understanding of a range of poems in a variety of forms and styles, making you both more confident when encountering unfamiliar poems and also more likely to be able to formulate advanced, well-informed arguments.

  - The final section on the A level paper also poses a comparative question and features poetry. Using your set poetry text (either the *Pre-1900 AQA Digital Anthology* or the *Post-1900 AQA Digital Anthology*) and a set prose text, you respond to one question from a choice of two – typically on a theme or aspect of characterization that is in some way connected with love. Part of the skill in answering is to select apt poems as well as apt material from your chosen novel.

- Component 2 'Texts in shared contexts' (which applies to A level only) takes a synchronic approach; the texts are drawn from a defined historical period. You choose one of two: either 'World War 1 and its aftermath' or 'Modern times: Literature from 1945 to the present day'. Within each period your choices are determined by the genre of the core set text that you pick; this is to ensure that you cover each of poetry, prose and drama, and that you study one text that was written after 2000. In the examination:

  - The first question invites you to examine a viewpoint in relation to your set text.

  - The second question focuses on an unprepared prose passage (which is either taken from a novel, or is a passage of literary non-fiction). You typically write about the presentation of a theme or idea in that passage in this question.

  - The third question asks you to write a comparative essay exploring how the above theme or idea is presented in two of your set texts.

- Component 3 'Texts across time' (which also only applies to A level) is tested by non-exam assessment (coursework): you produce a scholarly essay that makes connections between two texts and is around 2,500 words long. Here, you enjoy a high degree of freedom. While you must choose at least one text that was written before 1900 – and the texts must be by different writers and not featured elsewhere on the specification – everything else is up to you and your teacher. (An AQA adviser also works with your teacher to provide guidance and approve your question.) There are various ways in which you can approach the task, and the focus is very much on developing your personal interests in literature and fostering your skills of independent learning.

AS level

An AS level specification runs alongside the A level one. The rules for AS level and its relationship to A level are common to all subjects.

The AS level in this specification relates to Component 1 of the A level, so you will study 'Love through the ages'. There will be two exam papers:

- The first involves the study of a Shakespeare play and a poetry anthology.
- The second involves the study of two prose texts, and there is also a question on an unseen prose extract.

This means that there will be parts of this book (those devoted to Components 2 and 3) that are not strictly relevant to AS level. Nevertheless, all parts of this specification connect up, so even if you know that you are studying for AS level only, it is still worth looking at all sections of this book as part of your overall approach.

Texts and contexts

A text is not a sealed unit that exists in isolation and contains a single meaning. The word *text* itself derives from the Latin *textus*, which means 'woven'; think about other nouns from this word family, such as textiles and texture, and you gain a sense of the richly layered, woven qualities of a literary text. In addition, the word *sub*text reminds us of underlying meanings – what could be going on *beneath* the text. With all this potential for meaning, you can appreciate that there is room for you, the reader, to respond to and interpret a text as part of a process that is much more complex and interesting than that of a simple transmission model of communication (by which an unambiguous message is sent from a God-like author to a passive reader).

It's also worth remembering that whenever we read a text for the first time, we make sense of it by locating it within the network of texts that we already know: we apply our knowledge about how texts work to construct fresh meanings as we read. The word 'context' carries a sense of what goes *with* the text, and in literary studies we often use this word to denote how the text connects to – or goes with – wider ideas and circumstances that shape its meaning. Without any sense of their wider contexts, many texts would lose much of their significance. For example, wouldn't *Animal Farm* seem little more than a simple story of farm animals if we didn't know something about the history of the Russian Revolution or ideas of government?

Contexts can be more than just social, cultural or historical aspects. Think, for example, about how much more meaning we can draw from a text when we understand something about the **genre** in which it was written. Genre comes from a French word meaning 'type' and in its widest sense it refers to the main types of literature: poetry, prose and drama. Indeed, these are useful ways in which we might begin to think about texts when we first encounter them. However, genre also refers to the types within various areas of literature. For example, crime, romance, historical novel and so on are all genres – as

> **Key term**
>
> **Genre.** A way of categorizing texts. Genres can be arranged around ways of writing (such as poetry/drama/prose), around content (such as crime, politics) around purpose (such as satire) and so on. In a most general sense, genre involves grouping texts by type – and so connecting texts. There are many ways of grouping literary texts. They can be grouped in many ways through their connections with other texts, with which they have things in common. In most cases, generic groupings are not fixed, so thinking about genre involves connecting with other texts.

are comedy and tragedy. The genre into which we categorize a text helps to shape the ways in which we interpret it. For example, *Measure for Measure*, Shakespeare's seemingly dark and serious work that explores justice, morality and sexuality becomes a very different text if we view it in the light of its categorization as a comedy in its first published version (the First Folio of 1623). In what ways, you might ask, is it comic for a ruler to use blackmail in an attempt to extort sex from a novice nun? In the process of your investigation you are likely to uncover interesting ideas about the nature of genre in Shakespeare's theatre – in which a comedy meant something other than a play that is funny – as well as consider ways in which a director might want to stage the play today.

In poetry, genre also refers to specific types, or forms, of poem. A well-known example is the sonnet, which also has sub-genres, such as the Petrarchan sonnet and the English (or Shakespearean) sonnet. Knowing the conventions, both of form and of subject matter, can be helpful. Let's take Shakespeare's Sonnet 130 (below) as an example.

Activity

How does the following poem both conform to and flout (break) the conventions of the sonnet?

Did you know?

'Reeks' was a neutral term in Shakespeare's time; it meant 'emits vapours', which could even be pleasant. This older sense survived longer in some regional forms of English. For example, as Robert Burns (1759–1796) contemplates his supper in 'Address to a Haggis' he declares: O what a glorious sight, / Warm-reekin', rich!'

My mistress' eyes are nothing like the sun;
Coral is far more red, than her lips' red;
If snow be white, why then her breasts are dun;
If hairs be wires, black wires grow on her head.
I have seen roses damasked, red and white,
But no such roses see I in her cheeks;
And in some perfumes is there more delight
Than in the breath that from my mistress reeks.
I love to hear her speak, yet well I know
That music hath a far more pleasing sound;
I grant I never saw a goddess go;
My mistress, when she walks, treads on the ground.
   And yet, by heaven, I think my love as rare,
   As any she belied with false compare.

Possible response

In this poem the expected formal conventions are followed: it is an English sonnet, comprised of three quatrains and a couplet. But the conventions of subject matter seem, at first, to be flouted. Sonnets are usually associated with love and many praise a loved one, yet all three quatrains of this sonnet appear to point out the mistress's flaws. The accumulation of such details strengthens the reader's sense of the mistress's inadequacy; our impression is of a kind of mocking catalogue of her features as the speaker describes them in terms of what they are not. This interpretation is, however, overturned by the **couplet**: 'And yet, by heaven, I think my love as rare, / As any she belied with false compare'. In this way, we recognize our earlier preconceptions as being false: Shakespeare both praises his mistress and criticizes the false comparisons of other sonneteers who tell lies ('belie') by using inaccurate metaphors ('false compare').

Key term

Couplet. Two lines with the same metre that also rhyme.

Commentary

The above reading becomes even more interesting when we consider context – when we know more about the kinds of sonnets that were being written at the time. For example, the first quatrain of a 1596 sonnet by Bartholomew Griffin reads:

> My Lady's hair is threads of beaten gold;
> Her front the purest crystal eye hath seen;
> Her eyes the brightest stars heavens hold;
> Her cheeks, red roses, such as seld have been;

Griffin uses a technique called the **blazon**, which is a poetic praising of the loved one's various physical attributes. You could say that Shakespeare conforms to the convention of the genre by using this feature, but also surprises us by using it cleverly to mock, not his mistress but the clichéd poetic techniques of other poets.

Shakespeare's sonnet also plays with our generic expectations in its conclusion. There is a marked **volta** after the third quatrain. 'And yet' signals this shift, and the mild oath 'by heaven' intensifies the sense of a new and more sincere mood. This mood is more akin to what we expect of a sonnet about a lover, and it is far from the distant, arch or objectifying stance taken in the rest of the poem; in the couplet, the speaker's tone is loving and passionate. In his final comparison, which is the only one expressed in a positive form, Shakespeare declares that his mistress – now called his 'love' – is as rare as any woman who is praised by conventional and false comparisons. In this way the sonnet concludes by satisfying our generic expectations and giving us what we want from a sonnet: love.

This shows that genre is not fixed. While there are elements that we recognize as recurring between texts of the same genre, our enjoyment often depends on a text having features that are both recognizable and innovative – the interplay between the security of the expected and the surprise of the unexpected.

Intertextuality

Such readings, which are underpinned by our understanding of other texts, lead us to our final consideration of the word ***intertextuality***. As its prefix suggests, this denotes the meanings that accrue when we explore the relationships *between* texts. The discussion of Shakespeare's sonnet above begins as a discussion of genre, then becomes one of intertextuality. While this term is relatively recent – coined by the feminist theorist Julia Kristeva in 1969 – it can be usefully applied to texts of all ages and in all components of the course. Thinking about intertextuality helps us to progress from viewing texts as sealed units and enables us to explore the meanings that they gain from their relationships with other texts. For example, we might consider the overt intertextual connection between Michael Symmons Roberts' love poem 'To John Donne' and the poem 'To his Mistress Going to Bed' by John Donne, or the one between Wilfred Owen in 'Dulce et Decorum Est' and the poems of Jessie Pope.

> **Key terms**
>
> **Blazon.** A poetic listing of a loved one's beautiful qualities.
>
> **Intertextuality.** This denotes the meanings that accrue when we explore the relationships between and across texts. This can be done explicitly, through direct reference, or implicitly through the use of similar content and/or techniques.
>
> **Volta.** A turning point, or shift in mood or argument, of a sonnet.

Texts and contexts – a contemporary example

If any of the previous discussion about the concepts surrounding contexts or genre sounds unusual or unfamiliar, don't despair. The good news is that you already know a great deal about it and about how texts conform to or confound generic expectations. Let's broaden our discussion and bring together the elements we've been discussing in a final modern example.

The consumption and marketing of media products depends on our shared understanding of genre conventions and our ability to make intertextual links. When new books, films and television series are launched, the makers often try to reel in audiences by referencing or 'mashing up' previous hits. The American film and television producer Jerry Bruckheimer is a master of this sort of contextual linking. His *CSI* (*Crime Scene Investigation*) universe has developed from one original series into a global franchise, based on the premise that the audience which enjoyed the original *CSI* (set in Las Vegas) was likely to transfer its loyalties fairly easily to *CSI* spin-offs, set in Miami and New York. *CSI*'s success reveals that viewers enjoy these shows because of – not in spite of – their predictability. Long-time fans develop a powerful and expert working knowledge of the generic conventions of the forensic police procedural that influences their reception of *CSI* as a media text and shapes their future viewing expectations.

There are limits to their tolerance, of course; while accepting that, within the shared context of the *CSI* universe, detectives can cross from one fictional world into another as their cases overlap and their suspects make a run for it, no *CSI* fan would put up with the forensics team walking away from a crime scene at the end of an episode, admitting they haven't got a clue who did it. The show's established generic practices have given its fans too firm a benchmark against which to measure their responses. Thus the genre steadily self-replicates, with old episodes endlessly recycled on cable television, linked *CSI*-branded media products (such as comic books, computer games and novelizations) coming on stream, and copycat *CSI*-influenced television documentaries and forensic-based reality shows competing for air-time.

As an English literature student, you too need to work like a *CSI* armchair critic in order to understand how your linked texts work. Looking at generic patterns and structures within texts is a useful perspective from which to study writers' methods as you connect and cross-reference them. Being alert to the importance of genre conventions can help you to develop your own meanings as you examine the writer's ideas and intentions. Once you begin to study your set texts in detail, you will discover interesting issues located at key textual stress-points, when generic boundaries, limitations, rules and requirements come under pressure. One of the most interesting questions to ask as you study is: How do writers surprise, delight and make us think, while conforming to traditional practices and conventions?

Component 1:
Love through the ages

This chapter will:

- offer strategies for studying Shakespeare
- develop your understanding of plot, characterization and themes
- develop skills in close reading
- develop skills in using contexts to enrich your responses
- develop skills in making connections: connecting a passage to the play as a whole, to other texts and to the topic of 'Love through the ages'
- consider ways of responding to critical views.

The demands of the question

Let's begin with the end in mind: a reminder of the nature of the task in the Shakespeare section of the 'Paper 1: Love through the ages' exam, whether for AS or A Level.

For each of the four set plays, there is a passage printed in the question paper and a question. You answer one question only. The question invites you to write about both that passage and the play as a whole – as well as consider a critical viewpoint. In addition, you should use contextual information to help you develop your response and explore links to Component 1's overall theme of love.

While having to do so many things in just an hour might seem daunting, the question is actually there to help. Engaging with it fully will enable you to demonstrate the skills required by the Assessment Objectives (AOs) – and to do so in a fluent and natural way.

Let's consider each Assessment Objective separately, so that you can see how this works in practice.

- The whole task helps you to show your skills for AO1, which is concerned with your informed personal and critical response to the text, and how you organize that response using appropriate concepts and terminology, as well as accurate writing.

- Writing about the passage in particular enables you to demonstrate your abilities for AO2 by exploring Shakespeare's methods – his stagecraft, use of language, dialogue, dramatic form and so on. Thinking about the whole play helps you to make comments about those methods that work on a bigger level, such as dramatic structure, and so how meanings are made.

- Contextual elements (AO3) might arise in response to the critical viewpoint in the question, or naturally during the course of your answer. Your understanding of genre – the type of play it is and how Shakespeare has conformed to or developed this type – might be relevant, or perhaps some of the particular circumstances in Elizabethan or Jacobean England might inform your response to the passage or arise from your argument.

- Such work is going to involve connections (AO4) to the overall theme – love – and the passage might give rise to, for example, questions about how typical this presentation of love is. Connections to a range of ideas seen in other texts might be relevant: from ideas of chastity and fidelity in Shakespearean England, to notions of **patriarchal** authority in marriage.

- You meet AO5 when you respond to the critical viewpoint, consider others and explore the extent to which you agree.

Key term

Patriarchy / Patriarchal. A system of society or government controlled by men.

While the above comments separate out the Assessment Objectives to make it easy to recognize what you have to do to meet them, the good news is that, in practice, the AOs overlap and a strong answer which addresses the question directly is – as it develops – likely to be meeting many of them simultaneously. You are going to see this process in action as the chapter progresses.

Studying Shakespeare at A level

Your study of your set Shakespeare play has similarities to how you studied Shakespeare earlier in your academic career: as before, you will build your understanding of elements such as **plot**, themes and characterization. For the 'Love through the ages' exam, however, there are also other elements that demand your attention. For example, you'll foreground the ways in which love is presented. Of course you'll consider Shakespeare's methods, but you'll also consider other influences, such as how actors and directors have shaped the play's meaning, how audiences have responded, and how critics have offered interpretations. In addition, you'll be considering historical and literary contexts that can enrich your response to the text. For example, you might use Early Modern ideas about medicine to help you understand the symptoms of love in the plays, or you might explore the ways in which the play conforms to or develops aspects of its literary genre.

Preliminary reading

Your study of a Shakespeare play is like your study of a poem: you can't expect to grasp everything at once. Aim to build your understanding in layers. Your first encounter should be a preliminary reading for pleasure and plot. Read the list of characters and then the play.

For your first reading:

- Consider listening to a recorded version of the play.
- Focus on understanding the story and how it unfolds.
- Think about your first impressions of the characters.
- Use the footnotes, but not so much that you lose the thread of the story.
- Bolster your understanding by using a good-quality synopsis and by returning to it as you read. While this chapter contains a brief account of the plot of each set play, which focuses on the structure of the narrative, you should also read a detailed scene-by-scene synopsis.

After your first reading, watch or listen to a version of the play. If you are unable to see a production, watch a recording. For example, the BBC Shakespeare series has televised versions of all the set plays available on DVD.

More detailed study

Your third experience of the play should be a detailed reading, in which you study the text scene by scene. You are likely to work through at least parts of the play like this with your teacher, but don't underestimate the amount you need to do independently.

In your detailed study:

- Make full use of the footnotes.
- Write your own notes about aspects such as the presentation of characters and relationships, imagery and other linguistic effects, stagecraft and themes.
- As you take notes, pay particular attention to the presentation of aspects of love and related themes, such as the presentation of gender and ideas about courtship and marriage.

Key term
Plot. The events as they are sequenced in the text (in comparison with 'story', which is all of the events as they happen naturally and chronologically).

Link
The Oxford Companion to Shakespeare, for example, contains a helpful synopsis for each of the plays.

The more detailed your study, the better you are able to engage in class discussions and debates.

- By this stage you should also be making connections – for example, by appreciating elements in different parts of the play, such as **motifs** and recurring **image patterns**, character development and shifts in mood or atmosphere.

- As well as reading criticism, read about performances and the different interpretations they suggest. Carol Rutter's *Clamorous Voices: Shakespeare's Women Today*, for example, offers perspectives from leading female actors about roles such as Isabella from *Measure for Measure* and Kate from *The Taming of the Shrew*.

Link

See the Further reading section at the end of this chapter for details.

Key terms

Image patterns. Where an image or connected images are used more than once.

Motif. A recurring element that has symbolic significance in a text.

Significant / Significance. This involves weighing up all of the potential contributions to how a text can be analysed (such as the way the text is constructed and written, contexts which can be applied, aspects of genre, possible theoretical approaches) and then finding potential meanings and interpretations.

Dramatic methods: the structure of Shakespeare's plays

It is commonly known that Shakespeare did not invent stories. Much of his skill is in reshaping older tales to make them relevant to his audience. As well as shaping their content, he also shaped their construction. To help us explore Shakespeare's approach towards structure, it's worth noting a distinction that modern literary critics make between story and plot. Story is everything that happens: all the events as they happened naturally and chronologically. Plot refers to the events as they are sequenced in the text.

Let's consider an example of how the sequencing of plot events can help to create effects. In *Measure for Measure*, the importance of the first meeting between Angelo and Isabella in Act 2 Scene 2 is heightened by the way in which Shakespeare arranges the plot details: our expectations grow in Act 1 Scene 2 (when Claudio tells Lucio to go to his sister to ask her to plead to Angelo on his behalf), then further in Act 1 Scene 4 (when Lucio visits Isabella in the convent) and even more in Act 2 Scene 1 (when we are reminded of Angelo's determination to carry out the death sentence at both the beginning and the end of this scene). When the meeting between Angelo and Isabella does finally arrive, we feel both the hope that has been built up by what we have seen and heard of Isabella, plus the dread of knowing that, if she is unable to persuade Angelo, Claudio will surely die.

Plot

Analysing plot structure is helpful not only for developing textual knowledge, but also for considering the **significance** of particular moments to the play as a whole. Remember that the exam requires you to write about both a passage and the whole play. There are several models of how plots are arranged; the following is especially helpful. The main action of your chosen play can be separated into seven stages:

- *exposition* (important background information that we learn near the beginning of the narrative)
- *conflict* (what happens to produce discord)
- *complication* (how this grows worse, or more complex)
- *climax* (the peak of the drama)
- *suspense* (how the conclusion of events is delayed)

- *denouement* (how the events finally unfold)
- *conclusion* (the state of affairs at the end).

While the material that follows is organized via the set plays, it is intended to help you develop your understanding and skills for the examination, rather than provide discrete information about individual texts. Reading about all four plays will enable you not only to sharpen your skills, but also to bolster your contextual understanding and your confidence in making connections between Shakespeare's plays and also to themes and ideas relevant to the **historicist** literary concept of 'Love through the ages'.

Research idea

Research more about different ways to analyse the structure of plots. For example, you might find the five-part structure that Gustav Freytag explains in his *The Technique of the Drama* (1863) helpful. An Internet search for 'Freytag's Pyramid' should yield relevant results. ●

Othello

Plot structure

Exposition	Othello and Desdemona have married secretly.
Conflict	Discord occurs in several forms: Desdemona's father opposes her marriage; a war with the Turks threatens to separate Othello and Desdemona; and Iago's hatred of Othello is revealed.
Complication	Iago plots to destroy Othello by making him believe that Desdemona has been committing adultery with Cassio.
Climax	The play's psychological peak is Othello deciding to kill Desdemona.
Suspense	We anticipate the murder; we wonder if Iago will escape punishment.
Denouement	In common with other tragedies, the denouement involves death: Othello kills Desdemona, Iago kills his wife and Othello kills himself.
Conclusion	Cassio and Iago survive. Iago vows silence. The chief enemy of love remains mysterious and we are left pondering his motivations.

Further comments: the climax

Note the importance of Act 3 Scene 3. This pivotal scene is the longest and marks the play's inevitable descent to its tragic outcome. Unlike other Shakespearean tragedies in which there is a definitive single crisis point, there is none in *Othello*. Instead, there is a build-up of tension as Iago's case against Desdemona – constructed from weak and circumstantial evidence – gathers momentum to the point where Othello has accepted Desdemona's guilt and he pledges to act. Note Iago's role in the process of decision-making: rather than the decision to act coming from the tragic hero, it seems to come as a result of ideas planted in his mind by his **antagonist**.

Key term

Antagonist. The most notable character who opposes the **protagonist** (hero) of a narrative. Often the antagonist is the villain who wants to harm the hero/heroine or prevent him/her from achieving their goals.

THINK ABOUT IT

Some critics term this part of the play the 'temptation scene', recalling the temptation of Christ in the wilderness by the devil. In what ways might this be a helpful term?

Writing about an extract and the play

At this point, we'll explore an extract from the play for two reasons: firstly, to practise making links between it and the rest of the play and, secondly, to consider how Shakespeare uses dramatic methods. The extract below contains elements of both *exposition* and *conflict* and is the moment in Act 1 Scene 1 when Iago and Roderigo awaken Brabantio with the news that his daughter has eloped with Othello.

 Activity

1. In what ways is this extract **significant** to the play as a whole?
2. How does Shakespeare use dramatic methods in this extract?

Iago
…For, sir,
It is as sure as you are Roderigo,
Were I the Moor, I would not be Iago:
In following him, I follow but myself;
Heaven is my judge, not I for love and duty,
But seeming so, for my peculiar end:
For when my outward action doth demonstrate
The native act and figure of my heart
In compliment extern, 'tis not long after
But I will wear my heart upon my sleeve
For daws to peck at: I am not what I am.

Roderigo
What a full fortune does the thicklips owe
If he can carry't thus!

Iago
Call up her father,
Rouse him: make after him, poison his delight,
Proclaim him in the streets; incense her kinsmen,
And, though he in a fertile climate dwell,
Plague him with flies: though that his joy be joy,
Yet throw such changes of vexation on't,
As it may lose some colour.

Roderigo
Here is her father's house; I'll call aloud.

Iago
Do, with like timorous accent and dire yell
As when, by night and negligence, the fire
Is spied in populous cities.

Roderigo
What, ho, Brabantio! Signior Brabantio, ho!

Iago
Awake! what, ho, Brabantio! thieves! thieves! thieves!
Look to your house, your daughter and your bags!
Thieves! thieves!

Brabantio appears above, at a window

Brabantio
What is the reason of this terrible summons?
What is the matter there?

Roderigo
Signior, is all your family within?

Iago
Are your doors lock'd?

Brabantio
Why, wherefore ask you this?

Iago
'Zounds, sir, you're robb'd; for shame, put on
your gown;
Your heart is burst, you have lost half your soul;
Even now, now, very now, an old black ram
Is topping your white ewe. Arise, arise;
Awake the snorting citizens with the bell,
Or else the devil will make a grandsire of you:
Arise, I say.

Brabantio
What, have you lost your wits?

Roderigo
Most reverend signior, do you know my voice?

Brabantio
Not I what are you?

Roderigo
My name is Roderigo.

Brabantio
The worser welcome:
I have charged thee not to haunt about my doors:
In honest plainness thou hast heard me say
My daughter is not for thee; and now, in madness,
Being full of supper and distempering draughts,
Upon malicious bravery, dost thou come
To start my quiet.

Roderigo
Sir, sir, sir,--

Brabantio
But thou must needs be sure
My spirit and my place have in them power
To make this bitter to thee.

Roderigo
Patience, good sir.

Brabantio
What tell'st thou me of robbing? this is Venice;
My house is not a grange.

Roderigo
Most grave Brabantio,
In simple and pure soul I come to you.

Iago
'Zounds, sir, you are one of those that will not
serve God, if the devil bid you. Because we come to
do you service and you think we are ruffians, you'll
have your daughter covered with a Barbary horse;
you'll have your nephews neigh to you; you'll have
coursers for cousins and gennets for germans.

Brabantio
What profane wretch art thou?

Iago
I am one, sir, that comes to tell you your daughter
and the Moor are now making the beast with two backs.

Brabantio
Thou art a villain.

Iago
You are – a senator.

Commentary

In what ways is this extract significant to the play as a whole?

This scene is significant in many ways. An answer might, for example, discuss the following elements:

- Its *expository function*, providing information about the central love in the play: the **protagonist** and his wife, who have just eloped.

- *The development of Iago* as the **antagonist**. In the extract we witness Iago's easy manipulation of Roderigo. This anticipates similar behaviour later on towards Cassio and Othello. Our understanding of Iago's hatred of Othello colours later scenes between Iago and Othello with dramatic irony.

- In this scene we begin with the antagonist, but anticipate the introduction of the protagonist, Othello. Like Roderigo, the audience might be duped into an unfavourable impression of him. When we do meet Othello in the next scene, his calm, noble bearing and declarations of love make him seem very different from our earlier impressions gained from Iago. Thus, *duplicity emerges as an important theme*; the difficulty of making judgements and distinguishing between appearances and reality is enacted by the opening scene, which begins in dialogue and is dominated by a character who lies, plots and deceives.

- Importantly, this extract establishes the *conflict* that will lead to the protagonist's downfall. Many aspects of this are relevant to Shakespeare's exploration of love, including the following:

  ○ Iago's determination to use Othello's love to bring about his downfall.

Key term
Protagonist. The main character.

- Roderigo's sexual desire for Desdemona. Iago encourages this to sustain Roderigo's antipathy towards Othello, then uses it to provoke conflict between Roderigo and Cassio.

- Desdemona's father's opposition to the marriage. Iago inflames Brabantio's anger about the inter-racial union. Later in the scene, we discover that Brabantio had a nightmare about losing his daughter in similar circumstances, and in Act 1 Scene 2 he seeks retribution from the Duke, using language that echoes Iago's as well as making accusations that Othello has used witchcraft to win Desdemona's love.

- Links could also be made to several scenes in which sexuality and race are significant – for example, Act 3 Scene 3, in which Othello questions Desdemona's love in the 'haply for I am black' soliloquy. Here Othello considers how his race, age and perceived lack of social grace mean that Desdemona's love for him cannot be sincere. This scene culminates in the play's *climax*, when he vows to kill her – thus confirming the effectiveness of Iago's plan, which we see beginning in the Act 1 Scene 1 extract.

How does Shakespeare use dramatic methods in this extract?

As you study the play, and especially as you plan your answers, read the text carefully – imagining the action that it suggests. Visualize it happening, rather than just reading the words. Think about the setting of the scene in question – where other characters are on stage – and consider the relative positions of these characters. If there are stage directions, think about how they suggest action. Consider also alternative ways of playing the scene. Watching different productions of the play, including film versions of productions, would be valuable here. In an examination, you might remember how a given moment was played; if so, refer to that production.

Here are some suggestions:

- The night setting lends the action a secretive or sinister light (while dim lighting might be used by modern productions, darkness could be suggested by torches in daylight performances – as in its first productions at Court or at the Globe).

- Symbolically, night could help to suggest the darkness of Iago's character – literally, it allows him to conceal his identity while he allows Roderigo to be seen. As well as through lighting, the set affords opportunities for Iago to remain hidden on the lower level, while Brabantio speaks from the balcony.

- There is a contrast between the quiet of the first part of the scene and the clamour of the second – in which there is much noise and shouting to waken Brabantio and engender a mood of danger and emergency. This reflects what is happening in this part of the play: a state of order is being disrupted.

- There is a contrast in mood between the intimate first section, in which Iago speaks privately to Roderigo, and the public part in which the pair awaken Brabantio.

As well as exploring the dramatic potential of a scene, consider the ways in which Shakespeare's dramatic language works. There are many opportunities for that in this extract. For example:

- The racial slurs, such as 'thicklips', and the sexual insults involving bestial terms, such as 'black ram', 'Barbary horse' and 'the beast with two backs'.

THINK ABOUT IT

The 1995 film of *Othello*, directed by Oliver Parker, makes the cunning and ingenuity of Iago, played by Kenneth Branagh, abundantly clear in this scene. Iago hides, then pushes Roderigo forward while remaining out of Brabantio's sight; he shouts the coarse insults from a position of cover, so that Brabantio thinks that they have come from Roderigo.

- Some productions play the scene for comedy. Perhaps at this point (before we have met Othello or come to understand the extent of Iago's evil) the humour encourages the audience to admire Iago's skill, or to take pleasure in his villainy.

- Despite this, racial prejudice is present under the cover of humour. While there might, for example, be laughter at the **extended metaphor** of Othello being a Barbary horse, which includes comical internal rhyme with the remark 'you'll have nephews to neigh you', beneath this, there are disturbing fears of inter-racial marriage, which are presented here as bestiality. Some might argue, however, that such fears are being satirized by Shakespeare through the ridiculous images that Iago invents.

When analysing language, you don't need to pick out every detail. A better strategy would be to select the most significant features: the ones that are most important and that relate most closely to the question and to your argument. As well as writing about what you feel are the most significant elements, aim to explore how they work together to create meaning and effects.

Key term

Extended metaphor. A metaphor which is carried beyond a single comparison of two elements and is developed further.

Contexts: sex, race and magic

Consider how the following contextual details might enrich your readings of the text.

Iago depicts Othello in ways commensurate with Early Modern prejudices about black people being animalistic, sexually voracious or associated with witchcraft. Links could be made to elsewhere in the play, such as to witchcraft in the next scene, when Brabantio says to Othello, 'thou hast enchanted her', or to Othello's superstitions about the handkerchief and his claims to Desdemona that 'there's magic in the web of it'.

However, there were ambiguities in Elizabethan attitudes towards race. On the one hand, Elizabeth I wanted to drive black people from the kingdom – she decreed in 1596 that there were 'of late divers blackmoores brought into this realm, of which kind of people there are already here to manie…' and ordered that 'those kinde of people should be sente forth of the land' – yet, on the other hand, she employed a black maid and black musicians. In addition, outsiders were not always threatening or undesirable; they could be exotic and attractive. The Moorish ambassador and his retinue who visited the Queen in 1600–1 certainly fascinated those who saw them. The ambassador himself was dignified in manner and strikingly dressed in a rich turban and robes. Shakespeare performed at Court during his stay and some critics suggest that the ambassador could be a model for Othello.

The Moorish ambassador to Queen Elizabeth I's court, Abd el-Ouahed ben Messaoud ben Mohammed Anoun

Contexts: homosexuality and male friendship

According to Stanley Wells in *Shakespeare, Sex & Love* (2010) 'Male to male sexual relationships were common, even though later ages have often tried to submerge the fact. And there is good reason to believe that they were not regarded as subversive.' He also notes that it was not unusual for people of the same sex to share a bed.

Wells argues that 'the most explicitly homoerotic passage in the whole of Shakespeare is that in which Iago claims that the sleeping Cassio sought to make love to him as if he were Desdemona' (Act 3 Scene 3 Lines 423–30) and goes on to explain how, with this invented episode, Iago is 'poisoning Othello's imagination with images of homoerotic activity'.

Ernest Jones, a biographer of Sigmund Freud, argued that Iago's jealousy came neither from envy of Othello's social position, nor sexual desire for Desdemona, but 'because he himself possessed a subconscious affection for the Moor, the homosexual foundation of which he did not understand' (Lois Potter, *Othello: Shakespeare in Performance series*, Manchester: Manchester University Press, 2002, p.92; cited by Wells).

Extension activity

Why not watch the film version of *Othello*, directed by Oliver Parker (1995), with such homoerotic readings in mind? To what extent does the text support the view that Iago is sexually attracted to Othello and/or Roderigo?

Did you know?

In a 1985 RSC production, Iago (played by David Suchet) hurled himself onto the body of Othello (played by Ben Kingsley) after his suicide and had to be dragged off. Audiences understood that, in this production, this action was proof of Iago's homosexuality.

The Taming of the Shrew

Plot structure

Exposition	Kate, the elder daughter of Baptista, has a reputation as a shrew (an argumentative and unruly woman). Her younger sister can't marry before her. Petruchio, seeking a rich wife, decides to wed Kate.
Conflict	Baptista consents to the marriage. Kate behaves shrewishly towards Petruchio.
Complication	After the wedding ceremony, the marriage is not consummated. Petruchio mistreats Kate in various ways to gain control.
Climax	Kate submits to Petruchio on the way to her sister's wedding. She is obedient from this point onwards.
Suspense	At the wedding, everyone expects Kate to behave shrewishly but Petruchio bets that she's the most obedient wife.
Denouement	Kate extols the virtues of wifely obedience and Petruchio wins his bet.
Conclusion	Petruchio and Kate go to bed.

Further comments: the Induction

In addition, you should consider the framing narrative that introduces the main narrative above. Known as the Induction, this introductory story tells of Christopher Sly, a drunken tinker, who is picked up while asleep by a Lord and his huntsmen. They take him to the Lord's house, where, for fun, they dress him in fine clothes, feed him well and persuade him that he is actually a nobleman who has just awoken from a strange illness. Part of his recovery process is to watch a 'pleasant comedy', which is, of course, the rest of the play.

For many years, the Induction was omitted from performances. Some consider it superfluous and, since the action does not return to Sly at the end, it gives the play an unfinished feel. Some, however, feel it's vital that the Induction be retained, since, rather than allowing the audience to believe that the wife taming has restored order, they can then view the whole play as a kind of drunken fantasy on the part of Christopher Sly. Indeed, some performances – such as the 1978 RSC production directed by Michael Bogdanov – have emphasized this reading by having the same actor play both Sly and Petrucchio. Thus, sexist ideas of men triumphing and women being better off behaving submissively are presented as being forms of misguided wishful thinking.

Ways to approach interpretations

Your examination question will invite you to show how other interpretations can shape your response to the text. It would be useful to practise doing this, and you should find that exploring interpretations often helps you to address the other Assessment Objectives more sharply. For example, an interpretation may involve an element of context, which leads you to consider Shakespeare's methods or helps you to make a connection with another text or to the wider topic of love.

 Activity

To what extent do you agree that the extract below from the denouement of the play helps to form 'a satisfying conclusion to the play'?

Petruchio
Nay, I will win my wager better yet
And show more sign of her obedience,
Her new-built virtue and obedience.
See where she comes and brings your froward wives
As prisoners to her womanly persuasion.

Re-enter KATHARINA, with BIANCA and Widow

Katharina, that cap of yours becomes you not:
Off with that bauble, throw it under-foot.

Widow
Lord, let me never have a cause to sigh,
Till I be brought to such a silly pass!

Bianca
Fie! what a foolish duty call you this?

Lucentio
I would your duty were as foolish too:
The wisdom of your duty, fair Bianca,
Hath cost me an hundred crowns since supper-time.

Bianca
The more fool you, for laying on my duty.

Petruchio
Katharina, I charge thee, tell these headstrong women
What duty they do owe their lords and husbands.

Widow
Come, come, you're mocking: we will have no telling.

Petruchio
Come on, I say; and first begin with her.

Widow

She shall not.

Petruchio

I say she shall: and first begin with her.

Katharina

Fie, fie! unknit that threatening unkind brow,
And dart not scornful glances from those eyes,
To wound thy lord, thy king, thy governor:
It blots thy beauty as frosts do bite the meads,
Confounds thy fame as whirlwinds shake fair buds,
And in no sense is meet or amiable.
A woman moved is like a fountain troubled,
Muddy, ill-seeming, thick, bereft of beauty;
And while it is so, none so dry or thirsty
Will deign to sip or touch one drop of it.
Thy husband is thy lord, thy life, thy keeper,
Thy head, thy sovereign; one that cares for thee,
And for thy maintenance commits his body
To painful labour both by sea and land,
To watch the night in storms, the day in cold,
Whilst thou liest warm at home, secure and safe;
And craves no other tribute at thy hands
But love, fair looks and true obedience;
Too little payment for so great a debt.
Such duty as the subject owes the prince
Even such a woman oweth to her husband;
And when she is froward, peevish, sullen, sour,
And not obedient to his honest will,
What is she but a foul contending rebel
And graceless traitor to her loving lord?
I am ashamed that women are so simple
To offer war where they should kneel for peace;
Or seek for rule, supremacy and sway,
When they are bound to serve, love and obey.
Why are our bodies soft and weak and smooth,
Unapt to toil and trouble in the world,
But that our soft conditions and our hearts
Should well agree with our external parts?
Come, come, you froward and unable worms!
My mind hath been as big as one of yours,
My heart as great, my reason haply more,
To bandy word for word and frown for frown;
But now I see our lances are but straws,
Our strength as weak, our weakness past compare,
That seeming to be most which we indeed least are.
Then vail your stomachs, for it is no boot,
And place your hands below your husband's foot:
In token of which duty, if he please,
My hand is ready; may it do him ease.

Petruchio

Why, there's a wench! Come on, and kiss me, Kate.

Extension activity

Some critics term this part of the play the 'submission scene'. To what extent do you believe that this is an oversimplification?

Commentary

The above extract might be seen as 'a satisfying conclusion', but this very much depends on how the play is staged and on our critical perspective – how we choose to interpret Kate's monologue, reflects how we view the play as a whole. Let's look at three types of response to the above viewpoint: the first using *context*, the second using *genre* and the third using *performance*.

To consider the viewpoint from the perspective of *context*:

- We might consider this as a fitting denouement – the culmination of Petruchio's taming, with the result that the formerly shrewish wife is seen in public to be completely transformed. Such a view would be compatible with the opinion that the play reflects Early Modern beliefs that for a marriage to be happy, the woman must submit to the man's authority. This is commensurate with some Elizabethan ideas about women being inferior to men – ideas that were often given extra weight by male-centred readings of the Bible, which saw woman as being the source of woe for man in consequence of Eve's sin in the garden of Eden. This view is reflected even more strongly in an earlier version of the play (published anonymously in 1594 and entitled *The Taming of a Shrew*).

- Alternatively, we might refute this view – arguing that it is only true when the play is considered from a male perspective. The above reading might be seen as more akin to the view of the ignorant drunken tinker Christopher Sly – indeed, the whole play might be thought of as the drunken, wish-fulfillment dream of this character, as is the case in the earlier version of the story, *The Taming of a Shrew*.

Link

More details about *The Taming of a Shrew* and of John Fletcher's sequel to Shakespeare's play, *The Woman's Prize* or *The Tamer Tamed* (1611), follow on page 26.

Remember that, while you need to know about each of the Assessment Objectives, in a strong answer they work together. The examples above demonstrate how considering a viewpoint (AO5) can help you to meet the Assessment Objectives. They do this here largely through using context (AO3), which in this case is knowledge of *The Taming of a Shrew* and understanding of other writings and beliefs from Early Modern England. This leads to ideas about the play's structure (AO2) and its connections with other texts (AO4).

To consider the viewpoint from the perspective of *genre*:

- We might see the above extract as part of a satisfying conclusion from a generic perspective. We expect Elizabethan comedies to end with marriages and a restoration of order, and here we are given three marriages as well as Kate's monologue in praise of male authority, which restores the **patriarchal** order that earlier she was disrupting.

- Alternatively, this finale might seem unsatisfactory in the sense that, rather than the play ending with marriage, the main marriage took place in Act 3 Scene 2. Obstacles, which in this genre are usually overcome before marriage, continue to present difficulties after marriage. In addition, the inclusion of a long monologue, which slows the action down, seems anomalous in a comedy – a genre that more typically contains fast-moving action and speedy verbal exchanges between characters.

Finally, we might consider the viewpoint from the perspective of *performance*:

- Rather than being wholly satisfying to the male audience, we might consider Kate's words to be ironic and her behaviour to be consistent with her earlier rebellious qualities. Such a view might be satisfying to a modern audience, who could find the idea of a submission to **patriarchy** distasteful. Speaking of her role as Kate in Barry Kyle's 1982 RSC production, Sinead Cusack argues that 'At the end of the play I was determined that Kate and Petruchio were rebels and would remain rebels for ever, so her speech was not predictable. Having invited her to speak, he couldn't know what form her rebellion was going to take. He was very shaky indeed in that scene, not knowing what was coming.'

- The stage business of the throwing of the cap might also give evidence for whether we read the extract as being 'satisfying'. For those who read Kate as being submissive, it is likely to be a satisfyingly dramatic demonstration of her obedience, which is greeted by pleasure in the body language of Petruchio and shock on the part of the women on stage. The satisfaction on the part of Petruchio (and perhaps the men in the audience) might be made more overt at the conclusion of her monologue. At this point in the 1999 RSC production, Stuart McQuarrie, after a long pause, 'delivered his "Why there's a wench!" as a triumphant roar to the other men' (David Bevington and Peter Holland (eds.) *Shakespeare in Performance: The Taming of the* Shrew, London: Methuen, 2008, p.278).

- The action at the end of the speech can make the extract seem satisfying or unsatisfying, depending on how it is played. A submissive Kate is perhaps kneeling and placing her hand under Petruchio's foot as a sign of submission. However, some productions contest this reading by having Kate deliver her lines challengingly and standing apart from Petruchio. Similarly, there is no definitive way of playing the response to Petruchio's demand for a kiss. His lovingly said line could provoke a romantic kiss enjoyed by both characters and provide a satisfying conclusion, or his words could be met with an unsatisfying silent refusal, or perhaps a kiss could be taken by force, suggesting that the marriage is to be one of dominance on the part of the male and endurance on the part of the female.

Activity

Explain which view you find the more persuasive. Justify your choice by close reference to the text and, if possible, to performances.

Critical views

In 1888, George Bernard Shaw wrote a letter of complaint to the *Pall Mall Gazette* encouraging people to boycott the play: 'No man with any feeling of decency can sit it out in the company of a woman without being extremely ashamed of the lord-of-creation moral implied in the wager and the speech and put into the woman's own mouth.'

By contrast, Germaine Greer, writing in her seminal feminist text *The Female Eunuch* (1970) disagrees: 'Kate has the uncommon good fortune to find Petruchio who is man enough to know what he wants and how to get it. He wants her spirit and her energy because he wants a wife worth keeping… Kate's speech at the close of the play is the greatest defence of Christian monogamy ever written. It rests upon the role of a husband as protector and friend, and it is valid because Kate has a man who is capable of being both, for Petruchio is both gentle and strong.'

Did you know?

Many editors refer to the female protagonist as Katherine or Katherina, rather than Kate, because Kate is the name that she rejects when Petruchio first greets her by using it in Act 2 Scene 1. Note how her monologue in Act 5 Scene 2 is bookended by two versions of the name: Petruchio commands 'Katherine' to tell the women about the duty they owe their husbands, but 'Kate' to kiss him. The stage directions in the Folio of 1623 (the first reliable text of Shakespeare's plays) at first call her Katherina, but later Kate.

Other versions of the story

It's also useful to consider two plays with strong intertextual links to *The Taming of the Shrew*: the earlier *The Taming of a Shrew* (published anonymously in 1594) and *The Woman's Prize* or *The Tamer Tamed* (1611) the sequel to Shakespeare's play by his collaborator, John Fletcher.

> ### Activity
>
> Compare and contrast the following extract from *The Taming of a Shrew* with the corresponding part in Shakespeare's play.
>
> Two areas to consider are:
>
> - the significance of the Biblical references
> - how gender roles are presented.

> The King of Kings the Glorious god of heaven,
> Who in six days did frame his heavenly work,
> And made all things to stand in perfect course.
> Then to his image he did make a man.
> Old Adam and from his side asleep,
> A rib was taken, of which the Lord did make,
> The woe of man so termed by Adam then,
> Woman for that, by her came sin to us,
> And for her sin was Adam doomed to die,
> As Sarah to her husband, so should we,
> Obey them, love them, keep, and nourish them,
> If they by any means do want our help,
> Laying our hand under their feet to tread,
> If that by that we might procure their ease,
> And for a precedent I'll first begin,
> And lay my hand under my husband feet
>   *She lays her hand under her husband's feet.*

Research idea

Find out more about Early Modern attitudes towards control in marriage. You might like to read Thomas Dekker's *The Bachelor's Banquet* (1603). Excerpts and entertaining illustrations may be found at:

http://www.shakespearesengland.co.uk/category/marriage/

In *The Woman's Prize*, Petruchio is dominated by a new wife, called Maria. This play ends with a more overt moral than its predecessor; it argues for companionate marriage – marriage based on mutual affection. As Maria explains in the epilogue, the play's purpose is 'To teach both sexes due equality / And, as they stand bound, to love mutually.'

Contexts: attitudes to women and control

A 'scold' is an alternative term for a shrew: in 16th-century legal parlance 'a troublesome and angry woman, who does break the public peace'. An iron frame was fitted over the unpopular woman's head and padlocked. The punishment for scolding was to wear such a scold's bridle and be publicly displayed as both a humiliation and a deterrent.

> ### Activity
>
> Think about the ways in which any of the women in your set play might be presented in ways that draw on the stereotype of scold and consider how they are controlled by men.

You might consider the ways in which Julietta is paraded in the streets in *Measure for Measure*, how the male characters react to Paulina in *The Winter's Tale* or how Iago's wife, Emilia, is treated in *Othello*.

Extension activity

Find out about beliefs about illness and medicine in Early Modern England. Might we believe that Kate's shrewishness stems from an illness caused by an excess of choler? If so, to what extent do you believe that Petruchio's taming could be an attempt to cure her?

You might like to begin by visiting http://www.nlm.nih.gov/exhibition/shakespeare/taming.html

A scold's bridle

Measure for Measure

Plot structure

Exposition	Unenforced laws lead to a fall in moral standards and a rise in sexually transmitted diseases. The Duke decides to clean up the city by handing power to Angelo, a strict deputy. He secretly watches the results while disguised as a Friar.
Conflict	The newly enforced laws mean that Claudio, a man of good character whose fiancée Juliet is pregnant, faces death.
Complication	Isabella, Claudio's sister, who is training to become a nun, begs Angelo for mercy.
Climax	In a second meeting, Angelo offers to free Claudio if Isabella will have sex with him.
Suspense	The Duke offers to save Claudio if Isabella helps him. She persuades Angelo's former lover, Marianna, to hide in a dark place to have sex with him; Angelo will think she is Isabella, and Claudio will be freed.
Denouement	After the 'bed trick', Angelo reneges on the agreement and demands Claudio's severed head as proof of execution. The Duke has the head of another prisoner sent instead. This 'head trick' fools Angelo. The Duke arranges to return and hear grievances publicly.
Conclusion	The Duke reveals his identity. Angelo is forced to marry Marianna. Claudio is freed and able to marry Juliet. The Duke proposes to Isabella.

Further comments: Isabella's silence

The way we interpret the whole play is determined by how we interpret the ending. Does Isabella accept the Duke? As with interpretations of *The Taming of the Shrew*, we tend to give ourselves the *Measure for Measure* that our age desires – hence the numerous modern productions in which a strong, silent Isabella rejects the Duke. This is in keeping with a modern feminist sensibility that dislikes the idea of the disempowering of its female lead and the restoration of patriarchal order. One consequence of this, though, is that the play ends on a decidedly downbeat note.

Think about the effects of a more traditionally comic finale. If we go to see a comedy, don't we expect a happy ending – and one, in Shakespeare, that usually ends with marriages? In addition, audiences might see marriage to Isabella as a fitting reward for the Duke's actions throughout the play: he has gained first-hand knowledge of his subjects, has successfully tested his deputy and, in Act 5, returns triumphantly and, with the knowledge gleaned from his experiences, is ready to govern more effectively in the future. Moreover, is it possible to reconcile a rejection of the Duke with an allegorical reading of the play? In such a reading we might consider the marriage much less a physical union than a union between Church (Isabella) and State (the Duke). Indeed, we might argue that a definite show of acceptance and of mutual attraction in the main characters finally gives the audience what they expect and allows them to leave the theatre happy. Furthermore, scholars believe that the play was performed at Court before King James during the Christmas season of 1604; so, to have a gloomy ending for those performances, in which the character who most resembles the King is rejected, might seem unlikely.

Some productions use the private conversations between the Duke and Isabella and make the match seem convincing. For example, N. W. Bawcutt writes that, in the 1983 Stratford version, 'there was a sense of steadily ripening intimacy between [Isabella, played by Juliet Stevenson] and the Duke, and their final union came as no surprise' (N. W. Bawcutt (ed.) *Measure for Measure*, Oxford: Oxford University Press, 1991. p.40).

Further comments: tragedy and comedy

Like *The Winter's Tale*, *Measure for Measure* is very much a play of two halves: the mood and action shifts markedly at the midpoint. This happens in the middle of Act 3 Scene 1, when the image-laden, idea-driven and largely verse play becomes prose-heavy and dominated by action; the Duke, who was hiding for much of the first half, takes centre stage, and Isabella, who was formerly the play's most active and powerful character, becomes his passive agent. Like *The Winter's Tale*, the first half of *Measure for Measure* feels like a tragedy, while its second half – stuffed with improbable plot twists, instances of disguise and ending in marriages – feels like a comedy.

> ### Did you know?
>
> The term 'problem play' was coined by the Victorian critic F. S. Boas. The term 'problem' came from the new, socially engaged plays by writers such as Shaw and Ibsen, and this gives a sense of the demanding, serious nature of plays like *Measure for Measure*. Nowadays, we usually think of problem plays as dealing with powerful and conflicting arguments about moral issues, or use the term for plays whose genre is unstable – which, for example, deal with tragic themes, but contain much comic material.

> ### Activity
>
> 'Typically, Early Modern texts present women being dominated by aggressive males.'
>
> In the light of this view, how does Shakespeare present the relationship between Angelo and Isabella in the following extract and elsewhere in the play?

The following extract comes from what can be considered the climax of the play, when Angelo blackmails Isabella for sex.

Angelo
Admit no other way to save his life, –
As I subscribe not that, nor any other,
But in the loss of question, – that you, his sister,
Finding yourself desired of such a person,
Whose credit with the judge, or own great place,
Could fetch your brother from the manacles
Of the all-building law; and that there were
No earthly mean to save him, but that either
You must lay down the treasures of your body
To this supposed, or else to let him suffer;
What would you do?

Isabella
As much for my poor brother as myself:
That is, were I under the terms of death,
The impression of keen whips I'd wear as rubies,
And strip myself to death, as to a bed
That longing have been sick for, ere I'd yield
My body up to shame.

Angelo
Then must your brother die.

Isabella
And 'twere the cheaper way:
Better it were a brother died at once,
Than that a sister, by redeeming him,
Should die for ever.

Angelo
Were not you then as cruel as the sentence
That you have slander'd so?

Isabella
Ignomy in ransom and free pardon
Are of two houses: lawful mercy
Is nothing kin to foul redemption.

Angelo
You seem'd of late to make the law a tyrant;
And rather proved the sliding of your brother
A merriment than a vice.

Isabella
O, pardon me, my lord; it oft falls out,
To have what we would have, we speak not what we mean:
I something do excuse the thing I hate,
For his advantage that I dearly love.

Angelo
We are all frail.

Isabella
Else let my brother die,
If not a feodary, but only he
Owe and succeed thy weakness.

Angelo
Nay, women are frail too.

Isabella
Ay, as the glasses where they view themselves;
Which are as easy broke as they make forms.
Women! Help Heaven! men their creation mar
In profiting by them. Nay, call us ten times frail;
For we are soft as our complexions are,
And credulous to false prints.

Angelo
I think it well:
And from this testimony of your own sex, —
Since I suppose we are made to be no stronger
Than faults may shake our frames, let me be bold;
I do arrest your words. Be that you are,
That is, a woman; if you be more, you're none;
If you be one, as you are well express'd
By all external warrants, show it now,
By putting on the destined livery.

Isabella
I have no tongue but one: gentle my lord,
Let me entreat you speak the former language.

Angelo
Plainly conceive, I love you.

Isabella
My brother did love Juliet,
And you tell me that he shall die for it.

Angelo
He shall not, Isabel, if you give me love.

Isabella
I know your virtue hath a licence in't,
Which seems a little fouler than it is,
To pluck on others.

Angelo
Believe me, on mine honour,
My words express my purpose.

Isabella
Ha! little honour to be much believed,
And most pernicious purpose! Seeming, seeming!
I will proclaim thee, Angelo; look for't:
Sign me a present pardon for my brother,

Or with an outstretch'd throat I'll tell the world aloud
What man thou art.

Angelo
Who will believe thee, Isabel?
My unsoil'd name, the austereness of my life,
My vouch against you, and my place i' the state,
Will so your accusation overweigh,
That you shall stifle in your own report
And smell of calumny. I have begun,
And now I give my sensual race the rein:
Fit thy consent to my sharp appetite;
Lay by all nicety and prolixious blushes,
That banish what they sue for; redeem thy brother
By yielding up thy body to my will;
Or else he must not only die the death,
But thy unkindness shall his death draw out
To lingering sufferance. Answer me to-morrow,
Or, by the affection that now guides me most,
I'll prove a tyrant to him. As for you,
Say what you can, my false o'erweighs your true.

Commentary

Comments about a range of Shakespeare's *dramatic methods* might be considered in response to the above activity.

The *dramatic verse* is particularly rich and intense in the above extract, and arguments for Angelo's dominance could be made in numerous places throughout the text (for example, by analysing details from his speech 'Who will believe thee, Isabel?').

Significant details include the following:

- The imagery of measurement, which weighs Angelo's power and reputation against Isabella's accusation, which will 'smell of calumny'. Supporting links might be made to the ways in which male authority dominates women in the play.

- The riding image of Angelo abandoning himself to his lusts by giving his 'sensual race the rein', which shows not only his dominance but also the abuse of his authority for sexual gain. This image might be explored in contrast to his earlier use of riding imagery in Act 1 Scene 3, when the Duke told Friar Thomas that the people were like unruly horses that needed control. Here, the metaphor shows Angelo's sexual appetite being allowed to run wild, like a horse on a free rein.

- The balance between Angelo's lines and Isabella's, which might be more noticeable in a production. There is an ebb and flow to their lines: a mirroring effect that comes from some of the shared lines and the lines that are matched. This might suggest that – at some level – there is an attraction between the two. There is even a match when Angelo declares his love and Isabella seemingly rejects it: 'ANGELO: Plainly conceive, I love you. ISABELLA: My brother did love Juliet'. One short line matches another and indeed Isabella's line does not so much reject Angelo's love but change the subject.

- In addition, the way in which the scene is played has a major impact on meaning. For example, while one production could play Angelo as an aggressive tyrant who dominates Isabella, another – mindful of his Puritan credentials – might present him as naive and in the grip of emotions he does not really understand. Rather than being domineering, he could declare his love in a pleading and weak fashion, and his threatening speeches might sound more petulant than menacing.

A range of comments relating to *contextual issues* could also enrich the arguments. For instance:

- In the main source for the play – Cinthio's story and later play, *Epitia* – the Isabella figure (called Epitia) is much more overtly seductive than Shakespeare's Isabella. As N. W. Bawcutt writes, 'There is no suggestion that the official has resorted to sexual blackmail; on the contrary, remarks made about the power that female beauty has over men, convey some impression that Epitia has seduced him.' Perhaps it could be argued that, at times such as those in the heated exchanges of Act 2 Scene 4, a vestige of the source text remains and what is being dramatized is something more than dominance.

- If we were to go along with the reading of Angelo as being sexually naive and in the grip of emotions he does not understand and cannot control, we might refer to medieval medicine and the idea of the humours. Perhaps Angelo, after a long period of repressing his sexual feelings, now suffers from an illness characterized by an excess of the blood.

John Gielgud and Barbara Jefford as Angelo and Isabella in the 1950 Shakespeare Memorial Theatre production of *Measure for Measure*.

Activity

Study the still on the left from the 1950 Shakespeare Memorial Theatre production of *Measure for Measure*, starring John Gielgud and Barbara Jefford. Comment on the body language and facial expressions of both actors. To what extent might this image be used to substantiate the view that Angelo is presented as a man of virtue whose downfall comes as a consequence of him being tempted by a provocative Isabella?

To make comments that show *connections* with the **historicist** literary concept of 'Love through the ages', we could consider:

- the extent to which Angelo and Isabella resemble other representations of virtuous maiden and dangerous seducer
- the uneven distribution of power between men and women within a literary representation of a patriarchal society
- the high premium placed on the virginity of women in literature.

Different viewpoints have been considered in many of the above examples. Another that is relevant includes the view that Isabella might be played as more the aggressor in the exchange than Angelo: she, for example, could drive herself into a frenzy when considering what she would do rather than yield to Angelo, and her speech in which she talks of wearing 'the impression of keen whips' not only presents the ecstatic imagery of a virgin martyr, but includes sado-masochistic and provocative language that – whether she realizes it or not – inflames Angelo's sexual desires.

Contexts: prostitution

Southwark was not just famous for its theatres. Other forms of entertainment, such as bear-baiting, were available. The area also contained many brothels.

Contexts: marriage and sex

While the laws that Angelo reinstates might seem harsh and unlikely, it's worth noting that similar acts against a range of sexual crimes existed and were enforced. Sex before marriage – known as fornication or sexual incontinence – was a criminal offence. Such offences were dealt with by the Ecclesiastical Court (known popularly as the Bawdy Court, because of the high volume of sex-related cases that it handled).

The Winter's Tale

Plot structure

Exposition	Leontes, King of Sicily, has entertained his boyhood friend, Polixenes, King of Bohemia, for nine months. With the aid of Leontes' pregnant wife, Hermione, Polixenes is persuaded to extend his stay.
Conflict	Struck by jealousy, Leontes is convinced of adultery between Polixenes and Hermione. He asks his courtier, Camillo, to poison Polixenes.
Complication	Polixenes and Camillo escape to Bohemia; Leontes imprisons Hermione. She gives birth to a girl (Perdita) whom Leontes rejects, asking a courtier, Antigonus, to dispose of her; Antigonus' wife, Paulina, protests.
Climax	Despite assurances of her innocence from the oracle, Hermione is convicted of adultery. Leontes' son, Mammilius, dies. Hermione collapses, seemingly dead from the shock. Jolted to his senses, Leontes swears to grieve daily. Meanwhile, Antigonus, who went to Bohemia with Perdita, places her in a basket with a blanket and treasure before being killed by a bear.
Suspense	Sixteen years have passed. Perdita has grown up under the care of a kindly shepherd and lives as a shepherdess. She is in love with Polixenes' son, Florizel, who disguises himself as a shepherd. Polixenes opposes the marriage, so the couple flee to Sicily.
Denouement	Polixenes follows them. When Perdita's identity is discovered, his objections disappear. The noble families are reconciled. All go with Paulina to view a statue of Hermione, which comes alive; Hermione was never dead, but hidden.
Conclusion	Hermione and Leontes are reconciled. Florizel and Perdita marry, as do Camillo and Paulina.

Further comments: plot complexity

The above account of the plot elements reveals the complexity of this play, which stretches the bounds of believability. Even more distinctly than *Measure for Measure*, it is comprised of two halves: the first being tragic and the second comic. These sit uneasily together, with a massive 16-year gap being smoothed over by a chorus. The turning point at which tragedy tips into comedy comes in the form of an action which represents a horrific death, but which is almost always greeted in the theatre by laughter: 'exit pursued by a bear'.

While popular in its own time – as well as commercial performances, there were seven recorded Court performances before 1640, and it was selected as part of the entertainment for the marriage of James I's daughter, Elizabeth – the play has been viewed less favourably in other eras. In 1672, the poet and playwright John Dryden criticized *The Winter's Tale*, *Measure for Measure* and *Love's Labour's Lost* – declaring that these plays 'were either grounded on impossibilities, or at least, so meanly written that the Comedy neither caus'd your mirth, nor the serious part your concernment'.

Further comments: whose story?

How we interpret *The Winter's Tale* depends on whose story we think it is. The most obvious answer is that it is the story of Leontes and his separation from, and later reunion with, Hermione. Yet the play might also be seen as the story of male friendship and how boyhood friends are separated and then reunited. Alternatively, the main focus of the play might be seen as the younger generation, because – through the union of Florizel and Perdita – the wounds of enmity opened up by the older generation are healed.

Link

Further discussion of the ways in which the play might be viewed from a generic perspective may be found as we explore an extract below. See page 37.

Activity

'Typically, texts rarely present marriage for love as leading to happiness.'

In the light of this view, how does Shakespeare present the relationship between Florizel and Perdita in the following extract and elsewhere in the play?

The extract below comes from Act 4, when Florizel and Perdita are about to engage in the handfasting ceremony (which was part of marriage in Shakespeare's day).

Shepherd
Take hands, a bargain!
And, friends unknown, you shall bear witness to 't:
I give my daughter to him, and will make
Her portion equal his.

Florizel
O, that must be
I' the virtue of your daughter: one being dead,
I shall have more than you can dream of yet;
Enough then for your wonder. But, come on,
Contract us 'fore these witnesses.

Shepherd
Come, your hand;
And, daughter, yours.

Polixenes
Soft, swain, awhile, beseech you;
Have you a father?

Florizel
I have: but what of him?

Polixenes
Knows he of this?

Florizel
He neither does nor shall.

Polixenes
Methinks a father
Is at the nuptial of his son a guest
That best becomes the table. Pray you once more,
Is not your father grown incapable
Of reasonable affairs? is he not stupid
With age and altering rheums? can he speak? hear?
Know man from man? dispute his own estate?
Lies he not bed-rid? and again does nothing
But what he did being childish?

Florizel
No, good sir;
He has his health and ampler strength indeed
Than most have of his age.

Polixenes
By my white beard,
You offer him, if this be so, a wrong
Something unfilial: reason my son
Should choose himself a wife, but as good reason
The father, all whose joy is nothing else
But fair posterity, should hold some counsel
In such a business.

Florizel
I yield all this;
But for some other reasons, my grave sir,
Which 'tis not fit you know, I not acquaint
My father of this business.

Polixenes
Let him know't.

Florizel
He shall not.

Polixenes
Prithee, let him.

Florizel
No, he must not.

Shepherd

Let him, my son: he shall not need to grieve
At knowing of thy choice.

Florizel

Come, come, he must not.
Mark our contract.

Polixenes

Mark your divorce, young sir,

Discovering himself

Whom son I dare not call; thou art too base
To be acknowledged: thou a sceptre's heir,
That thus affect'st a sheep-hook! Thou old traitor,
I am sorry that by hanging thee I can
But shorten thy life one week. And thou, fresh piece
Of excellent witchcraft, who of force must know
The royal fool thou copest with, —

Shepherd

O, my heart!

Polixenes

I'll have thy beauty scratch'd with briers, and made
More homely than thy state. For thee, fond boy,
If I may ever know thou dost but sigh
That thou no more shalt see this knack, as never
I mean thou shalt, we'll bar thee from succession;
Not hold thee of our blood, no, not our kin,
Far than Deucalion off: mark thou my words:
Follow us to the court. Thou churl, for this time,
Though full of our displeasure, yet we free thee
From the dead blow of it. And you, enchantment, —
Worthy enough a herdsman: yea, him too,
That makes himself, but for our honour therein,
Unworthy thee, — if ever henceforth thou
These rural latches to his entrance open,
Or hoop his body more with thy embraces,
I will devise a death as cruel for thee
As thou art tender to't.

Commentary

Comments about a range of Shakespeare's *dramatic methods* might be considered in response to the above activity. For example:

- The ways in which the happiness between Perdita and Florizel is presented at the start of this extract and earlier in the scene.

- The presentation of the conflict caused by Polixenes' opposition to the marriage.

- In structural terms, this extract might present the attempted marriage as the major point of conflict in the second story of the play; we might think of the first part ending with the death of Antigonus and a new story beginning with Perdita and Florizel as new protagonists. Alternatively, we might view this point as being part of the bigger story of the play as a whole, with the Perdita/Florizel relationship being a crucial part in the healing of the rift between Hermione and Leontes, and between Leontes and Polixenes, with their eventual union forming part of the play's happy conclusion.

- We might also explore the favourable ways in which the couple are presented. For example, the **pastoral** setting and costumes may suggest a wholesome union for young love. The time of midsummer is also appropriate for a play that is moving from the sadness and winter of the first part to rebirth and happiness in its second.

- The handfasting ceremony is dramatically effective, with the love of the two characters having been seen during Act 4 as both chaste and natural. The audience anticipates it as the culmination of their courtship, but is shocked when Polixenes turns from one who watched in wonder, saying to Camillo 'How prettily th'young swain seems to wash/ The hand was fair before!' to one who suddenly rages against the union. His abrupt outburst of uncontrollable rage may recall the jealousy of Leontes in Act 1, which, it might be argued, is another example of a marriage that was happy, but which led to pain.

- At Polixenes' removal of his disguise, the play seems to shift from being a pastoral comedy to a tragedy as, in his kingly pride, he insists on class distinctions and pours scorn on those whose hospitality he had been earlier enjoying. As Florizel is about to make a contract to marry when Polixenes interrupts, commanding him to 'divorce', his pointed questioning scornfully juxtaposes a **symbol** of monarchy with one of shepherding, and the deterioration of their relationship is shown through an angry shift from the 'you' pronoun: 'Thou a sceptre's heir, / That thus affects a sheep-hook?'

- There are many instances where Shakespeare's dramatic verse might be analysed – for example, the enraged exit speech that threatens Florizel with disinheritance, insults the shepherd and culminates in a chilling death threat to Perdita.

A range of comments that relate to *contextual issues* could also arise. For instance:

- Ideas of handfasting and Early Modern customs surrounding marriage. Another love match that almost led to tragedy takes place in *Measure for Measure*. Claudio claims that upon 'a true contract' he gained possession of Juliet's bed, but that the marriage was not solemnized owing to a need to delay it to obtain part of a dowry. It might be argued that, while Claudio and Juliet's union was really a promise to marry in the future (*per verba de futuro* in the legal parlance of the time), Perdita and Florizel's was *per verba de praesenti* (by vows exchanged verbally in the present moment). In other words, their marriage was just at the point of being made legally binding when Polixenes interrupts. Knowing about such laws and customs makes their actions all the more serious and all the more dramatic.

- Links between sexuality and witchcraft. The widespread fears of, and interest in, the supernatural during the reign of James I are relevant, as are references to other Shakespeare plays such as *Othello*, in which the title character is accused of enchanting Desdemona. Note that in *The Winter's Tale* even the pure and gentle Perdita is called 'enchantment' and accused of being a 'fresh

Key terms

Pastoral. A mode of writing that typically presents rural people in an idealized way and uses natural imagery to create an impression of peace, innocence and contentment.

Symbol. This stands for much more than its literal meaning. Unlike a metaphor (in which one thing is compared overtly to another), with a symbol the significance is left more open. For example, the flowers in Blake's 'The Garden of Love' might be taken to symbolize pleasure and fulfilled desires.

piece of excellent witchcraft' by Polixenes in his rage at the idea of his son, Florizel, marrying beneath him.

The above examples also offer relevant comments that show how this extract *connects with other texts* and with the *theme of 'Love through the ages'*. Further examples include the following:

- Parental authority and the desire amongst the aristocracy to make socially advantageous marriages is also seen in other Shakespeare plays, such as *Othello* and *Romeo and Juliet*.

- A related link, which is played for comedy, could be made to the socially unequal marriage that is imposed upon Lucio in Act 5 Scene 1 of *Measure for Measure*.

Different viewpoints have been considered in many of the above examples. Others that are relevant include the view that true love does lead to happiness: the end of the play demonstrates the power of love and forgiveness.

Contexts: love as a dangerous passion

'Of Love' (1597) by Sir Francis Bacon

The stage is more beholding to love, than the life of man. For as to the stage, love is ever matter of comedies, and now and then of tragedies; but in life it doth much mischief; sometimes like a siren, sometimes like a fury… Amongst all the great and worthy persons there is not one that hath been transported to the mad degree of love: which shows that great spirits, and great business, do keep out this weak passion…

It is a strange thing, to note the excess of this passion, and how it braves the nature, and value of things, by this; that the speaking in a perpetual hyperbole, is comely in nothing but in love.

For there was never proud man thought so absurdly well of himself, as the lover doth of the person loved; and therefore it was well said, that it is impossible to love, and to be wise.

Men ought to beware of this passion, which loseth not only other things, but itself! For whosoever esteemeth too much of amorous affection, quitteth both riches and wisdom. This passion hath his floods, in very times of weakness and great adversity; both which times kindle love, and make it more fervent, and therefore show it to be the child of folly. They do best, who if they cannot but admit love, yet make it keep quarters; and sever it wholly from their serious affairs, and actions, of life; for if it check once with business, it troubleth men's fortunes, and maketh men that they can no ways be true to their own ends.

Activity

How might you apply some of Sir Francis Bacon's ideas about love to your set play?

Some areas to consider include the following:

- How far do you agree that Leontes' friendship with Polixenes is presented as a purer form of love than his passionate sexual feelings for his wife?

- To what extent are love and sex presented as leading to the downfall of the male characters in *Measure for Measure*?
- To what extent might Othello's behaviour be seen as that of a man brought low by love?
- How far do you agree with the view that Petruchio's success is in consequence of his ability to control his sexual feelings?

Themes and issues

As you will have noticed, the four set plays engage with a wide range of themes associated with love. These include:

- adultery
- courtship
- marriage
- perversion
- jealousy
- parental control
- the battle of the sexes

- young love and older love
- sex before marriage
- the control of women
- prostitution
- love and prejudice
- love and madness.

Activity

Which of the themes and issues listed above are concerns that feature in the play you are studying? Explore the extent to which each is significant.

Further reading

Books

David Bevington and Peter Holland (eds) *Shakespeare in Performance: The Taming of the* Shrew, London: Methuen, 2008.

Michael Dobson and Stanley Wells, *The Oxford Companion to Shakespeare*, Oxford: OUP, 2001.

Germaine Greer, *The Female Eunuch*, London: Flamingo, 1999.

Carol Rutter, *Clamorous Voices: Shakespeare's Women Today*, The Women's Press, 1988.

Emma Smith (ed.), *Shakespeare's Comedies: A Guide to Criticism*, Oxford: Blackwells, 2004.

Stanley Wells, *Shakespeare, Sex & Love*, Oxford: OUP, 2010.

Websites

http://podcasts.ox.ac.uk/people/emma-smith

http://www.rsc.org.uk/education/resources/bank/

Link

Advice on structuring answers is given later in the chapter on pages 55–57.

The demands of the question

Let's begin with a reminder of the nature of the task in the poetry section of the 'Paper 1: Love through the ages' exam. In the A Level there will be two unseen poems printed in the examination paper. (In the AS level you will write about a poem taken from the Anthology. In the AS exam you will work on unseen prose in Paper 2.) The A level question will invite you to compare and contrast the two unseen poems, as well as to consider a critical view – a statement or opinion from another reader.

Examination questions that feature unseen texts might at first seem odd. How are you supposed to comment on material that you haven't actually studied? Since you haven't studied the poems (or prose at AS) used in the exam, does this mean that you can't really revise for this section and that you should just concentrate on the set texts instead? Of course not. Ignore anyone who tells you that examinations involving unseen texts are more about luck than revision; they require just as much preparation as the other parts of the course. What the examiner is doing with the unseen texts is using them as a vehicle to test your knowledge and skills – and, in particular, how well you can apply them. If you have spent no time at all building your knowledge or skills in these areas, it will be as obvious to the examiner as if you were taking your driving test without ever having sat in a car.

So, how do you prepare for an examination that involves unseen texts? The answer is simple and in two parts:

- Read a wide range of literature.

- Practise writing about unseen texts.

Indeed, everything that you are going to learn or practise in this chapter is connected to that answer. Since the topic of the examination is 'Love through the ages', it makes sense to focus at A Level on poems that in some way explore love. This should not pose problems, though, since love is probably the most popular and enduring topic that poets explore.

A flexible approach to reading and analysing

Poetry is so broad a literary genre that it's impossible to adopt a one-size-fits-all approach towards reading and analysing poems. The following approach, which concentrates on close reading, is offered as a way for you to build up your ideas – not as a blueprint for an examination answer. There are three stages to follow:

1. Form initial ideas; see the big picture.

2. Build on initial ideas by analysing the details.

3. Re-read the whole poem.

Stage 1: Form initial ideas; see the big picture

Read the poem several times – ideally aloud. Even in an examination room, try to hear the sounds of the poem and its rhythms in your head; when you're working alone in a quiet place, actually read the poem out loud. The sounds and cadences of their verse are of vital importance to many poets. As you read and re-read, build a sense of the poem's main meaning.

You'll notice the emphasis on re-reading. This is deliberate. Because of the compressed nature of most poetry – the sense of a poem being a concentrated work of art – its full meaning is unlikely to be released on a single reading.

The following example, from Terry Eagleton, gives you a sense of how we recognize poetry as poetry:

> 'If you approach me at a bus stop and murmur "Thou still unravished bride of quietness", then I am instantly aware that I am in the presence of the literary. I know this because the *texture, rhythm* and *resonance* of your words are *in excess of their extractable meaning*'.

Terry Eagleton, *Literary Theory*, p.2 (my emphasis)

Think of a song that you like. In all probability, you will have listened to it repeatedly – gaining increased pleasure and perhaps understanding its meaning better as you've done so. Even if you didn't understand it all on first listening, you are likely to have responded to something – perhaps to the beat, a refrain or a chorus. The same is true of poetry. As T. S. Eliot (1888–1965) argued: 'genuine poetry can communicate before it is understood'.

So, don't worry about understanding everything at once, or strain over puzzling details. At this early stage, your reading should be about building a sense of the big picture – understanding what the poem is about. Use the punctuation to guide you: follow the poet's thoughts and feelings across whole clauses and whole sentences. While it might be tempting to read line by line and stanza by stanza, resist such temptations at this stage. Poems are comprised of sentences, and paying close attention to them is the easiest way to understand the poem's meaning. The poem might be complex, but it will also make sense. Stage 1 is about considering the overall significance of the poem – its main meaning. Aim to see the wood, rather than the trees.

As poems are so different, there can be no single strategy to make the main meaning obvious, but if you read and re-read, slowly, following whole clauses and sentences, it will emerge. Some of the following questions might be helpful for you to ask as you read and re-read:

- What is the main idea, or subject?
- Does the poem tell a story? If so, what happens and what is significant about the story?
- Does it express an attitude, or have a particular concern?
- Does the poem express the thoughts and feelings of a **speaker**?
- Is it addressed to someone in particular?
- Is the poem written in the voice of a character, who is clearly not the poet?

Note that, during the examination, you will have further help in responding to the big picture if the question includes a critical view. While you might complicate or disagree with this view, considering it will help you focus on one way in which to approach the poem, and should help you to form your own view.

> **Key term**
>
> **Speaker.** The voice that speaks the poem. This is the default term to use when writing about the person speaking in a poem. It is helpful to reserve the term *persona* for a speaker who is a character who is clearly not the speaker; for example, Carol Ann Duffy adopts the persona of Shakespeare's wife in 'Anne Hathaway'.

Activity

Following the advice above, form initial ideas about the following poem and gain a sense of the main meaning/the big picture.

Link

This poem is included in the *AQA Anthology of Love Poetry through the Ages: Post-1900*.

Timer

Gold survives the fire that's hot enough
to make you ashes in a standard urn.
An envelope of coarse official buff
contains your wedding ring which wouldn't burn.

Dad told me I'd to tell them at St James's
that the ring should go in the incinerator.
That 'eternity' inscribed with both their names is
his surety that they'd be together, 'later'.

I signed for the parcelled clothing as the son,
the cardy, apron, pants, bra, dress –

the clerk phoned down: *6-8-8-3-1?*
Has she still her ring on? (Slight pause) Yes!

It's on my warm palm now, your burnished ring!

I feel your ashes, head, arms, breasts, womb, legs,
sift through its circle slowly, like that thing
you used to let me watch to time the eggs.

Tony Harrison

A student's example initial response

At first I found myself a little put off, both by the beginning of the poem, which felt 'weighty' and almost mythical with its references to gold and ashes, and by parts that didn't seem to be connected. Why, I wondered, were parts of two lines in italics, and what was the speaker doing in the second half of the poem, which puzzled me further by being broken up into stanzas of unusual length?

However, I persevered, reading whole sentences and avoiding being distracted by certain unusual words and the unexpected stanza breaks. By reading it aloud in my room, I found it easier to 'tune in' to the speaker's voice and to follow the flow of his thoughts and the story he seemed to be telling. The poem began to make sense.

It seems to be about a man whose mother has died – he is the speaker of the poem. The poem tells of two main experiences. The first is the man looking at his mother's wedding ring – it is, for example, the gold of the first stanza, the 'burnished ring' of the fifth and the 'circle' of the last. The other experience is the story of the man being given instructions by his father and going to the crematorium; the italicized parts now make sense – they indicate another voice, which is that of the clerk in the crematorium.

As a whole then, the poem seems to be about a son's thoughts and feelings towards his mother and possibly his mother and father's relationship. It seems to be a poem about death and the enduring – and perhaps magical – qualities of love.

This is a promising response. The student has allowed herself to concentrate on forming an overview and has brought meaning very much to the fore. While she might revise or refine some of her ideas in the light of analysing the details, this is an excellent set of opening thoughts.

Using the title to point to the big picture

A poem's title can often be a helpful clue to understanding the main meaning and seeing the big picture. For example, Seamus Heaney's (1939– 2013) 'Act of Union' explores the consequences of both an act of parliament (the Act of Union that united Britain and Ireland in 1801) and a sexual act (between the speaker and the woman he addresses in the poem). Without its title, Ezra Pound's short **imagist** poem below might seem like a series of random images, but when we consider the title, we recognize these images as forming the picture seen by the speaker as he watches people emerge from an underground station.

> **In a Station of the Metro**
> The apparition of these faces in the crowd;
> Petals on a wet, black bough.

Some poems indicate the situation in their title. Marvell's 'To His Coy Mistress' allows the reader to recognize that a male ('His') speaker is addressing ('To') a female with whom he is romantically involved ('Mistress') and that she is shy, modest or pretending to be so ('Coy'). Some poems' titles match their subject matter, whilst others do not. An example of the former is Rochester's 'The Imperfect Enjoyment', which reflects upon a sexual experience that, owing to the speaker's over-excitement, ended prematurely. An example of the latter is Larkin's 'Wild Oats', which is narrated by a gloomy speaker whose dull and protracted relationship with a woman he doesn't love constitutes the opposite of him sowing his wild oats. (The phrase 'to sow your wild oats' means to indulge in youthful sexual behaviour.) While the second type might seem to be misleading, such a mismatched title can end up becoming more helpful for interpretations than some straightforward ones. Larkin's title – when we recognize its irony – helps us to respond to the poem as a whole. The speaker is poking fun at his old self by sharing how he did not sow his wild oats; such self-deprecating humour might, to some readers, seem an endearing quality, and there is a sense of regret that he did not find real love.

Remember, in most cases, titles carry significance, but be aware that some poems simply take their title from their first line or part of their first line – for example, Wordsworth's 'Strange fits of passion have I known' and Edward Thomas's 'And You, Helen'. It is inadvisable to read too much into titles like these.

> **Key term**
>
> **Imagism / Imagist.** A type of poem which is concise and uses hard, clear and concentrated imagery as its main way of creating meaning and achieving effects.

Activity

Consider the significance of the title 'Timer' in Tony Harrison's poem.

A student's example response to the activity

After I had a pretty good grasp of the big picture, I began to look more closely at the poem. The first thing that caught my attention was the title. It didn't seem an obvious choice – after all, the word 'timer' appears nowhere in the poem itself. I wanted to move on to something else, but it intrigued me: why did Harrison choose this title? So, I re-read the poem with the title in mind. At first, I thought, yes, it is good – the poem is all about the passage of time. The death of a parent is a time when you are forced to confront mortality, perhaps reflect on the past of the deceased and maybe your own sense of being next.

I realized that I was in danger of moving off the poem into a bit of speculation about the implications of time, so I went back to the text, and, in particular, the last stanzas. Of course, it struck me: an egg timer. That was the timer of the title. I looked at how this was appropriate in so many ways: not only is the image of the egg timer a homely and loving one, but it also reminds us of an hour glass – a symbol of passing time and of death.

This consideration of the title has helped the student to appreciate what is important to the poet and what wider implications arise from the personal experiences that inspired it. Overall, these ideas about the title should be invaluable when she comes to analyse details, such as the complex imagery and symbolism at the end of the poem.

Stage 2: Build on initial ideas by analysing the details

Study the poem closely, part by part. Keep following the punctuation, reading whole clauses and sentences, but allow your attention to be drawn to the details, paying attention to aspects to do with meaning (such as figurative language, i.e. similes, metaphors, personification, etc.) and positioning (such as the use of word order and the formation of **stanzas** and the organization of the experience within the poem). If you are not working under exam conditions, look up unusual words, or words used in an unusual way, in a good dictionary.

In rhetoric, techniques are subdivided into **schemes** and **tropes**. Schemes relate to positioning; tropes relate to meaning.

As you pause to consider a technique, ask yourself: how does it

- shape meaning?
- build on your initial idea?

As far as possible, relate each detail to the big picture.

Key terms

Scheme. Schemes are figures of speech, which deal with things like word order and sound, rather than the actual meanings of words.

Stanza. A stanza is a group of lines – a separate unit – that helps to break up and organize how the poem appears on the page; it is a place where the reader 'stands' and pauses.

Trope. A figure of speech which deals with meaning.

Advice on annotation

As you read, re-read, think and plan, annotate the poem to record your responses and make connections.

- Leave white space around the text. Don't obscure the poem – you need to see it throughout the whole writing and planning process.
- Use a pencil. This helps to keep the poem clear and means that, if you revise your thinking, you won't be distracted by earlier false starts. You can easily erase errors or changes of mind – something that is less easy if annotations are made with a fluorescent highlighter or a red pen.
- Underline sparingly. As well as noting larger parts – for instance, areas that you may wish to comment on later – pick out details. You could also use a faint line to indicate a turning point or a subdivision. For example,

a long block of text in a verse paragraph might be easier to explore when subdivided.

- Use lines and arrows to indicate connections. You want to build a convincing *overall* reading; this is likely to involve making connections between different parts of the poem and different features within it.

- Record an excess of ideas; have more ideas than you can use. Then you can *select* details that work together and pick those that are *most significant* to the poem overall and, of course, to the question.

It is important to comment purposefully on how a variety of techniques work together to create effects and shape meaning.

Also recognize that your sense of the big picture is likely to be modified in the light of your exploration of the details. This is a normal part of the reading, thinking and planning process.

Areas to consider as you analyse the details

The areas below are offered with a warning: use them, but remember that they are not to be followed slavishly; they are intended to be neither comprehensive nor prescriptive. The most significant aspects for exploration will be suggested by the poem itself. Avoid using the areas below as a checklist; all will not be relevant to every poem, and there may be areas not listed that are important when analysing some poems. You will, however, find it helpful to read and re-read systematically; by practising this method throughout the course, you will be training yourself to understand poems thoroughly and to analyse them in detail.

The areas for a detailed analysis of effects are grouped into three aspects:

1. Imagery
2. Aural effects
3. Structural effects

While these are numbered 1, 2 and 3, this is not a definitive hierarchy: you can use them in any order. As you read, you'll discover that, more often than not, imagery, aural and structural aspects work together.

Imagery and metaphor

As you re-read, consider the ways in which imagery and other related features work. Depending on the poem, some of the following elements might be relevant.

While most commonly used to suggest a visual picture, an **image** might suggest another sensory perception: an auditory image is as possible as a visual one. *Image cluster* is a useful term to use when writing about a grouping of nearby images that are related. Some images are easier to imagine clearly than others: the terms *concrete* and *abstract* are useful ways of differentiating between them.

Metaphor, in its various forms, highlights something through the use of comparison. Essentially, an item is made more evident to the reader through being described as something that it is not. Each of the following types of metaphorical use has been defined on the right: **conceit, personification**.

Study tip

Examiners sometimes advise 'Write a lot about a little, not a little about a lot'. This advice is relevant to this stage of the planning process; by the end of it, you should be able to select the most significant techniques to explore in depth when you write up your response.

Key terms

Conceit. An arresting or elaborate comparison that brings together two (typically dissimilar) elements in an unusual way. Such comparisons, while at first seemingly far-fetched, often prove to be apt.

Image. This is quite a vague, but useful, term that is often used to denote the many types of language that conjure sensory perceptions in the mind of the reader. Other features – such as metaphor, simile, personification and symbol – are sometimes considered as sub-divisions within imagery.

Metaphor / Metaphorical. A literary technique that involves the transfer of meaning, with one thing described as being another (e.g. education is a journey, as in the metaphor 'I'm stuck' or ' I am making good progress'). There are many types of metaphor, but in a broad sense metaphor involves the linking of something with something else that is otherwise not related to it.

Personification. Something non-human is described as though it is human. This might be, for example, an object or an abstract idea.

Link

The use of **conceit** is explored on page 52 when metaphysical poetry is considered.

Key terms

Caesura. A break within a line of verse, often indicated by a punctuation mark.

End-stopped. When a line of verse ends with a punctuation mark.

Enjambment. Used in poetry to describe the continuation of a sentence or a clause beyond the end of a line and on to the next one.

Octave. An eight-line verse.

Onomatopoeia. This is when the word chosen sounds like what it refers to. For example, the word plop is onomatopoeic in English.

Quatrain. A four-line verse.

Sestet. A six-line verse, often used to describe the second section of one form of sonnet.

Tercet. A three-line stanza.

Verse paragraph. Stanzas of poetry without any patterns of rhyme or rhythm, usually separated by a blank line.

Voice. The characteristics of the speaker, or the narrative voice used; the perspective taken by the narrative.

When you notice a prominent or significant feature being used, pause and consider its effects and how it helps to shape the meaning.

Aural effects

As you re-read the poem, consider the ways in which aural elements, or sound effects, work. Depending on the poem, some of the following elements might be relevant: **voice**, rhyme, sound repetition, sound replication (sometimes called **onomatopoeia**) rhythm and pace.

When you notice a prominent or significant feature, pause and consider its effects, how it helps to shape the meaning and how it relates to the whole poem.

Extension activity

By using a dictionary of literary terms or reputable websites, find out about metre. You may find the following quotations from a poem by Coleridge helpful: 'Iambics march from short to long'; 'Trochee trips from long to short'; 'With a leap and a bound the swift Anapests throng.'

Commenting on features

Keeping the focus on the meaning helps you to make relevant comments. Avoid spotting features and moving on. Anchor your observations in the text. Vague, general or assertive comments – particularly about areas such as metre and rhyme – should be avoided. For instance, examiners are used to reading remarks such as 'the rhythm helps the poem to flow', or 'the use of iambic pentameter gives a heartbeat in the poem, which helps to suggest a sense of love'. Rarely are such comments related closely enough to the text of the poem to support high marks. It is often more helpful to notice a change in the rhythm or rhyming pattern; this can make you consider why there has been such a change. What does a change draw your attention to; why might that be significant?

Structural effects

As you re-read the poem, consider the ways in which structural elements work (effects that relate to the whole poem, its organization, development and shape). Depending on the poem, some of the following elements might be relevant:

- Form. If the poem has a specific form – such as sonnet, ballad, or dramatic monologue – this is likely to influence how you read it. For some forms, there are critical terms that will help you to explore the poem. For example, a dramatic monologue usually has a defined persona, who speaks to an addressee and reveals aspects of his/her character as well as the situation or story as the poem progresses.

- The development of an argument.

- Narrative and the telling of a story.

- Stanza type, regularity (your vocabulary should include the main stanzaic forms, such as **couplets, tercets, quatrains, sestets, octaves and verse paragraphs**).

- Line length, shape, regularity.

- Sound breaks in **end-stopped** lines, **caesura**, and non-breaks in **enjambment**.

- Build-up, climax, anticlimax, contrast, turning point.
- Shift in mood or tone (when the mood of the speaker changes; for example, from despair to hope).
- **Motif** (a recurring metaphorical element within a text).
- Linear structure, cyclical structure.

Stage 3: Re-read the whole poem

Having annotated the poem and built up your ideas in the areas above, you are almost ready to write. You must, however, complete a further stage of planning first. Since you've just worked closely on the details, you risk losing sight of the big picture – so re-read the poem to unify it and remind yourself of its overall meaning and concerns. When you begin to write it's important to begin with the big picture, not the details.

Activity

Re-read 'Timer' on page 42. Begin by commenting on the poem's main meaning – the big picture – then explore one or two aspects or elements that seem to you to be of particular significance.

Commentary

In 'Timer', Harrison explores the enduring qualities of love in a tender poem that recounts the thoughts and feelings of the speaker caused by the receipt of his dead mother's wedding ring.

The ring is an important image: simultaneously ordinary and of almost magical significance. The 'wedding ring which wouldn't burn' that is taken from the envelope 'of coarse official buff' seems like something anyone would have; Harrison's choice of everyday vocabulary and simple description give us that impression. Yet the ring's power is palpable right from the start. The poem's rhythm is mostly iambic but, rather than beginning with an iamb, Harrison begins with a single stressed syllable –'Gold' – which makes the reader linger, giving prominence to that first word and its sense of being a precious – even magical-sounding – metal.

The ring is also a powerful symbol of love. It 'survived the fire' of the speaker's mother's cremation and it symbolizes the love that the speaker's parents have – a love that lasts beyond death. While its power may be felt throughout the poem, it is most potent at the end. In the 13th line, Harrison emphasizes its significance by using the poem's only single-line stanza: a wonderstruck sentence that delays the cause of the wonder until the very last word: 'It's on my warm palm now your burnished ring!' 'Burnished' seems an old-fashioned term among so many simple and common words; its sense of being polished and shining adds a sort of gleam. Its other meaning – having been perfected, like a well-crafted sword of the Middle Ages, adds impressive and magical associations. In addition, this line brings the poem full circle: back to the present tense of the experience in the first stanza when the son contemplates the ring.

Like a magical artefact, it conjures the experience of the final three lines – an experience that brings the son close to his mother. Rather than seeing her, he 'feels' parts of her slip through the circle of the ring, as grains of sand slip

Study tip

In choosing which elements to write about, *select* those that are most important – ones that make a significant impact. Comment on related effects and how they work together. Avoid spotting features. Explore effects and how they shape *meaning*. Analyse details, but consider the big picture: the writer's ideas and attitudes, as well as how they are presented.

through the centre of an egg timer. The gold ring has become the ring of glass in the centre of the timer. The final stanza – the poem's only tercet – mirrors this action through its shape: the words 'circle slowly' are positioned in the centre of its central line, allowing the reader to visualize the sands slipping through the glass – sands which, magically, are both the sands of the timer and the ashes of the mother.

Harrison uses simple and familiar objects to explore complex ideas and emotions. While the timer is a symbol of the finite nature of time, the ring is a symbol of the eternal nature of love. When these symbols merge in the final stanza, it is significant that at the heart of the timer (a symbol of the transitory) is the ring (a symbol of permanence). What 'Timer' suggests is that, though our lives may be brief, true love endures. The speaker's father does not communicate such ideas in complex or philosophical terms, but simply, sincerely and – for the reader – touchingly. The ring is an '"eternity"' engraved with his and his wife's names. For him, it is more than a symbol, the ring is his guarantee – his 'surety' – that they will be together 'later'.

Reading love poetry from throughout the ages

Practising forming ideas about poems in the manner suggested above is one important way in which you can develop your skills. Another is by reading a wide range of love poetry. This approach builds familiarity with the range of ways in which writers have responded to love, and to some of the typical features and concerns of different eras. By discovering more about each literary period and its related styles and conventions, you will be building up vital contextual understanding.

While it is beyond the scope of this book to offer a wide and detailed survey of periods of literature, and the full range of love poetry they produced, what follows are suggestions for purposeful directions which your independent reading might take. They begin with poetry written not long before Shakespeare, and end at the beginning of the 20th century.

Early Modern poetry

Depending on the books you consult, this period (encompassing the 16th and 17th centuries) might be called Renaissance, be named according to the English monarch on the throne at the time, or be termed the Early Modern period.

A celebrated poet from early in this period is Sir Thomas Wyatt (1503–1542). Once a diplomat for King Henry VIII, he was later imprisoned for an alleged improper relationship with the woman who would become King Henry's second wife, Anne Boleyn. He is also credited as the person who brought the sonnet form to England from Italy.

> **Link**
>
> Twentieth-century poetry is discussed in Chapter 4, pages 66–72.

> **Link**
>
> Thomas Wyatt's 'Whoso List to Hunt' has been selected for the AQA pre-1900 anthology for use in Section C.

> **Activity**
>
> Read the following poem and analyse it in the same way that you analysed Harrison's 'Timer' (on page 42).

I find no peace
I find no peace, and all my war is done.
I fear and hope. I burn and freeze like ice.

I fly aloft, yet can I not arise;
And nought I have, and all the world I seize on,
That locks nor loseth, holdeth me in prison,
And holds me not, yet can I scape no wise:
Nor lets me live, nor die, at my devise,
And yet of death it giveth me occasion.
Without eye I see; without tongue I plain:
I wish to perish, yet I ask for health;
I love another, and thus I hate myself;
I feed me in sorrow, and laugh in all my pain.
Lo, thus displeaseth me both death and life,
And my delight is causer of this strife.

Other poets of the period worth discovering include Fulke Greville (1554–1628) (his 'Chorus of Priests' from *Mustapha*, which explores self-division and hypocrisy, provides interesting contextual links with *Measure for Measure*), Christopher Marlowe (1564–1593), Ben Jonson (1574–1637) and Michael Drayton (1563–1631).

Sonnets

You might recognize the above poem by Wyatt as a sonnet. Poets have used this form to explore love for eight centuries, and sonnets are certainly worth studying to prepare for the 'Love through the ages' exam. These 14-line poems are ideally suited to developing a speaker's thoughts and feelings; the form also adds sufficient constraint to ensure creative tension. In addition to extolling the virtues of a loved one, there are a great many ways in which sonnets explore the subject of love. For example, as in 'I find no peace', sonneteers often wrestle with love's pains and they sometimes use the form for subjects other than love.

> **Extension activity**
>
> Find copies of Michael Drayton's, 'Since there's no help, come let us kiss and part' and Shakespeare's, 'Then hate me when thou wilt' (Sonnet 90). Re-read them alongside Wyatt's 'I find no peace'. Choose two of these sonnets and compare how the poets explore difficulties in love.

By the 1590s many of the techniques and imagery of sonnets had become clichéd. Think about how love poetry in general – and sonnets in particular – often suggest foolishness in Shakespeare's plays: Romeo experiments with paradoxical abstractions as he pines for Rosaline in *Romeo and Juliet*; the four lovesick lords in *Love's Labour's Lost* write comically bad sonnets; and Bourbon in *Henry V* mentions having written a sonnet in praise of his horse! The following example by Bartholomew Griffin (d.1602) is from *Fidessa, more chaste than kind* (1596).

My Lady's hair is threads of beaten gold;
Her front the purest crystal eye hath seen;
Her eyes the brightest stars the heavens hold;
Her cheeks, red roses, such as seld have been.
Her pretty lips of red vermilion dye;
Her hand of ivory the purest white;
Her blush AURORA, or the morning sky;

Her breast displays two silver fountains bright.
The spheres, her voice; her grace, the Graces three;
Her body is the saint that I adore;
Her smiles and favours, sweet as honey be.
Her feet, fair THETIS praiseth evermore.
But ah, the worst and last is yet behind:
For of a griffon she doth bear the mind!

Link

Shakespeare's Sonnet 130 is reprinted and discussed on page 8.

Activity

Read the sonnet above by Griffin and note the ways in which it seems unsubtle, exaggerated or insincere. How does it differ from other sonnets that you know and like? You might, for example, compare it with Shakespeare's Sonnet 130. Don't subject Griffin's poem to an in-depth critical appreciation; the aim is that you use it to appreciate the other, more accomplished, sonnet in greater depth.

Activity

Compile a list of some of the features of sonnets – stylistic, formal and in terms of subject matter – that you have identified in your reading of this form. To help you further you could read as many as possible of Shakespeare's sonnets (there are 154 in total). In Shakespeare's sonnets you could look for ways in which the speaker, his lovers and their relationships are presented. You could also consider Shakespeare's presentation of time and its effects.

Meredithian sonnets

The sonnet has also been extended beyond its usual 14 lines to 16, in a type of sonnet that has become known as the Meredithian sonnet (named after George Meredith; see page 60).

Pastoral poetry

Pastoral is a mode of writing that typically presents rural people in an idealized way and uses natural imagery to create an impression of peace, innocence and contentment. In pastoral poetry, the poet typically assumes the identity of a shepherd and casts his mistress as a shepherdess, whom he addresses using a pastoral name (often derived from earlier Roman pastoral models), such as Celia, Phyllis, or Phoebe. While a wish to escape from the pressures of city or court life seems a common fantasy, it is not always clear whether such escapist writing is wholly sincere, or at least partly ironic. Examples of Shakespeare's plays that use pastoral settings include *As You Like It* and the second half of *The Winter's Tale*. In these plays there is simultaneously an enjoyment of pastoral escape and a questioning of pastoral ideas.

This sense that pastoral poetry presents an idealized picture of love (and of the world its inhabitants live in) can be explored by comparing the following two poems. Christopher Marlowe (1564–1593) is writing within the conventional pastoral genre, whereas Cecil Day Lewis (1904–1972) is clearly using these conventions to make a very different point.

The Passionate Shepherd to His Love

Come live with me and be my Love,
And we will all the pleasures prove
That hills and valleys, dales and fields,
Or woods or steepy mountain yields.

And we will sit upon the rocks,
And see the shepherds feed their flocks
By shallow rivers, to whose falls
Melodious birds sing madrigals.

And I will make thee beds of roses
And a thousand fragrant posies;
A cap of flowers, and a kirtle
Embroidered all with leaves of myrtle.

A gown made of the finest wool
Which from our pretty lambs we pull;
Fair-linèd slippers for the cold,
With buckles of the purest gold.

A belt of straw and ivy-buds
With coral clasps and amber studs:
And if these pleasures may thee move,
Come live with me and be my Love.

The shepherds' swains shall dance and sing
For thy delight each May morning:
If these delights thy mind may move,
Then live with me and be my Love.

Christopher Marlowe

The Passionate Shepherd to his Love

Come, live with me and be my love,
And we will all the pleasures prove
Of peace and plenty, bed and board,
That chance employment may afford.

I'll handle dainties on the docks
And thou shalt read of summer frocks:
At evening by the sour canals
We'll hope to hear some madrigals.

Care on thy maiden brow shall put
A wreath of wrinkles, and thy foot
Be shod with pain: not silken dress
But toil shall tire thy loveliness.

Hunger shall make thy modest zone
And cheat fond death of all but bone —
If these delights thy mind may move,
Then live with me and be my love.

C. Day Lewis

First write an analysis of Marlowe's presentation of love, the lovers and the world they live in. Then comment on how Day Lewis reflects this original poem in his presentation of a very different world. What meanings can you find in Day Lewis's poem? To find out more about life at the time of Day Lewis's poem, you could visit the website of the National Archive to view some primary sources. http://www. nationalarchives.gov.uk/education/resources/thirties-britain/

Look at the painting 'Shepherd and Shepherdess Reposing' on the left. In what ways are its subject matter and atmosphere similar to those in Marlowe's poem?

The painting 'Shepherd and Shepherdess Reposing' by Francois Boucher (1761)

Metaphysical poetry (c.1600–1700)

Verse from the 17th and 18th centuries characterized by complex arguments and forms, as well as arresting comparisons (which typically link disparate elements in unusual, yet strangely apt, ways) has been termed metaphysical poetry. Think, for instance, of this metaphor from Donne's 'To His Mistress Going to Bed': 'O My America, my new found land'. While striking, and, at first glance, absurd, we could argue that this comparison is actually apt: it elevates the woman by comparing her to a recently discovered land – and the speaker is as overjoyed at being with her as an explorer would be on discovering a continent. Yes, the comparison is hyperbolic, but not in the 'your hair is "threads of beaten gold"' way of earlier clichéd love poetry. The reader's intellect is stimulated, and we assume that the lover who is addressed in this fictional scenario is flattered and impressed by the inventiveness of the metaphor, which extends through the rest of the verse paragraph. The idea of showing off the originality of your inspiration is very much a part of this poetry, with the term '**conceit**', or 'metaphysical conceit', used for such comparisons.

Like studying the sonnet, studying metaphysical poetry would be useful for the 'Love through the ages' exam. By doing so, you will come to understand typical metaphysical features, as well as becoming familiar with some poems which you might be able to connect to – and which might cast light on – some of the poems set on the question paper. Metaphysical poetry can seem difficult at first, but you can mitigate the effects of this difficulty by reading annotated editions of the poems and by making good use of your dictionary as you read. As you read more metaphysical poems, you will become accustomed to the style.

Metaphysical poetry has attracted a great deal of critical attention, and having some knowledge of some of the ways in which other readers have responded at different times to metaphysical poetry would be a helpful way to use context to inform your readings. Late-20th-century critics, for example, have often taken feminist approaches, with some criticizing the sexist and domineering attitudes that male speakers in these poems take towards women.

Activity

The following two metaphysical poems both use lovers being apart as a central idea. Work on a comparison of the two poems, using the techniques described with reference to 'Timer' earlier in this chapter. Your question is:

'It has been said that metaphysical poetry is a form of showing off, rather than a showing of sincerity.' Compare the ways in which Donne and Marvell write about being apart from their lover in the light of this comment.

Neither poem is easy, because complexity of argument is a feature of metaphysical poetry, so you will need to work hard at teasing out possible interpretations. When you have completed your preparations, read the section below on comparing poems (pages 55–57), and then write a full comparison of these two poems.

To help you start here are a few suggestions:

- Consider the significance of each of the titles.
- How does each poem show a development of argument?
- How would you describe the voice which speaks each poem?
- In what ways does each speaker claim that their love is special?
- How are these poems similar, both in overall argument and in use of **conceits**?
- And how are they different?

A Valediction Forbidding Mourning

As virtuous men pass mildly away,
And whisper to their souls, to go,
Whilst some of their sad friends do say,
'The breath goes now,' and some say, 'No:'

So let us melt, and make no noise,
No tear-floods, nor sigh-tempests move;
'Twere profanation of our joys
To tell the laity our love.

Moving of th' earth brings harms and fears;
Men reckon what it did, and meant;
But trepidation of the spheres,
Though greater far, is innocent.

Study tip

When using a critical view, either *evaluate* (that is, by close attention to the text, assess the extent to which it is valid), or *apply* that view (that is, take the critic's view and test how it works with the text). Don't just quote a critic and move on.

Did you know?

One of the earliest uses of 'metaphysical' as a literary term was by Samuel Johnson in 1779. He used it to indicate a difficult style shared by writers such as Donne (1572–1631), Herbert (1593–1633) and Marvell (1621–1678), and their manner of organizing thoughts, feelings or arguments.

Dull sublunary lovers' love
(Whose soul is sense) cannot admit
Absence, because it doth remove
Those things which elemented it.

But we by a love so much refin'd,
That ourselves know not what it is,
Inter-assured of the mind,
Care less, eyes, lips, and hands to miss.

Our two souls therefore, which are one,
Though I must go, endure not yet
A breach, but an expansion,
Like gold to airy thinness beat.

If they be two, they are two so
As stiff twin compasses are two;
Thy soul, the fix'd foot, makes no show
To move, but doth, if the' other do.

And though it in the centre sit,
Yet when the other far doth roam,
It leans, and hearkens after it,
And grows erect, as that comes home.

Such wilt thou be to me, who must
Like th' other foot, obliquely run;
Thy firmness makes my circle just,
And makes me end, where I begun.

                              John Donne

The Definition of Love

My Love is of a birth as rare
As 'tis for object strange and high:
It was begotten by Despair
Upon Impossibility.

Magnanimous Despair alone
Could show me so divine a thing,
Where feeble Hope could ne'er have flown
But vainly flapped its tinsel wing.

And yet I quickly might arrive
Where my extended soul is fixed;
But Fate does iron wedges drive,
And always crowds itself betwixt.

For Fate with jealous eye does see
Two perfect loves, nor lets them close:
Their union would her ruin be,
And her tyrannic power depose.

And therefore her decrees of steel
Us as the distant Poles have placed,
(Though Love's whole world on us doth wheel)
 Not by themselves to be embraced.

Unless the giddy heaven fall,
And earth some new convulsion tear;
And, us to join, the world should all
Be cramped into a planisphere.

As lines, so loves oblique, may well
Themselves in every angle greet:
But ours, so truly parallel,
Though infinite, can never meet.

Therefore the love which us doth bind,
But Fate so enviously debars,
Is the conjunction of the mind,
And opposition of the stars.

Andrew Marvell

Comparing poems

Before proceeding with our survey of periods and styles of love poetry, let's pause to consider an important aspect of technique: making connections between poems. Below are two different ways of structuring a response.

Structure A

Study each poem closely – in the light of the question being asked and the viewpoint that it contains. As you annotate, note areas of similarity and difference.

If your understanding of another poem, or a literary period or style, helps you to respond to the unseen poems, note this as you plan. You can use such contextual detail when you write your answer.

This model uses six paragraphs. The first (introduction) and the last (conclusion) are short; the paragraphs in the main body of the essay (paragraphs 2–5) should be well-developed.

1. **Introduction:** *set things up.* Address the question directly. Deal with the big picture, not the details; engage with the viewpoint and both poems. A strong first paragraph contains a confident argument that is going to be developed as the essay progresses.

2. **Poem A:** *analyse.* Build on your introduction by exploring a key aspect, or key area, of the poem; analyse some related details. Keep the meaning central; show how the poet's methods shape the meaning and create effects. Use critical terminology to help you articulate your response precisely. Do this in every main body paragraph.

3. **Poem A:** *analyse.* Explore another key aspect, or key area, of the poem; analyse a handful of related details.

4. Poem B: *analyse/compare.* Build on your introduction by exploring a key aspect, or key area, of the poem; analyse a handful of related details. *Explore similarities and differences to Poem A as you do so.*

5. Poem B: *analyse/compare.* Explore another key aspect, or key area, of the poem; analyse some related details. *Explore the similarities and differences to Poem A as you do so.*

6. Conclusion: *draw the strands of your argument together.* Engage the question (and the view) directly. Address important final comparisons or contrasts arising from your analysis of the poems; draw conclusions.

Questions to ask when writing a conclusion

- What is your considered, final response to the question – including the critical viewpoint; to what extent do you agree?

- What are your final thoughts about the ways in which each poet explored the topic, or communicated the experience?

- How might you analyse the implications of what your analysis and comparison have shown?

- How might you broaden the scope of your essay to leave the reader with a wider question or issue to consider that arises directly from the question posed?

Structure B

Instead of making the poems the organizing principle of your comparison, this method takes a topic-based approach.

Write about six paragraphs. (This model uses six, but you might write seven or eight.) The main body paragraphs – those after the introduction and before the conclusion – should be full and well-developed. Here, when following Structure B, you never spend more than a single paragraph on only one poem (and even then you are setting up a comparison).

1. Introduction: *set things up.* Address the question directly. Deal with the big picture, not the details; engage with the viewpoint and both poems. A strong first paragraph contains a confident argument that is going to be developed as the essay progresses.

2. Poem A or B: *topic i.* Analyse an important aspect or topic in the poems. Explore this aspect and how it is presented in one poem. For example, if a particular image is significant and it develops throughout the poem, you could explore this. Keep the meaning central; show how the poet's methods shape the meaning and create effects. Use critical terminology to help you articulate your response precisely.

3. Both poems: *topic i comparing and contrasting.* Compare the ways in which this aspect, or a closely related aspect, is presented in the other poem. Discuss comparisons and contrasts between both poems as you develop your analysis.

4. Poem A or B: *topic ii.* Analyse another important aspect of similarity or difference. Explore this aspect and how it is presented in one of the poems. Make sure that you address the meaning first, and show how

Study tip

Structure A is a dependable way of writing about poems in depth. But be careful: don't lose yourself in an analysis of a poem and neglect the question asked – or forget to compare. Your answer must be a thorough analytical comparison, not two mini-essays joined in the middle.

the poet's methods shape the meaning and create effects. Use critical terminology to help you articulate your response with precision.

5. **Both poems:** *topic ii comparing & contrasting*. Compare the ways in which this aspect, or a closely related aspect, works in the other poem. Discuss comparisons and contrasts between both poems as you develop your analysis. Consider the subject matter and poetic methods.

6. **Conclusion:** *draw the strands of your argument together*. Engage the question (and the view) directly. Address important final comparisons or contrasts arising from your analysis of the poems; draw conclusions.

Which method?

Both methods have advantages. For example, Structure A often produces thorough analysis of the poems, with strong argument and an apt focus on the big picture and the given viewpoint. However, sometimes students fail to make the second half of a Structure A essay sufficiently comparative. Structure B often produces very well-integrated comparisons, with good flexibility; but, if mishandled, this can come at the cost of analytical depth; there might also be a tendency to comment on features rather than overall meaning and a relative neglect of the overall argument.

The best advice therefore, is that you try both during the course of your studies and consider how the type of poems you write about might influence your choice. Often, for example, when writing about relatively short poems, students find it easier to develop more detailed and fuller analysis using Structure A and working through sections of the poems – staying with each poem longer – rather than moving between poems too freely and too frequently. Many students find it easier to adopt Structure A, particularly when they find the poems they encounter challenging.

Cavalier poets

Poets who supported the Royalist cause during the Civil War are known as Cavalier poets. They often wrote about aspects of upper-class life, such as gallantry and courtship. One of this group, who was not a courtier, Robert Herrick (1591–1674), is famous for a *carpe diem* ('seize the day') poem called 'To the virgins to make much of time'. Another, Richard Lovelace, was imprisoned in 1642 for presenting a Royalist petition to Parliament. While in prison, Lovelace wrote the following poem, which contains a line that has passed into common use.

To Althea: *From Prison*

I
WHEN Love with unconfined wings
    Hovers within my Gates;
And my divine *Althea* brings
    To whisper at the Grates ;
When I lye tangled in her hair
    And fettered to her eye ;
The *Gods* that wanton in the Air,
    Know no such Liberty.

Link

See the example student response to the use of the ring image in 'Timer', page 42.

Study tip

Structure B is flexible and allows you to weave in a new point that arises from your writing, rather than your plan. It is also useful when analysing a longer poem: you can be selective more easily than when working through such a poem part by part.

Study tip

Keep your exploration of the poems detailed and meaningful. The topics explored should relate to an overall reading of the poems in question; they should also be significant. If you simply choose features but neglect to explore their significance to the overall meaning, you are likely to write a superficial answer.

II
When flowing Cups run swiftly round
    With no allaying *Thames*,
Our careless heads with Roses bound,
    Our hearts with Loyall Flames ;
When thirsty grief in Wine we steep,
    When Healths and draughts go free,
Fishes that tipple in the Deep,
    Know no such Libertie.

III
When (like committed linnets) I
    With shriller throat shall sing
The sweetness, Mercy, Majesty,
    And glories of my KING ;
When I shall voice aloud, how Good
    He is, how Great should be ;
Enlarged Winds that curl the Flood,
    Know no such Liberty.

IV
Stone Walls do not a Prison make,
    Nor Iron bars a Cage ;
Minds innocent and quiet take
    That for an Hermitage ;
If I have freedom in my Love,
    And in my soul am free ;
Angels alone that soar above,
    Enjoy such Liberty.

Restoration poetry

When the monarchy was restored in 1660 and Charles II acceded to the throne, the oppressive puritan regime of Oliver Cromwell and his Parliament ended. Theatres re-opened (with women on stage for the first time), scholarship flourished and morals seemed to loosen. While immorality and frivolousness were not evident in every writer of the period – John Milton (1608-1674), for example, wrote the magisterial *Paradise Lost* (1667) – it is not for nothing that the children's television programme, *Horrible Histories*, refers to Charles II as 'the king who brought back partying'.

You could research Restoration poetry, such as that of John Wilmot, the Earl of Rochester. Another writer worth discovering is Aphra Behn. Her poems of female infidelity and male sexual inadequacy make a good antidote to the arrogant seductions of some male poetry. Poems to seek out include 'Love Arm'd', 'On her Loving Two Equally' and 'The Disappointment'.

18th-century satire

Much of the 18th-century poetry that we still read today is satirical – that is, it mocks with a moral purpose. For example, Alexander Pope (1688–1744) uses a barrage of techniques in 'The Rape of the Lock' to satirize the attitudes of fashionable women and their world. Jonathan Swift (1667–1745), who wrote *Gulliver's Travels*, makes Pope's humour seem positively gentle through his more biting – and bodily – **satire** in poems such as 'The Lady's Dressing Table'. Like the pastoral, satire is a literary style rather than a literary period.

Link

While some of Rochester's verse is too crude to publish in this book, a more heartfelt lyric of his, 'Absent from Thee' (1676), is included in the AQA pre-1900 anthology. See Chapter 4 for further details.

Key term

Satire. The mockery of various types of human behaviour, involving irony and exaggeration.

Romantic poetry (c.1780–1830)

Concerned with much more than what romance means today, Romantic poetry has political and philosophical dimensions that are worth studying, and which will certainly enrich your understanding of the verse. Typically, it is marked by a focus on the self, by intensity of experience and by an interest in imagination and its workings. Nature is a primary influence and inspiration, and the interaction between poet and nature often leads to a state of transcendence. While its ideas are often complex, its language is often simple.

Usually direct and sincere, love poetry from the Romantic period contrasts with the self-conscious cleverness of some earlier styles, such as the metaphysical. Poets whom you should consider exploring include Blake, Burns, Wordsworth (1770–1850), Coleridge (1772–1834), Percy Bysshe Shelley (1792–1822), Keats (1795–1822) and Byron (1788–1824).

Burns is an easy poet to read and to research: his birthday is marked annually by Burns suppers and there is an excellent BBC audio archive which includes films of poems being performed by well-known readers: http://www.bbc.co.uk/arts/robertburns/

Activity

The following poem by Lord Byron is a good example of Romantic love poetry. Consider the presentation of the lover in this poem and then compare it with the presentation of a lover in a poem you have researched from a different era.

Did you know?

The 18th century is also famous for another literary mode: sentiment. This style prizes feeling over reason and glories in emotions such as tenderness, compassion and sympathy. The 18th century saw the first major flourishing of the novel, many of which were sentimental, but also included salacious content; 'O Leave Novels' by Robert Burns pokes fun at the supposed damage such novels did to young women.

Research idea

Using your library or an Internet search, find Wordsworth's preface to the 1802 edition of *Lyrical Ballads*. In this, he explains why he chose to write about 'low and rustic life' and describes poetry as 'the spontaneous overflow of powerful feelings: it takes its origin from emotion recollected in tranquillity'. ●

She walks in beauty

She walks in beauty, like the night
   Of cloudless climes and starry skies;
And all that's best of dark and bright
   Meet in her aspect and her eyes;
Thus mellowed to that tender light
   Which heaven to gaudy day denies.

One shade the more, one ray the less,
   Had half impaired the nameless grace
Which waves in every raven tress,
   Or softly lightens o'er her face;
Where thoughts serenely sweet express,
   How pure, how dear their dwelling-place.

And on that cheek, and o'er that brow,
   So soft, so calm, yet eloquent,
The smiles that win, the tints that glow,
   But tell of days in goodness spent,
A mind at peace with all below,
   A heart whose love is innocent!

Victorian poetry (1837–1901)

While the term 'Victorian' is sometimes used pejoratively (connoting the perceived values of Victorian society, such as being earnest, respectable or even prudish), the poetry from this long period is incredibly varied. Accordingly, the following comments are meant only as a starting point for your study of Victorian love poetry. For further research, consult one of the many good anthologies of Victorian poetry – see, for example, Christopher Ricks (ed.), *The New Oxford Book of Victorian Verse*, Oxford: OUP, 2002. There is also a helpful and accessible chapter on love in Stephen Croft (ed.) *Victorian Literature Oxford Student Texts*, Oxford: OUP, 2009.

Alfred, Lord Tennyson (1809–1892) wrote a wide range of verse related to love, from the Middle Ages-inspired 'Lady of Shalott' to the poems of grief for his friend, Arthur Hallam, such as 'In Memoriam'. Elizabeth Barrett Browning (1806–1861) produced a moving sequence entitled *Sonnets from the Portuguese* for her husband, Robert Browning (1812–1889). Robert Browning is famous for dramatic monologues in which he explores abnormal states of mind – which are often affected by love. Several of Christina Rossetti's (1830–1894) poems explore aspects of love that are melancholy, delayed or frustrated. Her brother, Dante Gabriel Rossetti (1828–1882), was also a Pre-Raphaelite painter and wrote poems of emotional and erotic power. George Meredith (1828–1909) is remembered chiefly for *Modern Love*, his sequence of sonnets – each of which has 16, rather than the usual 14 lines – inspired by the breakup of his marriage. (An example is printed below.) It makes an interesting contrast to an earlier popular sequence of poems by Coventry Patmore (1823–1896) *The Angel in the House*. Amongst Irish poets of the Victorian age, the most prominent was W. B. Yeats.

Activity

Read the following sonnet from *Modern Love* and consider how Meredith uses time to organize his feelings of love and loss.

XVI

In our old shipwrecked days there was an hour
When in the firelight steadily aglow,
Joined slackly, we beheld the red chasm grow
Among the clicking coals. Our library-bower
That eve was left to us: and hushed we sat
As lovers to whom Time is whispering.
From sudden-opened doors we heard them sing:
The nodding elders mixed good wine with chat.
Well knew we that Life's greatest treasure lay
With us, and of it was our talk. 'Ah, yes!
Love dies!' I said: I never thought it less.
She yearned to me that sentence to unsay.
Then when the fire domed blackening, I found
Her cheek was salt against my kiss, and swift
Up the sharp scale of sobs her breast did lift:–
Now am I haunted by that taste! that sound!

Activity

Create a timeline that includes the major periods of literary history, including all the texts you have studied throughout the course. Here are some details that you might like to include for each text: author, title of text, date of composition or publication, genre, stylistic features (if relevant) or link to literary movement. The British Library has an excellent multi-media timeline, which may be found at:

http://www.bl.uk/englishtimeline

Link

Material on love poetry from the 20th century is included on pages 66–72 of Chapter 4.

Further reading

Literary terms

Chris Baldick, *The Oxford Dictionary of Literary Terms*, Oxford: OUP, 2008. This is an excellent resource, with full but accessible entries on literary styles and movements as well as terminology.

John Lennard, *The Poetry Handbook*, Oxford: OUP, 2005. This book contains detailed discussions of all aspects of poetry and is an excellent resource for more advanced criticism.

Poetry

Deborah West (ed.), *Oxford Student Texts: William Shakespeare: Complete Sonnets* Oxford: OUP, 2007.

Julia Geddes and Helen Ince (eds), *Love Through the Ages Oxford Student Texts*, Oxford: OUP, 2009 and Julia Geddes and Anna Merrick (eds), *More Love Through the Ages*, Oxford: OUP, 2012.

The above anthologies of verse, as well as prose and drama extracts, offer a range of love poetry accompanied by accessible commentaries.

Jon Stallworthy (ed.), *The New Penguin Book of Love Poetry*, London: Penguin, 2003. This anthology is arranged by theme and includes a range of poems in various styles from a variety of periods.

John Stammers (ed.), *The Picador Book of Love Poems*, London: Picador, 2012. Chosen by contemporary poets, the poems in this anthology cover a wide range of emotions associated with love. They are arranged in pairs, which makes it easier to trace intertextual relationships and to make connections.

Websites

http://web.cn.edu/kwheeler/lit_terms.html

This is an excellent site, with clear and detailed explanations of terms and their use as well as a section of literature resources that includes a useful 'Periods of Literary History' document that would be helpful when drawing up a timeline.

www.shakespeares-sonnets.com

This site provides a wealth of information about the sonnets in an easy-to-follow format that includes illustrations.

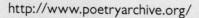

http://www.poetryarchive.org/

Readings of poems by all of the poets mentioned in this chapter are available on The Poetry Archive, an excellent resource, which also contains a glossary, comments on poetic form and further links to other good websites.

http://www.english.cam.ac.uk/classroom/index.htm

A site from Cambridge University that includes very detailed guidance on practical criticism (close reading) as well as a helpful glossary of terms.

http://www.bbc.co.uk/programmes/b00cbqhq

This excellent 'In Our Time' radio discussion places metaphysical poetry in its historical context and explores features of that style. It also offers close readings of specific poems. Immediate and engaging in places, it reaches high levels of complexity and depth.

The nature of the questions for A level

Each of the two questions in Section C of the exam paper invites you to compare how an aspect of love – typically a theme or an idea – is treated in two texts. Both texts are from the list of chosen comparative set texts: one is prose, the other poetry; one is written pre-1900, the other post-1900. Your choice of poetry text is between the *AQA Anthology of Love Poetry through the Ages: Pre-1900* and the *AQA Anthology of Love Poetry through the Ages: Post-1900*. You may take a clean copy of each of the set texts you have studied into the exam.

Studying poetry and comparing texts for AS level

If you are taking the one-year stand-alone AS level qualification, there are separate poetry and prose tasks – each one in a different exam paper.

- For Paper 1, after answering the Shakespeare question, you will write a response to a view about one poem that you have studied from your chosen anthology (this poem will be reprinted in the examination paper). The two anthologies are exactly the same as those for A level.

- For Paper 2, after answering a question on unseen prose, you will compare how an aspect – typically, a theme or an idea – is presented in two novels. All of the novels set for A level are included for study at AS level, plus two additional texts: Jonathan Coe's *The Rotters' Club* (2001) and George Eliot's *The Mill on the Floss* (1860). At AS level, you have a free choice from the list of set texts; there is no requirement to pick pre- or post-1900 texts.

Studying a novel for Section C

You are likely to concentrate on one novel from the list of chosen comparative set texts, although you could study two if you wanted to develop a broader knowledge base and have a wider choice for the exam. Your chosen text should be studied thoroughly before the examination. Ideally, read it three times: once quickly for pleasure and overall sense; once closely; and then once more – to unify it and ensure that you have a full and considered understanding as well as a strong sense of how the details fit into the big picture.

Remember that the tasks for the examination are comparative, so don't wait too long before you consider the relevant poetry anthology. Read the poems no later than after your first reading of the novel. That way, as you study the novel closely, you can think about possible ways in which it connects with the poems. When you come to study the poems more closely, such connections are going to emerge even more clearly.

Love through the ages: themes and ideas

Some themes, ideas and concerns that you are likely to encounter include, but are not limited to:

- Romantic love – in all its aspects, including meetings, courtship, seduction, partings, difficulties, strong feelings associated with love, physical encounters and emotional attachments

This chapter will:

- introduce the set novels
- offer strategies for studying your chosen comparative set novel
- introduce the set poetry texts
- offer strategies for studying your chosen comparative poetry text
- develop skills in making connections between novels and poems
- consider ways of responding to critical views and contexts.

- Marriage
- Love, money and social class
- Love and society
- Adultery and infidelity
- Gender
- Love and identity
- Love and growing up
- Sexuality
- Time and its effects on love

As well as themes and ideas, think about **motifs** – recurring elements – that are relevant to love.

> **Activity**
>
> As you study your chosen comparative prose set text, make notes on themes, ideas and motifs related to love. Use the list above as a starting point. Some questions to consider as you read include the following:
>
> - In what ways is the writer interested in each theme?
> - How does the text make readers think and feel about that topic?
> - In what ways does the writer explore the theme? (As well as **plot** and characterization, consider authorial methods such as imagery, symbolism and so on.)

Note that, while preconceived lists of themes and ideas (like the one above) are helpful in stimulating thought, you must allow the novel itself to suggest the areas that are **significant**. Avoid forcing it to conform to preconceived ideas. Several texts might include an exploration of a given theme, but it might be more significant in some than in others. For example, female sexuality is explored to some degree by Hardy in *Tess of the d'Urbervilles*, but many would argue that this theme is of more central importance to Kate Chopin in *The Awakening*. As you read and think about themes, ideas and motifs, include page numbers and brief quotations in your notes. Even if these are rough jottings, they will be helpful when you return to more focused study and when you think about connections as you study the poems from your chosen anthology.

Introducing the chosen comparative set texts: pre-1900 prose

Jane Austen, *Persuasion* (1817)

Anne Elliot once rejected a proposal from Captain Wentworth, on the advice that both his fortune and character were lacking. Now, at 27, her prospects for love in Regency England seem limited, but circumstances conspire to place the now wealthy Wentworth within her social orbit. Austen's narrative viewpoint – including the use of irony and **free indirect speech/thought** – as well as subtle symbolism and aspects of the Romance genre would all repay further exploration.

Key terms

Free indirect speech. This refers to speech that is embedded in a narrative, so it is unattributed (free) and a report of the speech rather than the actual words (indirect).

Free indirect thought. This is a narrative technique where a character's thought processes form part of the narrative, but are not attributed to him or her.

Charlotte Brontë, *Jane Eyre* (1847)

Orphaned, Jane is sent away to school and later becomes a governess to the daughter of the mysterious Mr Rochester, with whom she falls in love. On the eve of their wedding, Jane's veil is ripped by an intruder who is later revealed to be Rochester's insane wife, Bertha, who is usually confined to the attic. Jane flees but, years later, feels compelled to return. She finds the house has burned down and that Rochester has been blinded and injured in an attempt to save Bertha, who jumped to her death from the roof. Jane and Rochester marry. As you read, consider Brontë's extensive use of imagery and symbolism as well as setting. Think also about the ways in which she uses genres such as romance, gothic and **Bildungsroman.**

Emily Brontë, *Wuthering Heights* (1847)

At its simplest level, the story concerns Catherine and Heathcliff (the orphan her father brought to live with her family). After her father's death, Heathcliff is cast out and made to live like a labourer. Despite loving Heathcliff, Catherine marries rich Edgar Linton. Heathcliff goes away and returns, years later, a rich man bent on revenge. Largely a narrative of the housekeeper's memories, and framed by the observations of Heathcliff's tenant, the novel's unusual form renders events ambiguous and our responses to characters uncertain. Accordingly, any study of the novel should pay heed to the effects of narrative point of view. Like *Jane Eyre*, *Wuthering Heights* has a **Byronic hero**, and Brontë makes significant use of gothic elements as well as imagery, symbolism and settings.

Kate Chopin, *The Awakening* (1899)

Edna Pontellier tires of her life of leisure and her roles of wife and mother. While holidaying with her family at Grand Isle, she meets Robert, but before they can act on their feelings, he leaves for Mexico. Back at home in New Orleans, Edna takes a lover; her sexuality awakens, but she feels no love. She moves into a flat on her own and pursues her passion for painting. Robert returns, but Edna leaves to help a friend give birth. When she returns, Robert has left. Edna goes to Grande Isle, swims out to sea and drowns.

While written towards the end of the Victorian period, this short novel feels almost **modernist** in its interest about the interior world and its complexity. It is worth considering the ways in which Chopin uses the narrative to both suggest objectivity and to encourage sympathy with the **protagonist**. Her use of symbolism is subtle and the use of imagery is richly patterned. Think, for example, about the ways in which water imagery flows throughout the novel.

Thomas Hardy, *Tess of the d'Urbervilles* (1891)

Sent by her penniless father to seek help from the d'Urberville family, Tess Durbeyfield receives work, but also unwanted advances from her 'cousin', Alec, which culminate in the loss of her virginity. After the birth and death of her child, she works as a milkmaid and attracts the attentions of the gentleman farmer, Angel Clare. She marries him, but, on her wedding night, reveals her past. Angel flees. After much hardship, Tess becomes Alec's mistress. When Angel returns, she kills Alec and is later hanged for her crime. Rich in natural imagery and symbolism, it makes subtle use of foreshadowing and aspects of the genres of Bildungsroman and tragedy.

Research idea

Feminist approaches

The presentation of Rochester's wife, Bertha, helped to inspire the title of one of the most important works of feminist literary criticism, *The Madwoman in the Attic* by Gilbert and Gubar (1979; 2000). Rather than viewing Bertha as being of unsound mind, they treat her as a marginalized figure in Victorian society, and show how female characters in literature are often categorized as angels or monsters. Even if you aren't studying Charlotte Brontë, you may find that you can apply some of their approaches to your chosen texts. ●

Key terms

Bildungsroman. A novel that deals with one person's formative years and moral or spiritual development (a German critical term).

Byronic hero. An emotionally complex, mysterious and tormented male character, who is arrogant, cynical and contemptuous of normal society, but, despite such anti-heroic qualities, manages to be alluring to some of the other characters and many readers.

Modernist / Modernism. A trend in literature, the high point of which was from 1910-30. Modernist texts tend to be impressionistic and fragmentary, blurring genres and drawing attention to their own construction.

! REMEMBER

As you study your novel closely, foreground elements that relate to poems in the relevant anthology. Such elements might relate to subject matter, themes, ideas or concerns, as well as to authorial methods. Aspects that are typical of writing about love are also worth considering.

Studying a poetry anthology for Section C

The poems in your chosen anthology should be read often. It would be helpful to read the entire selection a few times – one after the other – to build your familiarity with them and to gain a sense not only of the main meaning of each poem, but also of the range of themes and styles. You should also note down your thoughts about possible ways in which the poems connect to your chosen comparative set novel. Your detailed study of the anthology should take the form of a close reading of each poem. Use the strategies suggested in Chapter 3, and use dictionaries to look up all unfamiliar words and to check that you have understood the nuances and connotations of some others. After reading each poem, or after reading a few, undertake more detailed work on comparisons – exploring the extent to which each poem might relate to aspects of your novel in terms of subject matter, themes and authorial methods. Think also about how it contains aspects that are typical of writing about love.

It would be helpful to undertake secondary research to find out about the poets and their contexts. For example, it would be useful to research the 1920s when studying Edna St Vincent Millay and the 1930s when studying MacNeice. It is often interesting and productive to compare how writers from different times explore similar experiences, such as courtship, marriage, adultery, or leaving a lover.

Introducing the chosen comparative set texts: post-1900 poems

'Love and a Question' by Robert Frost

'Love and a Question' (1913), by Robert Frost (1874–1963), is a narrative poem, in which a poor stranger seeks shelter in a house where a man and a woman are about to consummate their marriage. The 'Question' of the title refers to the groom's dilemma: is it right to ruin a night of romantic passion by showing brotherly love? No conclusive answer is offered, and the poem's deceptively simple style belies thematic complexity. Its straightforward story and use of character types lend the poem the air of a parable, but – unlike those of the Bible – its message is not spelled out. It is interesting to read the poem's events and descriptions symbolically. For example, what might the stranger represent, and why has Frost chosen this dramatic time for him to arrive? Look also at the details: How is the weather used in the second stanza, and what is the significance of the heart image in the third? As you re-read, ask yourself how the poem's situation and events reflect ideas about marriage, intimacy, fear, jealousy and possessiveness?

'A quoi bon dire' by Charlotte Mew

'A quoi bon dire' (1916), by Charlotte Mew (1869–1928), is an enigmatic lyric from a speaker to her dead lover. Ask yourself why Mew keeps the details vague: the lover didn't speak definitely, but said 'something that sounded like Goodbye'; the speaker disagrees with everybody else who thinks the addressee is dead; and, while everyone thinks that the speaker ages, the addressee does not. Perhaps the speaker is deluded, but we may appreciate the charm of a love that lasts, which keeps its lover youthful and which seems to be embodied by new lovers in the final stanza. Make connections between this poem and other love poems that share an interest in time and the ways in which it affects love.

Also ask yourself to what extent time is **significant** in your chosen novel. Note the poem's form. What are the effects of the two cross-rhymed **quatrains** which end abruptly with a short line that closes the stanza with an assertion of difference between the couple and everyone else? Consider the variation in stanzaic form: in what ways do these variations create effects and add to the poem's meaning?

'I being born a woman' and 'Love is not all' by Edna St Vincent Millay

One of the most rebellious and liberal literary voices of the 1920s, Edna St Vincent Millay (1892–1950) was popular, critically-acclaimed and rich. Both of these sonnets reflect her radical voice.

'I being born a woman' (1923) subverts earlier phallocentric (male-centred) love poetry, in which a male speaker leaves his silent lover to seek new adventures. Millay's female speaker doesn't dress up a parting in terms of fake gallantry: she uses the **octave** to disentangle love's physical and spiritual components; then, in the **sestet**, makes it clear that the man can't even expect verbal intercourse the next time they meet.

'Love is not all' (1931) reflects on the qualities of love. The first six lines define love in terms of what it is not: it can't provide basic needs such as food, water or shelter. Then the poet turns to consider that lack of love can also cause death and develops a personal example in which the speaker asks whether she would – in difficult circumstances – give up her love for the addressee. The **couplet** closes the poem with a half rhyme and without a definite answer. It would be interesting to compare Millay's sonnet to others that address love directly, such as Shakespeare's 'Sonnet 116'; you might like to consider the extent to which Millay's poem uses elements of both the Shakespearean and the Petrarchan sonnet.

'Meeting Point' by Louis MacNeice

'Meeting Point' (1939), by Louis MacNeice (1907–1963), is a celebration of love. An ordinary situation of a couple meeting in a coffee shop is charged with extraordinary power; it seems that temporal laws are suspended. Think about the ways in which the poem's form and structure reinforce its ideas (consider, for example, the use of refrain and repetition). Think also about how the poem uses imagery. For instance, you might think about the unusual use of natural imagery in this urban setting as well as the beauty of the metaphors, such as the one in the third stanza in which the bell transforms into a flower.

'Vergissmeinnicht' by Keith Douglas

'Vergissmeinnicht' (1943), by the soldier poet Keith Douglas (1920–1944), recounts a story from a tank battle in North Africa during World War II. Returning to the battlefield, the speaker sees in a blown-up German tank a photograph of a young woman with the inscription Vergissmeinnicht (don't forget me). The speaker empathizes with this woman, wondering how she would feel to see her dead lover. It is worth considering how this powerful poem generates such pathos. Consider, for example, narrative strategies, the use of rhyme (which changes subtly at different points in the poem), the use of contrasts and the use of imagery and personification.

THINK ABOUT IT

Exploring biographical readings of poems can be useful, but avoid allowing such readings to simplify the poems – biographical readings are just one of many critical approaches. For example, some think that 'Love is not all' was written to Millay's husband, Eugen Boissevain, with whom she was said to have had a sexually open relationship. Frost's early work is also considered by some to be autobiographical, or at least triggered by people and events close to home.

Did you know?

Thomas Hardy is said to have remarked that America produced two great things in the 1920s: the skyscraper and Edna St Vincent Millay.

THINK ABOUT IT

Discover more about 'Meeting Point' by visiting the website of the writer and broadcaster, Clive James. His engaging interpretation reads the poem as a superior kind of Brief Encounter (a film set in the 1930s, directed by David Lean, in which the central couple share their most intimate moments over a cup of tea in the refreshment room of a railway station). You might also like to research the poem's biographical and historical contexts. Many, for example, believe that the poem was written about a specific lover (the American writer, Eleanor Clark).

Activity

Review the poems from the anthology that have been mentioned so far. Make notes which help you to see connections between your chosen comparative set novel and these poems, and between the poems and writing about love in general. You might like to generate a mind map using an A3 page, with the title of your novel in the centre. It would probably be most productive to establish connections first by means of subject matter or theme, before developing further branches that consider how these ideas are shaped by the writers' methods.

'Wild Oats' and 'Talking in Bed' by Philip Larkin

Philip Larkin (1922–1985) wrote a range of poems that explore love in a wide number of ways. 'Wild Oats' (1963) narrates the story of the speaker admiring a beautiful woman, but settling for her 'friend in specs [he] could talk to'. Note how Larkin suggests the dullness of the relationship: think, for example, about the speaker's use of listing and humour. Think also about the speaker's voice; behind the colloquial language, the irony and the sarcasm (such as 'Well, useful to get that learnt') can you detect a sincere voice – one that suggests self-pity or wounded self-esteem? How do you respond to the ways in which the speaker views the two women whom he juxtaposes as 'bosomy English rose / And her friend in specs'? Consider the sounds of the words he chooses, as well as their meaning. Think about the poem's final image and about the strength of its final rhyme. Do you feel pity for the speaker, or are you repelled by his having kept the photos ('snaps') for so long? How might feminist ideas be applied to this poem? Finally, to what extent might the poem explore wider English attitudes towards love and sex?

In 'Talking in Bed' (1964) a couple lie in bed silent. Outside, the world seems indifferent and the weather is turning wintery. The couple finds it hard to use truthful or caring words, or to speak in ways that are not untruthful or uncaring. The poem has a feeling of sparseness: note the white space caused by the three-line stanzas, the images of separation and distance. Consider these aspects in more detail and explore how they create effects and shape meaning. Think about rhyme: in each of the first three stanzas, the poem uses envelope rhyme (in which an unrhymed line is sandwiched between two lines that half-rhyme); but in the last a **triplet**, rather than a **tercet**, is used. Do these three rhyming lines suggest that the feelings they communicate are more certain? Yet consider what the speaker is certain about: the difficulties of communicating and of doing so truthfully and without offence. Consider the effects of the accumulation of terms in a negative form in the last line.

'One Flesh' by Elizabeth Jennings

'One Flesh' (1966), by Elizabeth Jennings (1926–2001), considers the speaker's parents' relationship as they lie in separate beds. Over time their love has cooled. Consider the way in which the experience is structured. The first **sestet** centres on images of the couple in their separate beds, the second develops from cooling passion to growing coldness, then celibacy or a total absence of sexual relations. The final stanza expands on the implications of the first two, considering the paradoxes of their seeming closeness and actual separateness, as well as the coldness that has resulted from the initial fire that produced the speaker.

Link

See Chapter 3 page 43 for a discussion of the poem's ironic title 'Wild Oats'.

Key term

Triplet. a stanza of three lines in which every line rhymes.

You might like to explore the ways in which Jennings uses imagery. Consider, for example, the more abstract images of 'flotsam from a former passion' and the 'thread' and 'feather' in the final stanza. Think also about Jennings' use of biblical diction. Note the changes in the final sestet. The perspective shifts: in the last three lines it is revealed that the speaker is not a dispassionate onlooker, but the old couple's daughter. Consider the effects of the variation to the established form; rather than having a half rhyme with the third line, as in the previous two stanzas, Jennings uses a full rhyme linking the final line with the fourth. As you explore these effects, ensure that you consider the meaning of the final sentence.

What do you think the poem is saying about love and the extent to which it endures? You might like to compare your responses to the poem with your responses to Larkin's poems. To what extent do you feel that 'One Flesh' and 'Talking in Bed' share similar ideas about love?

'For My Lover, Returning to His Wife' by Anne Sexton

The work of Anne Sexton (1928–1974) is often seen as **confessional** poetry, in which life experiences that are taboo, or which would usually remain private, are explored directly. In such writing, the distance between the speaker and the author is probably reduced.

Ironically, the title 'For My Lover, Returning to His Wife' (1968) sounds like one from an Anne Bradstreet (1612–1672) poem. Often considered the first American female poet, Bradstreet's poems include 'To My Dear and Loving Husband' and 'For the Restoration of my Dear Husband from a Burning Ague'. They often use biblical language to express a Puritan sensibility and a deep love for her husband. However, there is nothing Puritan about this 20th-century American female poet as she confronts head on the complicated thoughts and feelings of a mistress as her lover returns to his marital home.

You might want to consider how the speaker presents the wife; you might, for example, look at images of domesticity and solidity. How does the speaker present herself and her feelings towards both the wife and the husband?

Consider the ways in which Sexton creates a voice and think about its tonal range. Are there parts of the poem that you consider to be controlled, or resigned, or which seem angry, bitter or sad? What does Sexton gain from choosing a free form and writing in **free verse**? For example, how does she use shorter lines to create impact, and what are the effects of the two two-line stanzas in the poem?

Think about the poem's wider themes and ideas. For example, how does it explore gender relations, marriage and adultery?

'Punishment' by Seamus Heaney

The consequences of sexual relationships that are forbidden by society are also explored in 'Punishment' (1975), by Seamus Heaney (1939–2013).

The speaker describes an Iron Age woman who was executed by her people for adultery. As the poem progresses, it becomes clear that she represents a Catholic woman who has been tarred and feathered by those in her community as punishment for her relationship with a British soldier.

Consider the speaker's position towards the subject. To what extent is he an 'artful voyeur': seeing the results of a savage act from a safe distance and using

> **Did you know?**
>
> The title of Jennings' poem comes from the Bible: 'Therefore a man shall leave his father and mother and be joined to his wife, and they shall become one flesh' (Genesis 2:24). Research the possible implications of the term 'one flesh' and then consider the extent to which the biblical ideals of marriage are reflected in the poem.

> **Key terms**
>
> **Confessional.** Confessional writing is deeply personal and intimate in its details.
>
> **Free verse.** Poetry that conforms to no regular metre or rhyme scheme.

them for his own artistic ends? What does he feel about those who mete out the punishment, and what do you think he feels about his own stance as a passive bystander?

Think about Heaney's structuring of the experience: the tender words and descriptions of the Iron Age body blend in the eighth stanza into the tarring and feathering incident, which is in full focus in the final two **quatrains**. How does the early part (about the body from the bog) affect the ways in which you respond to the later part (about Northern Ireland)?

The speaker digs deeper into his own conscience at the close of the poem. He admits that he would 'connive / in civilized outrage' at the act of punishment, but also understands 'the exact / and tribal intimate revenge'. This ending has attracted much critical comment. Do you think that, by both feeling for the victim and understanding the punishers, the poet is sitting uncomfortably on the fence, or even offering a justification for violence? Or is Heaney refusing courageously to simplify moral, emotional and tribal complexities, and bravely laying bare his own mixed feelings — however unpalatable they might be?

'Timer' by Tony Harrison

'Timer' (1978), by Tony Harrison (born 1937), is explored in Chapter 3, page 42.

'Long Finish' by Paul Muldoon

'Long Finish' (1998), by Paul Muldoon (born 1951), is a tribute to the poet's wife – celebrating ten years of marriage. Muldoon plays with an intricate and demanding form: the **ballade**. It is a double ballade – the first, third, fifth, seventh and ninth stanzas share one refrain; while the second, fourth, sixth, and eighth share another. The tenth stanza forms a kind of postscript (or envoi) to each ballade: it opens with an address to the poet's prince (in this case, the poet's wife, referred to as 'Princess of Accutane'). While sounding like the Princess of Aquitaine, who was one of the world's most powerful and wealthy women in the 12th century, the Accutane in 'Princess of Accutane' is actually a prescription drug taken for ailments such as eczema. The tenth stanza's fourth line ends with one refrain, and its final line with the other. Further complexities may be found in the poem's abrupt shift from the appreciation of the wife to, in the fifth and sixth stanzas, anecdotes of violence in Northern Ireland and, later, the references to the Japanese play *Matsukaze*.

Think about the ways in which love is presented in the poem and how the poem fits into traditions of love poetry (including the ballade) that celebrate a loved one. To what extent do you feel that marriage is presented in a playful and exciting way? Consider the presentation of the wife, including images of her body and comments on shared experiences. Think about the effects of the final stanza and consider the extent to which the poem, like a fine wine, produces a long finish.

Key term

Ballade. A French form that was popular in the 14th and 15th centuries. It usually opens with an address to the poet's prince, and it uses eight-line stanzas (rhyming ababbcbc). The last line of the first stanza recurs as a refrain in the last line of the subsequent stanzas. A ballade ends with an envoi – a kind of postscript, which begins with an address to the poet's prince and is a quatrain (rhymed abab).

Did you know?

The title refers to the persistent flavour of wine that lingers on the palate after swallowing wine; it is usually an indicator of high quality.

Activity

Research *Matsukaze* and the characters Maksuke (Pining Wind), Murasami (Autumn Rain) and Yukihira (the poet). In what ways are the allusions to this play appropriate to this poem, which celebrates lasting love?

'After the Lunch' by Wendy Cope

'After the Lunch' (2002), by Wendy Cope (born 1945), expresses a speaker's thoughts and feelings after a romantic lunch, when she realizes that she has fallen in love. The experience is communicated directly in three quatrains, which are rhymed aabb. The diction is everyday, and the poet seems to be exploring love in a down-to-earth way. That said, there is much subtlety to consider. Look, for example, at how the emotion intensifies and self-awareness grows as the poem develops. In the first stanza, emotion is masked as the speaker explains her tears of passion as having been produced by the 'weather conditions'. In the second, she 'is trying to think' and the voice of logic and reason seems, to begin with, to be dominant: 'This is nothing. You're high on the charm and the drink'. However, the final two lines offer a less logical mode of experience: 'a song' is playing inside her. In the last stanza, the voice of logic and reason resurfaces temporarily – 'You're a fool' – only to be silenced with: 'I don't care'. The penultimate line forms a conclusion, which articulates a more general truth arising from the specific incident detailed in the poem: 'The head does its best, but the heart is the boss'.

Consider the effects of the metaphor of 'the juke-box inside me' at the centre of the poem. How does the refrain 'On Waterloo Bridge' create effects? To what extent might this setting –the place, the name and the idea of being on a bridge – have symbolic significance?

'To John Donne' by Michael Symmons Roberts

'To John Donne' (2004), by Michael Symmons Roberts (born 1963), uses love to explore other issues. While written in the loving voice of one describing a woman stripping as a couple prepare for bed, it also addresses a scientific issue: the effects of the mapping of the human genome (the complete set of genetic information encoded in a person's body). While this information could be beneficial for medicine, what is contentious is the idea that a company could patent such information. The poem seems to ask the reader to consider the implications of someone owning the internal workings of their body.

The poem's title draws attention to its heavy **intertextual** debt to Donne's 'To his Mistress Going to Bed', whose speaker expresses the joy at discovering his lover and delight watching her undress.

> **Did you know?**
>
> The numbers in the final stanza are actually part of the human genome: a part that has already been patented.

> **Activity**
>
> Find a copy of Donne's poem – it is widely anthologized and readily available online, for example on http://www.poetryfoundation.org/poem/180683 – and think about the similarities and differences between the two poems. Consider point of view. What are the effects of Symmons Roberts using third person and Donne first person? Which words and phrases from Donne does Symmons Roberts use, and how do these affect the way we respond to the new poem? To what extent are they debased by their new context? Consider form and the different effects created by Donne's **verse paragraphs** and Symmons Roberts' **tercets**.

'The Love Poem' by Carol Ann Duffy

'The Love Poem' (2005), by Carol Ann Duffy (born 1955), explores love by incorporating fragments from famous love poems into her writing. Despite its beautiful and joyful language, the poem is ambiguous. Each stanza begins with a subordinate clause – 'Till love . . .' – but lacks a main verb. Whilst this is in keeping with the poem's collage style, some may find this unfinished quality dissatisfying. For example, what does 'Till love exhausts itself, longs for the sleep of words' mean? Is love about to fall asleep in a post-coital languor, or has it been used up so that it is no longer there except in the words of others? Could it be said that the poem is much more about poetry than it is about love? You might consider the poem in the tradition of poems that explore love directly and compare it to other poems that refer to previous love poetry.

Activity

Explore the poem's rich **intertextuality** by discovering the sources of its poetic borrowings and then considering, first, the effects of each one in the poem and then of the borrowings as a whole. Find sources for the following (one is from the Bible):

- 'my mistress' eyes'
- 'let me count the ways'
- 'come live / with me'
- 'one hour with thee'
- 'dear heart, / how like you this?'
- 'look in thy heart / and write'

- 'there is a garden in her face'
- 'O my America! / my new found land'
- 'behold thou art fair'
- 'the desire of the moth / for the star'

Planning and writing your answer

Planning your answer

Examination-style question: 'Compare how the authors of the texts you have studied present barriers to love.'

This question is open enough to allow you to select whichever prose text you have studied. Most, for example, explore barriers that spring from circumstances, family and/or society; the demands of a romance plot also often require obstacles to be placed between the protagonists before they are united at the climax of a novel. Less tangible types of barrier might include those of time, distance or internal barriers – something within a character that prevents a couple from being together.

You can generate a range of ideas if you adopt the following systematic approach:

A Place the novel's title in the centre of a page, then spend a minute or so jotting down notes about what springs to mind as you consider 'barriers to love'. Then channel your thoughts, by making notes on each of the following in turn:

- *Characters* and the barriers they might be associated with.
- *Themes, ideas, concerns* – how they are related to barriers.
- The writer's *methods* – how he or she uses literary techniques to suggest barriers.
- *Contexts* – and how these might relate to the idea of barriers to love.

B Consider the poems in your anthology. Remember that you will have a clean copy of this, and also of your prose text, in the exam. Which poems spring to mind first? Note the ways in which they involve 'barriers to love' and their connections to your novel. To avoid overlooking useful material, remind yourself about each poem in turn – jotting down notes and making possible connections to your prose text. For each relevant poem, write notes and *make connections to the novel* in the following areas:

- *Speaker* and *addressee*, or other *characters*.
- *Themes, ideas, concerns.*
- The poet's *methods*.
- *Contexts.*

C You should now be ready to select your best material. Aim for a balance between the novel and the anthology. You can structure your answer by following an adapted model of the ones suggested in Chapter 3.

One example of structure could be:

1. Introduction (explore how the topic is addressed in both the novel and the anthology)
2. Poem A
3. Poem A and the novel
4. Poem B
5. Poem B and the novel
6. Poem C
7. Poem C and the novel
8. Conclusion

The above structure is one that helps you to cover both the novel and the anthology in a balanced way, and also allows for detailed exploration of the methods used in each poem. Remember, too, that an answer should, at some points, use both contextual information and alternative viewpoints to enrich its argument. (Alternative approaches might take the form of critical views or approaches, or alternative readings.)

Remember that you could cover two or three poems in detail or range more widely. The former approach is more straightforward and an easy way for you to explore poems in depth. The latter approach offers more scope for a conceptual, sophisticated response, but – handle it badly – and your essay could sound superficial.

Introducing the chosen comparative set texts: post-1900 prose

The Great Gatsby by F. Scott Fitzgerald (1926)

The Great Gatsby is narrated by Nick Carraway, who recalls the summer of 1922, when he rented a house next to Jay Gatsby's mansion, which was on the opposite side of the bay from his distant cousin, Daisy Buchanan. Gatsby and his relationship with Daisy are at the heart of Carraway's story. Unreliable, but fascinating, the narrative offers no easy answers to questions such as how Gatsby made his money, and whether his and Daisy's love was as idyllic as we are led to believe. Any study of Fitzgerald's authorial methods should consider his use of narrative: how we view Nick determines how we view everything else. Symbolism, settings and imagery are also important, as is the extent to which we read the novel as a **modernist** text.

A Room with a View by E. M. Forster (1908)

Set amongst the English upper middle class, E. M. Forster's *A Room with a View* narrates the story of Lucy Honeychurch, who holidays in Florence (where she is kissed by the unconventional George Emerson). Back in England, Lucy is torn between her feelings for George and her obligations to her fiancé, Cecil. She sends George away then breaks off her engagement, but, after a chance meeting with George, she overcomes her repression and the two elope to Florence. Some authorial methods for you to explore include symbolism, setting and imagery, as well as **satire** and the genres of comedy and romance.

The Go-Between by L. P. Hartley (1953)

The Go-Between by L. P. Hartley is framed by the thoughts of a man in his 60s who discovers a diary written when he was 13. The story concerns the summer of 1900, when Leo stayed with the aristocratic Maudsley family and became a messenger for the beautiful Marian Maudsley and her lover, Ted, the local farmer. Leo grows uncomfortable delivering the messages, but is pressurized into continuing. Events reach a climax when Marion's mother and Leo discover Marion and Fred *in flagrante delicto*. Ted shoots himself and Marion has a breakdown. Back in the present, elderly Leo visits Marion, who asks him to take a final message – of how much she loved Ted – to her grandson. The authorial methods for you to analyse include Hartley's narrative structure and point of view, as well as the heavy symbolism and foreshadowing and the use of the romance and **Bildungsroman** genres.

> ### Link
>
> Aspects of *Atonement* (see below) are reminiscent of *The Go-Between*. *Spies*, one of the novels set for the 'Modern times' option (see page 148) also owes it a large **intertextual** debt.

Rebecca by Daphne du Maurier (1938)

Daphne du Maurier's *Rebecca* is told from the perspective of a diffident woman from a modest background who marries the wealthy Maxim de Winter. The novel reveals details about her predecessor, the elegant socialite Rebecca de Winter, and we gradually discover that she was far from being the perfect upper-class wife that we imagined. The novel draws on genres such as gothic and crime or thriller. Setting – as well as symbolism and imagery – is an important authorial method, as are narrative structure and point of view.

Atonement by Ian McEwan (2001)

In Ian McEwan's *Atonement*, 13-year old Briony Tallis witnesses her elder sister Cecilia cavorting naked in a fountain in front of Robbie, a Cambridge graduate and son of their cleaning lady. Later, she opens a letter from Robbie to Cecilia and is outraged at what she considers the outpourings of a 'sex maniac'. In a separate incident, Briony stumbles upon a sexual assault on her cousin at night in the grounds of the house. Falsely, she claims to have seen the perpetrator clearly. As a result, Robbie is sent to prison and Cecilia's life is ruined. Some of McEwan's methods for you to explore include narrative structure and point of view – at the end we learn that the whole book is the construction of the mature Briony, written in atonement for her actions as an adolescent.

Introducing the chosen comparative set texts: pre-1900 poems

'Whoso list to hunt' by Sir Thomas Wyatt

Sir Thomas Wyatt (1503–1542) is credited with bringing the sonnet form from Italy to England. A courtier to King Henry VIII, he was once imprisoned for an improper relationship with the King's then mistress, Anne Boleyn.

In 'Whoso list to hunt' the lover is cast as a huntsman and the beloved a female deer (hind). Note the hopelessness of the relationship; for example, consider the effects of the metaphor in which the speaker is like someone trying to catch the wind in a net. Look at the subtle structural effects: for example, how we move closer to the deer until, in the **couplet**, we are so close that we can read the inscription around her neck. Consider this conclusion and the extent to which you consider it a climax or an anti-climax.

In the first eight lines, despite each **quatrain** moving the poem forward, the central couplet seems to draw the reader's attention back. In the first quatrain, the emphasis is on the speaker being tired chasing his beloved: 'But as for me, alas, I may no more. / The vain travail hath wearied me so sore'. You might also like to consider the poem as being divided into an **octave** and a **sestet**. The octave explains the problem and the speaker's feelings in general terms, then the sestet provides a vivid example, culminating in the image of the writing on the collar. A biographical reading in which the reader sees the deer as Anne Boleyn is possible, but also consider what the poem might be saying about wider issues like unattainable love and possessive, controlling love.

'Sonnet 116' by William Shakespeare

Shakespeare's (1564–1616) 'Sonnet 116' explores the qualities of love and its enduring nature, with each of the three quatrains building on this idea. You might explore the use of imagery. How, for example, does Shakespeare use nautical language in the second quatrain, and what are the effects of the **personification** of time in the third?

While 'Sonnet 116' is a resounding endorsement of the power of love (indeed, it is a poem that is often read at weddings), it is a particularly high-minded type of love. Throughout, we are reminded of the difficulties that love has to withstand. For example, it doesn't alter 'when it alteration finds'; the language is deliberately vague – we might take the 'alteration' to be anything from a temporary absence to an infidelity. Similarly, love is presented as being able to withstand 'tempests' – might this, pessimistically, suggest that love is going to have to endure turbulent times? Finally, doesn't 'bear[ing] it out until the edge of doom' sound rather grim – more so than the 'till death do us part' in the Anglican marriage vows? Rather than the joy of love, Shakespeare seems to show us its endurance: what it can put up with. If we consider the poems that follow it in Shakespeare's sonnet sequence – Sonnets 117, 118, 119 and 120 all deal with infidelity – we might wonder if 'Sonnet 116' presents an unattainable form of love.

You might also consider the sonnet's **couplet**. To what extent do you think it boastful – does it show the poet to be someone who is a little too insistent – protesting too much – or one who is overly pleased at the strength of his argument and his facility with his craft?

'The Flea' by John Donne

In 'The Flea' by John Donne the speaker uses a flea to present arguments to the addressee in favour of them having sex. In the first stanza, he argues that denying him sex is as trifling as the flea, and – since it bit them both and contains their blood – it is as if they have had sex already. In the second, the speaker asks the addressee not to kill the flea; this would be sacrilegious, because the flea (which contains the blood of them both) is like their bed or temple. In the final stanza, the speaker responds to the addressee's action of killing the flea. The line of argument shifts: to give herself to the speaker would cause no more harm to her honour than was caused to her by the death of the flea. There are many aspects to explore in the poem: from the metaphysical **conceit** involving the flea to the development of the speaker's argument – and the witty way in which he develops it – to the elaborate form used (each stanza is comprised of a quatrain, made up of two couplets, and a triplet).

'To His Coy Mistress' by Andrew Marvell

Andrew Marvell's (1621–1678) 'To His Coy Mistress' is another metaphysical poem in which a speaker uses logic and wit in the service of seduction. Firmly in the *carpe diem* tradition, the poem's speaker invites the addressee to 'seize the day' by sleeping with the speaker before it is too late. The argument proceeds in the form of a syllogism (two premises followed by a conclusion). First, if the couple had endless time, there would be nothing wrong with the woman's shyness; the speaker would spend long periods courting her and praising her. Secondly, time is hurrying forwards and threatens, for example, to turn her beauty to dust and his desire to ashes. So, the speaker concludes, they should take their opportunity to express their love physically while they still can.

Like Donne's work, Marvell's poem is marked by wit. Note, for example, the amusing idea and the amusing rhyme in the first **verse paragraph** that – without the constraint of time – their chaste courtship could go on, literally, for ages: from ten years before the flood (in 1656 BC) she could, if she wanted, decide to 'refuse / Till the conversion of the Jews (an event foretold as taking place just before the Second Coming of Christ). Note also the way in which Marvell uses numbers as he makes novel use of the **blazon** by moving down her body with incremental attention: first praising the addressee's eyes for 'a hundred years' then spending four times as long on her breasts, before reaching her lower regions and lavishing 'thirty thousand' years on them. Consider how the mood of the speaker changes as the poem progresses, and how readers might respond to his wooing. Are there times when you feel that he is making a serious point, or do you feel that he is manipulating the woman he is addressing? How do you think the following elements develop as the poem progresses: the types of imagery, the pace of the poem, the persuasiveness of the examples?

'The Scrutiny' by Richard Lovelace

In 'The Scrutiny' by Richard Lovelace (1618–1657) the speaker addresses an unnamed woman to whom he promised fidelity the previous night. After arguing that it is impossible to keep his promise to her, he explains that he must seek other partners, but concludes that, afterwards, he might return to the addressee. Note the poem's immediacy: it begins, seemingly in the middle of an argument, by posing a question, and it uses the present and future tenses as the speaker uses his powers of rhetoric to argue out of commitment (offering the possibility of a reunion to clinch his case). Despite being open about his desire to seek others, at the heart of the poem, in lines 10 and 11, are images of him being able to 'dote' upon the addressee's 'face' and find 'joy in (her) brown hair'. Think about the ways in which the speaker and his attitude to women (including the addressee) are presented in the poem. Is his attitude simply offensive to a modern reader, or might he exhibit redeeming qualities? How do you respond to the language he uses? For example, consider the heroic diction and imagery and the way in which the search for promiscuous sex is presented in terms of discovery and warfare: the speaker must 'search the black and fair' and he compares himself to a mineralist who sounds 'for treasure'; the joys of love are termed 'spoils' with which he will be 'crowned'. Also consider the significance of the title.

Absent from Thee' by John Wilmot, Earl of Rochester

'Absent from Thee', by John Wilmot, Earl of Rochester (1647–1680), shares similarities with 'The Scrutiny'. It also expresses an attempt by a rake to explain his compulsion for infidelities, but perhaps it also conveys the emotional damage that such behaviour inflicts – though only the man's pain is considered. Consider the ways in which infidelity is presented. Note, for example, all the unfavourable words used to describe the man who strays and his feelings at having done so. You might like to contrast such feelings with those in the penultimate quatrain, in which he imagines his feelings upon being welcomed back by the addressee. Think also about the ways in which the poem uses pace to enhance its meaning, and consider the effects of the imagery of both heaven and hell.

Some other lyrics, again of undetermined date, have been hailed as timeless and exquisite. One often held in such esteem is the song 'Absent from thee, I languish still', with its nicely understated irony and plaintive modulations of the language of religious yearning.

'The Garden of Love' by William Blake

This poem contrasts what Blake sees as the natural human instincts of love and sex, with the repression of these instincts by the institutionalizing effects of organized religion. You could focus on many details in this simple – yet at the same time complex – poem. Note, for example, the story that the poem tells, and the way in which it uses repetition.

'Ae Fond Kiss' by Robert Burns

'Ae Fond Kiss' (1791) is a song that Robert Burns sent to Agnes 'Nancie' McLehose (a sophisticated woman who was separated from her husband and lived a quiet, genteel life in Edinburgh). She enjoyed a passionate, but chaste, friendship with Burns, but later decided to leave Edinburgh to join her husband who was working in the Caribbean. 'Ae Fond Kiss' is Burns's account of their parting. Note the simplicity of the language and the sincerity of its sentiment. Consider the effects of the cluster of uses of the word 'love' at the heart of the poem and how it is framed by two near-identical quatrains.

Activity

Find out more about John Wilmot, Earl of Rochester and the literature of the Restoration (named after the time when the monarchy was restored in 1660). Under King Charles II, the theatres were reopened and women appeared on the stage for the first time. Attitudes towards love and sex became much more liberal than in the preceding years, when the country was ruled by Cromwell and Parliament. In what ways might issues of the time be reflected in the poem?

Did you know?

The pure feelings celebrated in the poem belie the messiness of Burns's actual life. For instance, while he was enjoying intellectual stimulation with Nancie, he slept with her servant, who, in 1788, bore him a son.

'She Walks in Beauty' by Lord Byron

'She Walks in Beauty', by Lord Byron (1788–1824), expresses admiration for a woman who unites beauty of body, mind and spirit. There is a biblical ring to the first phrase; however, the woman does not walk in the law of the Lord, but in beauty. She seems simultaneously a person and something spiritual or emblematic. Note how Byron uses opposites throughout the poem to suggest the harmonious nature of her beauty. Her beauty is not only physical, but also mental. The second part of the second stanza makes this clear: her thoughts are 'serenely sweet' and her face is 'pure'. The ideas of balance continue in the final stanza, where the inner beauty is revealed to be spiritual and there is harmony between the mind and the heart. Consider the ways in which Byron presents the woman. To what extent do you think he simply objectifies her, or does he do more than admire her physical features?

'La Belle Dame Sans Merci' by John Keats

In 'La Belle Dame Sans Merci', by John Keats (1795–1821), a knight meets a beautiful woman who is half-human, half-fairy, and falls completely in love. After loving her, he falls asleep to awake on a hillside in the cold, where he sees 'other pallid and wasted figures' who have been enchanted, just like him. Many read this as a poem about obsession: once the knight has experienced the power of love with an immortal creature, he is doomed to loiter miserably, unable to take pleasure from life again. Note how Keats uses the **ballad** form to tell the story dramatically and directly. The first three quatrains are speech from the speaker, who has noticed the miserable and sick-looking knight and wants to know what is wrong with him. The next eight tell the story of his encounter with the fairy, and the last concludes the poem by confirming that the experience recounted is the reason for his state of health and temperament. To comment on the poem's presentation of love and sexuality, look closely at the descriptions of the fairy and her actions. The fifth stanza might be read as **pastoral** love, but it can also be seen as depicting acts of sex. Comment on the presentation of the fairy throughout; in what way is she presented as both highly desirable and deadly? What does the framing effect of the conversation between knight and speaker add to the poem? Include a comment on the repetition of words from the first stanza in the final one.

'Remember' by Christina Rossetti

'Remember', by Christina Rossetti (1830–1894), is a Petrarchan sonnet addressing a loved one and how he should feel about her after her death. On a first reading, it seems like a delicate poem that expresses a tender and considerate form of love. Used five times, the word 'remember' reverberates throughout the poem, but the thoughtful speaker reconsiders in the **sestet** and instructs the addressee to forget her if remembering would make him sad. That, however, is not the only way to read the poem. Some readers might feel that the speaker's volte face is undermined by the previous four uses of the word 'remember'; perhaps, whatever she says at the end, she has a powerful wish to be remembered. The poem is ambiguous in other ways too: is the love between the man and woman presented as being imperfect? The world to come, some might argue, is more of an attraction to the speaker than the addressee: it is 'the silent land', that she 'half turn[s]' towards; and religious belief seems at least as strong as love – the speaker seems to feel that the world is a place of 'darkness and corruption' and she is concerned that the addressee has sufficient time to

Key term

Ballad. A long poem that tells a story, and usually has a fast pace, with repetition a common feature 'pray'. Looking at the relationship more cynically, perhaps it is not so satisfying as first it seemed. Despite the gentle tone and the fragile speaker's focus on the addressee, it seems that he might be seen as domineering in the relationship. Look at the grammar of the sentences; the man always seems to be in control. The speaker writes of the time 'When *you* can no more hold *me* by the hand' and speaks of how 'You tell *me* of *our future* that *you planned*'. In both examples, he is the subject and she the object; the first one could show him leading her, and the second shows him controlling their future. How do you read the speaker's tone of voice: are there times when you think she is tender and loving; are there times when you think she is callous or nonchalant?

> **Activity**
>
> Find out more about Christina Rossetti. Consider how a more detailed understanding of her deeply held religious beliefs, or her ill-health, might shape your reading of the poem. Find out about the position of women in Victorian society and use this to inform your response to the poem and the ones by Hardy that follow.

'The Ruined Maid' and 'At an Inn' by Thomas Hardy

The two poems by Thomas Hardy (1840–1928) included in the anthology offer contrasting experiences of love. 'The Ruined Maid' is a comic poem, which imagines a 'fallen woman' returning to the village of her youth and having a conversation with a friend in which the reader realizes that the fallen woman is leading a much more comfortable life than the woman who stayed in the village. 'At an Inn' is more serious, and the voice of its speaker is muted and reflective. Using the first person plural, it narrates the experience of a couple who were not – as those at the inn thought – conducting a sexual affair; now, in the present, ironically, they yearn for the kind of relationship that was attributed to them.

Consider how 'The Ruined Maid' presents the different lives lived by the two women, and reflect on how Hardy creates two separate characters and his reasons for this. You might like to comment on, for example, the use of dialogue, accent and dialect. Discuss the effects of these features and how they work together. Think about how your response to the poem can be shaped by context. For example, some readers believe that the 'ruined maid' is a mistress, while others believe that she is a prostitute.

You might like to explore the ways in which Hardy's narrative creates drama in 'At an Inn'. For example, think about the use of an inn as a location; how is this appropriate and how does Hardy use it in the narrative? Consider the presentation of those at the inn, including the use of direct speech. Comment on how the story builds and on its anti-climax, which comes right at the heart of the poem. You might also think about the uses of figurative language, such as the imagery of the chilled breath and the buzzing fly on the window in the poem's central stanza and the personification of love.

'Non sum qualis eram bonae sub regno Cynarae' by Ernest Dowson

'*Non sum qualis eram bonae sub regno Cynarae*' (I am not as I was in the reign of the good Cynara), by Ernest Dowson (1867–1900), is a poem of yearning for a purer love. It is set on the morning after a night which the debauched speaker spent with another woman (presumably a prostitute) and when he experienced powerful feelings for his former love, Cynara. The poem is dramatic, full of emotion and wonderful to read aloud (a YouTube search should reveal performances of the poem by famous actors, such as Richard Burton). Notice how the poet uses an elaborate stanzaic form: all but the fifth line in each stanza are Alexandrines (a line of twelve syllables comprised of six iambs); in the last three lines of each stanza, a line of iambic pentameter is enveloped between the refrains, which rhyme. This shorter line adds a breathing space before each stanza's dramatic conclusion: 'I have been faithful to thee, Cynara! In my fashion.' Note the poetic use of the archaic pronoun 'thee' (usually denoting special intimacy) and the exclamatory utterance of the lost love's name. Think about the experiences and emotions conveyed in the poem and how they are structured. For example, how does Dowson make the emotions of the speaker in the last stanza seem even more intense than those of the previous ones?

Consider the presentation of Cynara. You could view her as being a woman he left, but only recognizes as his true love in retrospect – something that he tries to blot from his mind through self-destructive behaviour. But if we consider Cynara as a former lover who died – perhaps her 'pale lost lilies' suggest death – are we more sympathetic to the speaker? You might also consider the use of the Roman name Cynara. To what extent might Cynara be symbolic rather than real?

Did you know?

Used as the title of a book and film set during the American Civil War, 'gone with the wind' is one of the two most famous quotations from Dowson. The other is from a poem entitled 'Vitae Summa Brevis...': 'They are not long, the days of wine and roses'.

Further reading

Books

Gilbert S. and Gubar S. (1979; 2000) *The Madwoman in the Attic*, New Haven: Yale University Press.

Websites

http://pemberley.com/

This useful website offers online annotated versions of all the Jane Austen novels, including *Persuasion*, plus family trees, pictures of locations and much more.

http://www.bbc.co.uk/arts/robertburns/

This BBC website offers recorded readings of 'Ae Fond Kiss', as well as comments on the poem and a range of excellent supporting material about Burns.

http://www2.warwick.ac.uk/fac/arts/english/writingprog/archive/writers/muldoonpaul/180102/

On this website a selection of poems are read aloud by Paul Muldoon; the introductions offer insights into his work.

http://sheerpoetry.co.uk/

A website to which Carol Ann Duffy and other contemporary writers contribute.

http://www.bl.uk/romantics-and-victorians/articles/

The British Library website offers a range of relevant resources for literature, including essays on decadent writers.

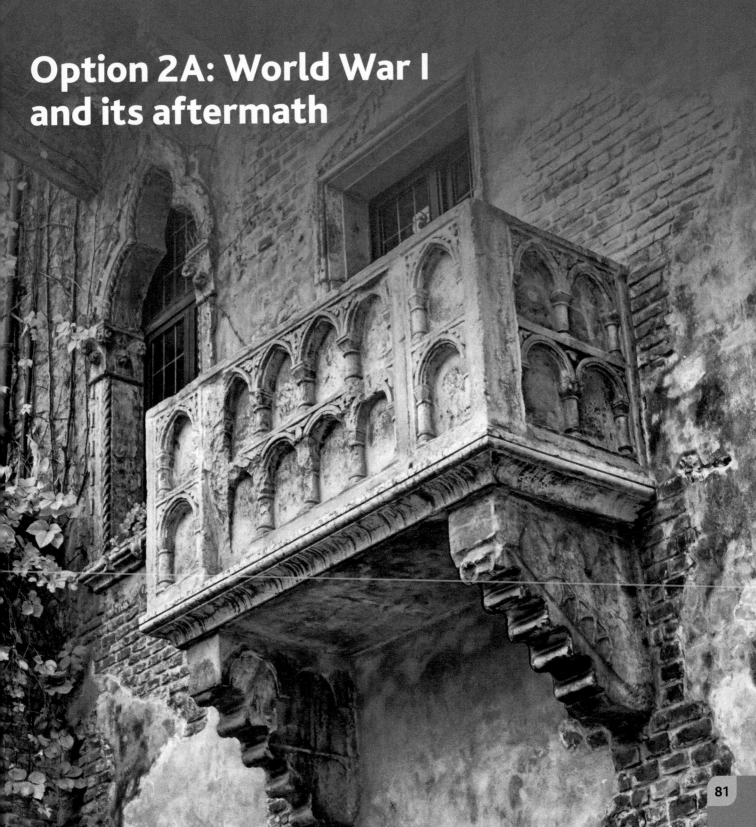

Component 2: Texts in shared contexts

Option 2A: World War I and its aftermath

This chapter will:

- explore the idea of studying texts in a shared context
- review the texts available for study within this shared context.

The poetry, prose and drama that you will study for the option on 'World War I and its aftermath' was published from the time of the conflict, throughout the remaining years of the 20th century, and into the early years of the 21st century. These works of literature range from those directly involved in the conflict – who wrote during, soon after and much later than the events themselves – through to modern and contemporary writers, who relied on research. Attitudes towards the conflict changed – sometimes rapidly and in complex ways – from 1914 to 1918. The same can be said for the 100-year period since the war. The social, political and cultural landscape has also changed throughout the last century, sometimes directly or indirectly as a result of the war. All of these factors have contributed to changing attitudes towards World War I, and these attitudes are reflected in the literature you will study.

Activity

Listen to a recording of a modern anti-war song, such as 'War' (originally performed by Edwin Starr and also covered by Bruce Springsteen and Frankie Goes to Hollywood), and also to James Thompson's poem 'Rule Britannia' (printed below), which was set to music by Thomas Arne and adopted as a national song in the 18th century (these are the original lyrics). What are the key messages expressed by each song about war? Do these different messages apply to all wars? Based on what you know already about World War I, to what extent do they apply to that conflict too?

Rule Britannia

When Britain first, at Heaven's command
Arose from out the azure main;
This was the charter of the land,
And guardian angels sang this strain:
'Rule, Britannia! rule the waves:
'Britons never will be slaves.'

The nations, not so blest as thee,
Must, in their turns, to tyrants fall;
While thou shalt flourish great and free,
The dread and envy of them all.
'Rule, Britannia! rule the waves:
'Britons never will be slaves.'

Still more majestic shalt thou rise,
More dreadful, from each foreign stroke;
As the loud blast that tears the skies,
Serves but to root thy native oak.
'Rule, Britannia! rule the waves:
'Britons never will be slaves.'

Thee haughty tyrants ne'er shall tame:
All their attempts to bend thee down,

Will but arouse thy generous flame;
But work their woe, and thy renown.
'Rule, Britannia! rule the waves:
'Britons never will be slaves.'

To thee belongs the rural reign;
Thy cities shall with commerce shine:
All thine shall be the subject main,
And every shore it circles thine.
'Rule, Britannia! rule the waves:
'Britons never will be slaves.'

The Muses, still with freedom found,
Shall to thy happy coast repair;
Blest Isle! With matchless beauty crown'd,
And manly hearts to guard the fair.
'Rule, Britannia! rule the waves:
'Britons never will be slaves.'

James Thomson (1763)

World War I and its aftermath: key issues

The specification identifies 13 suggested issues, some of which may have arisen already in your discussion about the two songs. They are:

1. Imperialism and nationalism
2. Recruitment and propaganda
3. Life on the front line
4. Responses on the home front
5. Pacifism
6. Generals and soldiers
7. Slaughter
8. Heroism
9. Peace and memorials
10. Writers in action and writers looking back
11. The political and social aftermath
12. Different and changing attitudes to the conflict
13. The war's impact on combatants, non-combatants and subsequent generations – as well as its social, political and personal and literary legacies

Activity

Discuss the extent to which the above issues are reflected in the two songs you listened to. How does your current knowledge of World War I relate to these issues?

World War I: overview

World War I is a key event in 20th-century history and in shaping our view of the modern world. Because this option is so bound up with one historical event, it would be a good idea to start with an overview of that event. The following summary is structured around seven key historical points, and can be used as a framework for reference as your study develops.

1. World War I, also known as the First World War or The Great War, began on 4 August 1914 and ended on 11 November 1918.

2. Britain entered the war as part of the Triple Alliance with two of the other long-established powers of Europe, France and Russia. Initially, their aim was to protect the neutrality of Belgium, following its invasion by German forces under Kaiser Wilhelm II. Germany, a newly emergent power, was in turn allied to the other established power in Europe, the Austro-Hungarian Empire, as well as to the Ottoman Empire, which included Turkey and much of the Middle East.

3. In total, the war was responsible for around 10 million deaths and over 37.5 million casualties.

4. The war was fought by land, sea and air, and was concentrated on two main fronts: the Western Front (so called because it was to Germany's west), centred around Ypres and later also the Somme; and the Eastern Front, centred around the Russian border and, to the south, the frontier with the Ottoman Empire.

5. The American entry into the war, in April 1917, ultimately proved decisive in bringing about Allied victory, and helped to stem the German breakthrough attack on Paris on the Western Front. The US-assisted counter-attack by Britain and France led to the collapse of the German army and to Germany's request for an armistice. Many Germans considered themselves humiliated by the harsh terms of the final peace treaty, and it can be argued that Germany's desire for revenge led ultimately to the rise of Hitler and World War II.

6. Initially, volunteers were sought to swell the ranks of the British Expeditionary Force, as the British army of professional soldiers sent to fight in France and Belgium was known in 1914. As Britain was primarily a naval power, her professional army was a relatively small one of around 100,000 men. A volunteer army of around 1 million men soon followed but, as the war dragged on and the casualties mounted, conscription had to be introduced in January 1916 (where men were 'called up' and ordered to fight). The BEF was led at first by Sir John French, who was later replaced by Field-Marshall Sir Douglas Haig.

7. Following the war, a flu pandemic – probably spread by large numbers of troops living and receiving hospital treatment in close proximity, before then returning home – infected 500 million people worldwide, and up to 100 million died as a result.

The literature of World War I and its aftermath includes a great variety of writing, covering four genres: poetry, drama, prose fiction and prose non-fiction (newspaper reports, letters, diaries, journals, memoirs and autobiographies). Texts about World War I and its aftermath have the following in common:

- The circumstances and events of the conflict itself.
- The thoughts, feelings and attitudes it generated at the time.
- The thoughts, feelings and attitudes it continues to generate to this day, as society reflects on the impact and legacy of the war.

Arguably, it is the nature of the links that connect texts on this subject – the shared context – that is the most compelling aspect of studying this body of work.

Looking at literature **synchronically** involves the scrutiny of discrete historical periods and how they can be understood in the context of time. Literary study always involves appreciation of both when the work was written (known as the **context of production**) and when the work is understood (the **context of reception**). However, synchronic study makes this consideration of time the primary focus. If we consider the extent of what might be meant by 'aftermath', then the time period under consideration stretches from the four years and three months of the war right up to the present day. Therefore, it is important to be aware of the full extent of the time period that is relevant here, and the significance of precise points in that timeline. Furthermore, at any one time, a range of different individuals, groups, ideas and attitudes need to be considered.

> **Key terms**
>
> **Contexts of production and reception.** Contexts are all of the various circumstances that can be taken into account when reading a text (*con* means with, *text* means something that has literally been woven together). **Contexts of production** are the various circumstances that can be considered as relevant at the time the text was written and first published/ first performed. **Contexts of reception** are the various circumstances that can be considered as relevant at the time the text is being read or watched, which might be many years later (in the case of World War I, maybe a century later).
>
> **Synchronically.** Looking at something within the concept of a particular time period.

World War I and its aftermath: requirements

Six core set texts and 14 chosen comparative set texts can be studied in this option. You will focus on *one prose text, one drama text* and *one poetry text*, one of which must have been published after 2000. The texts are all introduced below. The core set texts are introduced in some detail, while the chosen comparative set texts are discussed more briefly.

- **Core set texts:** You must study *at least one* of these in order to answer a question in Section A of your Paper 2 exam.
- **Chosen comparative set texts:** You must study *two* texts in order to answer the comparative context question in Section B of your Paper 2 exam. (*One* of the texts can be from the core set text list, if you *do not* use it in your Section A answer.)

Core set texts

Prose: *Regeneration*

The text

Regeneration by Pat Barker (1991) forms the first part of a trilogy. The two sequel novels are *The Eye in the Door* (1993) and *The Ghost Road* (1995), winner of the Booker Prize. *Regeneration* is set mainly at Craiglockhart Hospital in Edinburgh, and concerns shellshock victims and their treatment.

A central character is Dr William Rivers, who treats a variety of patients using pioneering, compassionate methods such as talking therapy and regressive hypnotherapy, alongside other doctors, such as Brock, who encourage creative and practical interests to help patients rediscover their real selves. Rivers' dilemma is that his official military role is to 'regenerate' men for a return to combat by treating their nerves, and yet he does not believe that treating men like broken machines is either in their interests or humane. Nor does he agree with the debasement of clinical psychology to speed broken men back to the front to die. His methods are set against those of Yealland, a brutally pragmatic therapist, who uses electroconvulsive methods and conditioning involving the use of fear of pain, to force patients back into being functioning soldiers. How Rivers deals with this dilemma, and how it will shape his future life and career, is a main feature of the novel.

Within this frame, Barker presents a variety of patients afflicted by war trauma. They include Burns and Billy Prior – two particularly intriguing creations who represent complex extremes of response to 'trigger' events. Prior's relationship with Sarah Lumb, a local munitions worker (or munitionette), is of central importance. Other patients include the well-known poets Siegfried Sassoon and Wilfred Owen. Barker presents a version of their meeting and friendship, including Sassoon's poetic mentoring of the young Owen.

The writer

Born in 1943 in Thornaby-on-Tees in North Yorkshire, Pat Barker quickly developed a reputation as a chronicler of working-class life. This is a recurrent interest, and she presents a cross-section of social and military life during the war. In *The Regeneration Trilogy* she specializes in writing based on research into real lives, blended with her fictional creations. In later novels too, such as *Life Class* (2007) and *Toby's Room* (2012), she threads her work with recurring characters and different perspectives on aspects of the conflict.

Themes

- Stress disorder: Barker presents a variety of complex conditions and a range of treatments (drawing in different ways on Freudian and other approaches).
- Male friendship and love: Bonds between soldiers, between patients, and between Rivers and his patients are all examined.
- Parenthood: A range of dysfunctional parents are set against Rivers as 'male mother'.
- Communication: Finding a voice is explored both literally and metaphorically across a range of characters.

Methods

Barker blends real characters (such as Rivers, Brock, Sassoon, Owen, Graves and Yealland) with fictional characters (such as Prior, Burns, Anderson and Sarah). She also uses real events, such as the meeting of Sassoon and Owen, and then improvises on them in order to offer imagined re-creations.

The variety of characters presented means that each one has his or her own narrative, which overlaps with others as the novel develops. Although writing in the third person, Barker explores individual points of view and thought processes to present complex characters who sometimes confuse the readers' sympathies and defy easy labelling. Despite the setting on the home front, Barker's presentation of patients' regressions and anecdotes embeds some narratives of trench warfare into the novel. Barker's methods also involve using other texts, such as Sassoon's *Finished with the War: A Soldier's Declaration*, and numerous poems by Owen and Sassoon.

Contexts

- Time: The text gives a 1991 perspective on the events of 1917. The historical time setting is dictated by the real-life people and events featured. The fictional characters and events portrayed reflect the horror of war and the resulting cynical attitudes prevalent in 1917, which are echoed in Barker's 1991 context as the orthodox view of the conflict: that it was a futile waste and the cause of enormous human damage.

- Genre: The novel emerged as the dominant genre for reflection on World War I. Barker's blend of detachment and sympathy is achieved through a broadly chronological division into four parts, but within this frame the point of view shifts in order to present ambiguous portraits of complex characters, events and issues.

- Gender: A female author presents a largely male cast of characters involved in a 'man's' war; but emasculation is one of its most significant physical and psychological consequences. Barker also presents a range of female characters on the Home Front. The late-20th-century context perhaps enables her to present masculinity and sexuality honestly and openly from the perspectives of both sexes.

- Location: The Craiglockhart setting adds much to the novel, but other settings in the Edinburgh area, Rivers' visit to Burns in Suffolk, Yealland's treatment room in London, and the various accounts of frontline experiences all enable Barker to depict life outside, even if the suggestion is that the war the individual characters keep in their heads is the ultimate setting.

> **Further reading**
> Find out more about *The Eye in the Door* and *The Ghost Road*. Aim to produce your own notes, using the framework of headings used in this chapter.

Prose: *Birdsong*

The text

Birdsong by Sebastian Faulks (1993) is the first part in a loose trilogy: it was followed by *The Girl at the Lion d'Or* and *Charlotte Gray*. The novel is concerned with Stephen Wraysford – before, during and after World War I. The first section, set in Amiens in 1910, deals with Stephen's passionate affair with Isabelle Azaire and the unravelling of her marriage when she discovers that she is pregnant with Stephen's child. The novel then jumps to the Somme in 1916 and then Ypres in 1917, as it follows Stephen's war career. In between these two episodes, Faulks introduces a parallel story of a year in the life of Elizabeth Benson, Stephen's granddaughter, and her enquiry into her grandfather's life. Her affair and subsequent pregnancy echo Stephen's experience two generations before.

Stephen's involvement in major conflicts with appalling casualties forms the main focus of the novel. Ultimately, Stephen is involved in the underground war of mining and counter-mining. This section of the novel is dominated by the character Jack Firebrace, who learns that his young son is dying of diphtheria, then dies himself before providing a possible escape for Stephen. Stephen survives, but only with the help of a German Jewish soldier; here, Faulks is clearly echoing Owen's poem 'Strange Meeting'. If this is Stephen's moment of epiphany about the preciousness of life, Elizabeth's comes when she visits the Thiepval Memorial to the Missing of the Somme. Stephen finds a new life beyond the war with Isabelle's sister, Jeanne, and Elizabeth makes a life with Robert and their child.

The writer

Sebastian Faulks was born in Berkshire in 1953. After studying English at Cambridge, he became a journalist. His first novels gave him an initial reputation as a historical novelist specializing in French settings and major 20th-century events. He often explores how external events and pressures impact on the inner life.

Themes

- Love: Faulks's subtitle 'A Novel of Love and War' foregrounds his exploration of the range of human love experiences, including sexual passion, adultery, friendship, parental love, patriotism, and so on.

- Death and destruction: Faulks presents an extraordinary number of sudden, often random deaths – after deliberately establishing sympathetic characters whom the reader wills to survive.

- History and forgetting: The novel makes the act of remembrance and research central to events, through the character of Elizabeth, while Stephen risks forgetting and remaining silent about a range of experiences and former friends.

- The horror of war: The recreations of the first day of the Somme, the Battle of Messines and the underground war are studies in graphic realism.

Methods

Faulks's novel is traditional in the sense that it follows the fortunes of a central protagonist in a chronological narrative. However, the novel is distinctive in its manipulation of time in that there are (a) significant leaps forward in time, and (b) a parallel narrative focused on Elizabeth. Both give the novel a 'time-slip' function that enables Faulks to create both harmony and dissonance. His use of key place and time settings, such as the first day of the Somme, Messines, the mines and, later, Thiepval Memorial in the 1970s, enables Faulks to present a story that is both personal and epic. Given the subtitle of the novel, the reader is perhaps struck most of all by the juxtaposition of the love affair with Isabelle and the documentary realism of suffering and death.

Contexts

- Time: The two time frames are clearly crucial to the novel's effect. The time of composition means that Faulks can look from the 1990s back to the 1970s – two important periods in the development of thinking about the war – and through both of these 'lenses' look back to the war itself, and even further back to the **pre-lapsarian** world of 1910.

- Genre: Elements of various genres are presented here: the historical novel, the **Bildungsroman**, romance, documentary epic, the 'time-slip' novel. The length and sweep of *Birdsong* suggest that Faulks is aiming for some kind of definitive statement about the war. The way in which he presents the sexual experiences of Stephen links *Birdsong* with the other World War I novels of this period. However, the section in the mines is an unusually distinctive attempt to explore a less well-known aspect of the war.

- Gender: A male author presents a central narrative about men in warfare. However, Faulks's presentation of Isabelle, Jeanne and Elizabeth arguably redresses any imbalanced perceptions that war is about men. Faulks leaves the reader in no doubt about the importance of these characters and their emotional impact.

- Location: Faulks locates most of the action in France, on the Somme front or close by. However, he also incorporates the Battle of Messines, close to Ypres in Belgium. This is perhaps both to acknowledge the two main Western Front locations for British soldiers, and to reflect a common experience they had – of being moved back and forth between these two locations.

> **Key term**
> **Pre-lapsarian.** Before the loss of innocence.

> **Further reading**
> Read the interview with Sebastian Faulks about the genesis of the novel, published in the *Independent*. This can found at http://www.independent.co.uk/arts-entertainment/books-interview--sebastian-faulks-the-bitter-taste-of-vichy-bottled-out-1174730.html

Drama: *Oh! What a Lovely War*

The text

The idea for this 1965 play has its origin in a piece for radio by Charles Chilton (1917–2013) about his father's experiences in the war. It uses a collage of non-fiction sources to assemble facts, songs and recollections into a whole that is touching yet, above all, an ironic critique of the war. It was developed with Chilton's cooperation into an epic satire for the theatre by the company of the Theatre Royal, Stratford East, and shaped primarily by its lead director, Joan Littlewood, using ensemble methods to research and improvise a series of fragments that made up a loose narrative entertainment. Another source was *The Donkeys* (1961) by Alan Clarke, and some scenes from that book were adapted in the drama. The plot is broadly chronological but it is impressionistic, giving snapshot scenes from, on the one hand, the lives of ordinary people on the home and Western Fronts, and on the other, the activities of politicians and generals.

The author

Although often named as the 'author', Joan Littlewood (1914–2002) oversaw this collaborative piece of writing. She brought together Charles Chilton and her collaborator Gerry Raffles (1924–1975), along with an ensemble cast, to develop the play. Littlewood had established the Theatre Workshop's base at the Theatre Royal, Stratford East in 1953. She was avowedly political in her approach, and a former member of the Communist Party.

Her influences were often from European theatre practitioners, such as Bertolt Brecht (1898–1956), and she applied their ideas to catering for British audiences.

Themes

- Ordinary people as victims of incompetence and ignorance: Littlewood offsets real-life figures, such as Sir John French and Douglas Haig, against often generic archetypes of soldiers, bystanders, suffragettes, and so on, to suggest a broad sweep of society. Scenes involving ordinary people with generic character names often portray an honest and/or humorous response to the absurdity of war. Littlewood engages the sympathy of the audience but without resorting to sentimentality.

- Futility: The use of set-piece scenes, intercut with statistics, headlines, songs and narrator's interjections, invariably stresses the pointlessness of military conflict by holding the apparent objectives up for ridicule.

- Military leaders as 'donkeys': French and Haig are presented as caricatures of stubborn, vain careerists – unaware of, or unconcerned about, the human costs of their tactics.

- Disconnections between classes, fronts and the powers involved: Littlewood presents the breakdown of communication as a basic characteristic of the whole conflict, so that lack of knowledge leads to lack of empathy, and all but the 'lions' and the innocent back home lose their common humanity.

Methods

Littlewood was keen to use the techniques of documentary epic and alienation that are often associated with the German dramatist Bertolt Brecht, who used them to distance the audience from what happens on stage. In this case, such techniques prevented the play from becoming a nostalgic trip down memory lane for the first audiences – many of whom would have felt chronologically and personally close to the events.

Oh! What a Lovely War achieves cohesion through:

- the presence of the narrator
- the running commentary of projected newspaper headlines and statistics
- the repertoire of popular songs
- the premise that the audience is watching a musical-hall variety performance led by clowns.

Key term

Agitprop. An art form with an explicitly political message.

This play is unique, in the sense that the subject matter and methods are inseparable, the result being an **agitprop** tour de force where the audience is almost forced to laugh at the horrific ridiculousness of this and all wars.

Contexts

- **Time:** The time setting involves an elliptical narrative of the whole conflict. This enables Littlewood to show the ways in which attitudes on all fronts changed as the war continued. The 1960s context is shaped by the publication of Clark's *The Donkeys* and the use of different media, including radio and television, to collate a version of events that reflects the concerns of the time; there was a widespread consciousness that propaganda and the nature of war involve enormous cost for very little gain.

- **Genre:** Littlewood explores an altogether different approach to representing the war on stage – combining the theories of European practitioners (such as Brecht) with working-class theatrical traditions (such as the music hall). The play reflects a new appetite for satire at the time, which combined anger and wit to challenge conventional British social attitudes.

- **Gender:** Littlewood was originally sceptical about any production that provided a stage – and therefore a voice – for patriarchal military power and methods. The result is a compromise, where tin hats and occasional explosions are tempered by Pierrot (clown) costumes and the sensibilities of the music-hall tradition. Her presentation of the suffragettes alongside traditional female stage stereotypes (such as chorus girls) clearly reflects questioning 1960s attitudes.

- **Location:** The panoramic sweep of the drama deliberately intercuts clashing locations on the home and fighting fronts for ironic effect, in an attempt to represent the totality of the war experience for all involved.

> **Further reading**
>
> Read the review of the original production written by famous drama critic Kenneth Tynan. You can find this at: http://www.theguardian.com/stage/2014/jan/31/kenneth-tynan-on-oh-what-a-lovely-war

Drama: *Journey's End*

The text

Journey's End by R. C. Sherriff (1928) deals with the four days' occupation of a front-line trench prior to a German offensive in 1918. In many ways, this countdown forms the structural and thematic basis for the play. Stanhope's company has taken charge of the trench, and the play deals with Stanhope's relationships with his subordinate officers.

All of the characters can be seen as war archetypes: Stanhope, a respected but battle-weary commander, who is tortured by inner demons; Raleigh, a naïve recruit, eager to please and impress; Osborne, a quietly authoritative public-school teacher; Hibbert, who is battle-shy and in need of coercion and coaxing; Trotter, cheery and lugubrious by turns; the Colonel, who is spokesman for the Brigadier, another 'donkey'. Sherriff also reveals complexities and surprises as Stanhope negotiates a series of crises but cannot escape his and the company's final doom.

The author

R. C. Sherriff (1896–1975) was an 18-year-old insurance clerk in 1914 when he first volunteered to join the BEF. Finally accepted in 1915, he arrived in France in 1916 and saw action at Messines and Vimy Ridge (the latter is referenced in the play). He later took part in the Third Battle of Ypres, otherwise known as Passchendaele, where he was seriously wounded for the second time.

His injuries meant that he served the remainder of the war as part of the Home Service of the East Surrey Regiment. His war record, then, gave him excellent qualifications for his best-known play about front-line combat. He returned to insurance work before seeking a new career as a scriptwriter in Hollywood.

Themes

- Camaraderie: The play presents close relationships between soldiers from the perspective of realism, rather than propaganda. Therefore Sherriff explores the challenges, complexities and peculiarities of men living in close proximity under very challenging circumstances. Stanhope's dilemma is how to balance closeness and sympathy with military discipline.

- Stress disorder: Each of the central characters has his own response towards stress, involving a coping mechanism that is in danger of becoming dysfunctional.

- The responsibilities of leadership: Sherriff presents Stanhope's priority as the welfare of his men (even though he can express this in harsh and manipulative ways), in contrast to the Colonel and the Brigadier (two remote figures who are more concerned with the efficiency of the war machine).

Methods

Perhaps Sherriff's most striking method is to restrict the setting of the play to a claustrophobic dugout. Action above is represented through stage directions and entrances and exits connected with the stages of combat leading up to and including the final barrage. Within this frame, Sherriff orchestrates a series of encounters, including public meetings and private, more intimate confessionals. His stage directions make use of subtle and symbolic lighting effects.

Contexts

- Time: Set in spring 1918, the play reflects the prevailing attitude at the time that the war appeared to be never-ending and doomed to destroy all those involved. At the same time, the presence of Raleigh keeps alive the spirit of 1914, which regards the war as an exciting and necessary conflict likely to end in victory. Much of the play's dynamic comes from the conflict between these attitudes.

- Genre: Sherriff is an exponent of realism and naturalism. These traditions are reflected in his presentation of flawed and complex characters and situations. The result is serious and compelling, but with moments of dark humour, surreal reflection and whimsy as his characters strive to escape and, failing that, cope with extraordinary stresses.

- Gender: This is a play by a combatant about other combatants in a frontline crisis. The absence of women is an interesting feature, almost a theme. Raleigh's sister, Madge, is engaged to Stanhope and assumptions about her sharply affect his behaviour and fuel his psychosis; Osborne and Trotter think and talk about their wives; Hibbert's pin-up postcards and sexual boasts are intended to impress his colleagues and distract from his failings as a soldier.

- Location: Sherriff is specific in locating his play near St Quentin, a crucial battlefront in the southern Somme area and the focus of intense fighting in the last phase of the war. The war was almost lost, then finally won, in this part of France.

> **Further reading**
>
> Read about the controversy the play created in *The Spectator*'s review of *Journey's End: The Classic War Play Explored* by Robert Gore-Langton. You can find the review at: http://www.spectator.co.uk/books/9097932/journeys-end-by-robert-gore-langton-review/

Poetry: *Up the Line to Death*

The text

Up the Line to Death, edited by Brian Gardner (1964), is a survey of 141 poems by male writers covering a range of views and experiences from at home and abroad. It is arranged roughly chronologically, and set out in themed sections reflecting locations (such as 'To Unknown Lands') or attitudes (such as 'A Bitter Taste'). The title is taken from Sassoon's 'Base Details', where complacent majors 'speed glum heroes up the line to death', and this announces Gardner's focus on fighting men.

The author

The editor, Brian Gardner, was a noted author, historian and biographer who specialized in World Wars I and II. The choice of poets represents a relatively early attempt to define a canon of key poets (Gardner has been criticized by more recent editors for his omissions and inclusions), but his focus on soldiers and soldier-poets also allows him to include lesser-known writers worthy of a place in his depiction of the war 'journey'. Gardner's choice is heavily based on biographical research, hence his brief descriptions of the poets' lives at the end of the book.

Themes

The themes are mostly defined by Gardner in his named sections. For example, his selection of patriotic verse is assembled under the title 'Happy is England Now', whereas poems accepting the grim reality of war in practice are framed in sections such as 'Death's Kingdom'. This arrangement enables students to see the broad as well as the more nuanced changes in attitude as the war developed.

Methods

Some of Gardner's editorial methods have been outlined above. Others include his use of a 'Prelude' and 'Epilogue', each of one poem, and a selection of reflective poems variously about armistice and the human cost, called 'At Last, at Last!'. The use of quotations from poems as titles for sections (such as 'O Jesus, Make it Stop', from Sassoon's poem 'Attack') encourages cross-referencing between poems and sections. The poems themselves represent diverse poetic methods.

Contexts

- Time: First published in 1964, the anthology coincided with that crucial period when the potent myth of 'lions led by donkeys' emerged; most of the poems are written by soldiers directly involved in action. Arguably, it introduced a new generation to reading World War I poetry, and became part of the anti-war movement of the time – as part of which World War I emerged as powerful evidence of the futility of all wars. As the first poem is from 1914 and the last from 1918, it defines its time frame specifically. However, only some of the poems are dated, so it is not easy to track a simple journey from idealism to cynicism.

- Genre: Given the nature of the poets included, there is a prevalence of traditional and lyric forms and styles. Some modernist poets (such as Richard Aldington, E. E. Cummings and David Jones) are included, but Gardner's focus on soldiers excludes experimentalists such as Ezra Pound and T. S. Eliot.

- Gender: As with *Journey's End*, this appears to be an exclusively male text, but there are some explicitly female points of reference, for example Kettle's 'To my daughter Betty'.

- Location: The 'Prelude' and some of the early poems are set on the home front and written by non-combatants, but the majority are set on the Western Front and written by experienced soldiers. There is a section dealing with other fronts and war arenas, 'To Unknown Lands', but the anthology is dominated by Somme and Ypres poems.

Activity

Read the poem 'Base Details' by Siegfried Sassoon, the poem from which this anthology takes its title. Discuss the significance of the phrase in the poem itself, and consider why Gardner may have chosen it as the title for his anthology.

Poetry: *Scars Upon My Heart*

The text

Scars Upon My Heart, edited by Catherine Reilly (1981), is a survey of 126 poems by female writers covering a range of views and experiences, mainly written from an autobiographical and home front perspective. It is arranged alphabetically and not divided into sections. The title is taken from Vera Brittain's 'To My Brother', written about Brittain's fears for her brother Edward, a veteran of the Somme who was now fighting on the Italian front. The main subject, then, is male suffering and the impact on women.

The author

The editor of the collection, Catherine Reilly (1925–2005), was a bibliographer and anthologist who specialized in researching the extent of women's writing in both World Wars. In many ways, Reilly's research sought to balance earlier anthologies dominated by male poets and even – as with *Up the Line to Death* – containing no women writers at all. Like Gardner, however, her aim was to include a wide range of poets and poems to demonstrate as full a picture as possible of their chosen perspective on the war. Both considered themselves pioneers whose research 'discovered' poets and brought them to public attention.

Themes

In her study of the link between male and female suffering, Reilly explores grief, loneliness, anxiety, nostalgia and the pleasures as well as the pains of a world without men. The alphabetical arrangement of poems means that the reader is constantly surprised by the variety of different subject matters, tones and methods.

Contexts

- Time: First published in 1981, this anthology coincides with a second period of reflection about the futility of the war – extending the prevailing myth of the 1960s. It reflects a new interest in discovering and publishing or republishing women writers in danger of being forgotten. All of the writers anthologized lived through the war, and the majority were directly involved and affected.

- Genre: Like Gardner, Reilly includes many lyric poems that are straightforward and traditional in form and content, to represent a broad typicality in women's poetry. The anthology is perhaps dominated by poems that are relatively short and represent accessible anecdotes or reflections of a personal nature.

- Gender: This is as explicitly female as Gardner's anthology is male. The editor's thesis is supported both by a preface written by Judith Kazantzis, the poet and prominent civil rights and peace activist, and by the integrity of the Virago Press, founded in 1973 to promote the work of women writers. Many of the poems reflect on traditional women's roles, but others describe the new opportunities that became open to women. Some explore the possibility of writing in male voices.

- Location: Some poems are by those with active service experience as Voluntary Aid Detachment (VAD) nurses abroad, and there are some attempts to write from the point of view of male combatants in Europe. However, the majority are written from the point of view of the writers themselves on the home front. The writers often position themselves in domestic, social or natural settings, in order to reflect on the contrast between themselves and the fighting men.

Activity

Read the poem 'To My Brother' by Vera Brittain, from which this anthology takes its title. Discuss the significance of the phrase 'scars upon my heart' in the poem itself, and consider why Reilly may have chosen it as the title for her anthology.

The chosen comparative set texts

Prose: *The Return of the Soldier*

The Return of the Soldier (1918) is Rebecca West's debut novel. It deals with the return of shell-shocked Christopher Baldry from the front. His trauma has resulted in a psychological time-shift to 15 years earlier, when he had a passionate relationship with an older woman, Margaret. He cannot remember his wife Kitty or their dead son. The novel is narrated by Chris's cousin, Jenny. Now that Chris has returned physically, the women seek a way of bringing him back psychologically. Just as Chris cannot accept the reality of his present, due to battle stress, so Kitty cannot process her grief for her son and preserves his nursery as a shrine.

Jenny and Kitty consult a psychoanalyst, Dr Gilbert Anderson, who devises a treatment using Margaret to make Chris accept Oliver's death so he can return to his marriage with Kitty and to the life of the soldier. West's rejection of a chronological narrative to reflect Chris's displaced sense of time, and her use of Jenny as an unreliable narrator, establish the novel's modernist credentials and enable her to critique attitudes to the social order and moral values underpinning relationships. The novel's presentation of women as characters central to men's lives and the social order is in stark contrast to Remarque's and Hemingway's work, where women hardly feature. The theme of psychoanalytical treatment foreshadows *Regeneration* and its exploration of conflicting treatments.

Prose: *All Quiet on the Western Front*

Im Westen nichts Neues, which translates as 'In the West (Front), nothing new', by Erich Maria Remarque (1929), is closely contemporary with *Journey's End* and *A Farewell to Arms*. Like both of those texts, it was written by a former combatant and draws indirectly on personal experience. It is a third-person narrative – telling the story of Paul Baumer – who, encouraged by his schoolteacher Kantorek, volunteers aged 19, along with a group of friends and schoolmates, soon after the start of the war. As a new recruit, he is mentored by an older veteran, Kat, who becomes an important influence.

The novel focuses on their endurance of awful living and fighting conditions at the front through a series of unnamed battles and campaigns, described in shockingly graphic detail. They soon turn into old men who struggle to survive. The soldiers' feelings of disillusionment and displacement are confirmed by Paul's visit home on leave, where he feels disconnected from the other villagers, including the schoolteacher, and his own father.

Following his return to the front, he kills a man in hand-to-hand combat and witnesses his slow, agonizing death. Kat is also killed and Baumer himself dies at the end of the novel. Remarque's realism about the nature of war and its futility paved the way for later novelists such as Faulks and Barry. Just as Hemingway's novel fell foul of the censor for its language and openness about sex, so Remarque's novel was outlawed in Nazi Germany for its alleged lack of patriotism.

Prose: *Strange Meeting*

Susan Hill's three-part novel *Strange Meeting* (1971) chronicles the shared experiences of two contrasting types. Hilliard is a quiet, introspective and increasingly bitter young veteran; Barton is outgoing, charming and new to the war. The novel is one of the first fictional responses following the reappraisal

Did you know?

The translated title *All Quiet on the Western Front* is probably inspired by a report from the Potomac River, a key frontier of the American Civil War (1861–1865). 'All quiet along the Potomac tonight' became the title of a best-selling poem of the time and was then turned into a popular song.

of the war that took place in the 1960s and the rediscovery of Wilfred Owen's poetry. Hill parallels their growing friendship and their mutual discovery of the true horror of war through a series of close encounters with the fear and death of their colleagues, often reflected upon in letters home.

When Barton goes missing in action in the final battle, Hilliard, his leg amputated, takes it upon himself to pay a consolatory visit to Barton's home. Feeling disconnected from his own family, Hilliard must struggle to return and connect: a familiar theme in war literature.

Activity

Read Wilfred Owen's complex poem 'Strange Meeting'. Discuss the significance of the title and why Susan Hill may have chosen it for the title of her novel.

Prose: *A Farewell to Arms*

A Farewell to Arms by Ernest Hemingway (1929) is another novel that focuses on the aftermath of combat. Frederic Henry is an American volunteer in the ambulance corps of the Italian army, who is injured by a mortar shell and then nursed in a Milan hospital by an English nurse, Catherine Barkely. Over the course of the summer they fall in love, Henry recovers his health and Catherine becomes pregnant.

After the Battle of Caporetto, when the Austrians break through the Italian line, Henry flees the brutal Italian enquiry into the betrayal they assume to be responsible for the defeat. Henry and Catherine escape to Switzerland, but their idyll is destroyed when their baby is stillborn and Catherine dies from a haemorrhage.

The novel is divided into five books, each narrated by Henry. Unlike Jenny in *The Return of the Soldier*, Henry is a reliable narrator, but the straightforwardness of his voice belies Hemingway's experimentation with what would become his hallmark 'degree zero' style or '**existential** realism'. The novel is partly inspired by Hemingway's own combat experience in Italy and a love affair he had with a nurse there, which is also explored in some of the short stories of *In Our Time*.

Prose: *Goodbye to All That*

Goodbye to All That by Robert Graves (1929) is an autobiographical memoir written when Graves was 33. As well as his war experience, it gives an account of his childhood, schooling at Charterhouse, and first marriage. It was intended as a farewell to that phase of his life and perhaps all that went with it: England, Edwardian attitudes, the public school system, institutionalized cruelty, physical injury and emotional pain.

The most pertinent sections of the book regarding World War I deal with his experiences in the Royal Welch Fusiliers, alongside Siegfried Sassoon. Graves chronicles the Battle of Loos and the first part of the Somme offensive, when he was very badly injured in severe fighting and at one stage presumed dead. The text was initially controversial in that Sassoon, Edmund Blunden and Graves's own father took exception to the ways in which people, events and opinions are portrayed. Just as Graves is keen to account for the past and bid farewell to his version of it, he also appears to welcome new ways of living and writing in the modern world that was heralded by the war.

Key term

Existentialism. A philosophy that stresses individual action and responsibility. This broad term emerged in the late 19th and early 20th centuries, and is often associated with feelings of disorientation and confusion in the face of a world that seems to be meaningless and absurd.

Did you know?

In 1929, Robert Graves and the American poet Laura Riding settled in Deià, Mallorca, building a house there. Fellow writer Gertrude Stein had said to Graves: 'Mallorca is a paradise, providing you can stick it.' Apart from a period during the Spanish Civil War, Graves lived there until his death in 1985.

Prose: *A Long, Long Way*

A Long, Long Way by Sebastian Barry was first published in 2005 and, in terms of presenting living and fighting conditions, it blends the realism of Hemingway, Remarque and Faulks with the lyricism of Owen and Rosenberg. Barry finds, as Graves puts it, 'beauty in death' and in horror.

The novel follows the fortunes of Willie Dunne from innocent recruit to his death on the final page; his life, like the text layout, is reduced to nothing. He is the son of a loyalist police commissioner who, at 6'6", sets a physical, political and moral standard that the diminutive Willie can never reach. His journey develops – much like Paul Baumer's – from a swift initiation into a frighteningly new world of war. There is the horror of battles and atrocities, but there is also the camaraderie of his colleagues.

Over time, Willie has crucial moments of growth – sexual transgression and sympathy for the IRA back home in the Easter Rising – then harbours guilt and the need to confess, which finally alienates him from his ties at home. Four years of brutal experience take their toll, and he becomes displaced from his former colleagues as the casualty toll breaks up the Royal Dublin Fusiliers, the remnants being flung to a variety of foreign fields.

Prose: *The First Casualty*

In *The First Casualty* (2005), Ben Elton returns to the subject of World War I, following his work as co-scriptwriter of *Blackadder Goes Forth*. The novel tells the story of a police inspector, Douglas Kingsley, who is first disgraced and imprisoned as a conscientious objector and then given the opportunity for 'redemption' in the form of an elaborate mission to solve a crime at the front. His death is faked and an alternative identity – Captain Christopher Marlowe – is provided so that he can investigate the death of the war hero, poet and closet homosexual Viscount Abercrombie. Kingsley even has a sidekick in the form of Nurse Kitty Murray.

The crime is solved and Kingsley's reputation is restored. Elton uses this premise to explore a variety of themes: attitudes on the home front, heroism, homosexual love, shellshock and the ways in which the slaughter changed attitudes to the conflict. The fact that his central character is investigating a crime at Ypres gives Elton the opportunity to survey the horrors and degradations of the front line. He blends the detective, adventure and war-reportage genres here. The literary career of Abercrombie enables the reader to reflect on parallels with the real war poets.

Prose: *Life Class*

In *Life Class* (2008), Pat Barker returns to the subject of World War I, this time from the perspective of three art students at the Slade School of Art in 1914 under the tutelage of Professor Henry Tonks. Tonks was a real-life artist and surgeon who pioneered plastic surgery to treat disfigured soldiers. When war breaks out, Kit Neville (loosely based on war artist Christopher Nevinson) and Paul Tarrant leave for the Belgian front, while Elinor Brooke (loosely based on artist and Bloomsbury acolyte Dora Carrington) remains at home.

Did you know?

In 1914, to be 'loyalist' in Dublin was to support the continuation of British rule, at a time when many Irish people were seeking independence from Britain.

Did you know?

Barry's title is taken from the music-hall song 'It's a Long Way to Tipperary', which became popular with soldiers as a marching song conveying their yearning to return. In the novel it is the return trips to Dublin that prove so ironically painful for Willie. Like so many real soldiers, he dies unable to experience the anticipated joyful return.

Did you know?

The title of Elton's novel refers to the variously attributed proverb that the first casualty of war is the truth.

Both Neville and working-class northerner Paul are suitors of Elinor's, and the three are also linked by their pursuit of detachment in art. Barker uses this love triangle to reflect changing attitudes to class, sex and gender. Central to the novel is a debate between Elinor's traditional belief that art should celebrate beauty – and therefore cannot respond directly to the horrors war – and Paul's radical view that art has a responsibility to scrutinize and reflect the truth of conflict. Barker uses techniques familiar to readers of *The Regeneration Trilogy*: blending historical and fictional characters; presenting society in a state of change; and using striking imagery to convey the horrors of the front and the effects on individuals.

Activity

Look at the Nevinson painting and discuss the significance of the title. Why do you think the censors were alarmed by the potential effects of exhibiting works of art like this?

◄ 'Paths of Glory' by Christopher Nevinson, painted in 1917

Extension activity

Research other works by Nevinson and war artists such as Paul Nash, John Singer Sargent, Wyndham Lewis, Eric Kennington and Walter Bayes. How do they depict war?

Drama: *The Accrington Pals*

The Accrington Pals by Peter Whelan (1982) was inspired by the famous, true story of the 700-strong battalion – part of the East Lancashire Regiment – which lost 585 men on the first day of the Battle of the Somme. In chronicling the first years of the war up to that point, Whelan is as much concerned with the women of the town as he is with those men who volunteered for Kitchener's New Army in 1914.

Did you know?

Pals battalions became a phenomenon of Lord Kitchener's quest for volunteers after the outbreak of war in 1914. These volunteers became known as 'Kitchener's Army'. Another veteran soldier, General Sir Henry Rawlinson, suggested that men would be more inclined to enlist in the army if they knew that they were going to serve alongside their friends and work colleagues. In the end there were over 200 pals battalions.

Although the large cast reflects a panoramic portrait of a working-class community, Whelan focuses the audience's main attention on stall owner May, on Sarah and on Eva – all women struggling with the pressures of their working lives and the demands on their affections as they worry and wait for news of their menfolk at the front.

The play relies on juxtaposition for its powerful effects: men and women, home front and fighting front, solidarity and individualism, naivety and cynicism, the old morality and the new, propaganda and truth. Reflecting the Thatcherite 1980s, the play places May – the individualist building her business dream – against her cousin Tom's socialist idealism. Tom thinks he has found his utopia in the camaraderie of fighting men. Whelan identified the play's central concern as 'the eternal double-edged question: How much am I for others, how much am I for myself?' Although naturalistic, the play also features an eerie fantasy sequence where May appears to meet unrequited lover Tom in battle.

Drama: *Blackadder Goes Forth*

Blackadder Goes Forth, by Richard Curtis and Ben Elton (1989), is the fourth and final series of the TV sitcom with recurring characters. It provides an irreverent and satiric re-working of *Journey's End*, with Blackadder in the Stanhope role as a front-line captain of a company on the Western Front in 1917. Just as Stanhope reluctantly deals with the orders of the Colonel and Brigadier, so Blackadder must negotiate General Melchett, who is mad as well as misguided. However, rather than a flawed and mentally vulnerable hero, Blackadder is a selfish coward intent on self-protection. His hapless lieutenant George, and batman Private Baldrick, are seen as irritations and comic foils rather than charges for whom Blackadder feels responsible.

Although farcical in style, the series was not perceived as disrespectful in practice, partly owing to the clear bias towards direct combatants and also to the poignancy of the final episode, where the company go over the top. It has attracted criticism, however, for its exaggerated portrayal of the 'lions led by donkeys' viewpoint. Curtis and Elton clearly criticize attitudes associated with British nationalism generally and the British Army's tactics in particular, albeit without sentimentalizing the 'Tommy'.

Drama: *My Boy Jack*

My Boy Jack by David Haig was written and first performed before 2000, but its most definitive public performance was on television in 2007. This performance was followed by publication of the prescribed version by Nick Hearn Books, also in 2007. It is the result of Haig's research into the famous story of Rudyard Kipling's son John, who was declared missing in the Battle of Loos in 1915. Kipling was prominent both as a best-selling writer and as a self-appointed political spokesman of Empire, and this is a poignant true story of loss, grief and changing attitudes to war.

The time setting of the play extends from 1913 – when the audience first see Rudyard and John discussing how John's severe myopia might be hidden when he goes before the Army Medical Board – to 1933 and the announcement that Hitler had become Chancellor of Germany. There is also a flashback scene (Act Two Scene Two) to 1904, featuring Rudyard with his children, presumably to

---

Did you know?

Blackadder Goes Forth was blamed by former Education Secretary Michael Gove for belittling Britain and clearing Germany of blame for World War I.

THINK ABOUT IT

Read about the 2014 Blackadder debate and consider your own views. See http://www.dailymail.co.uk/news/article-2532923/Michael-Gove-blasts-Blackadder-myths-First-World-War-spread-television-sit-coms-left-wing-academics.html and http://www.theguardian.com/world/2014/jan/05/tony-robinson-michael-gove-blackadder-first-world-war

---

Did you know?

Other writers of the time had similar experiences. Sir Arthur Conan Doyle (creator of Sherlock Holmes) had, like Kipling, been a staunch establishment figure and advocate of the war. His son Kingsley was wounded on the first day of the Battle of the Somme, then contracted Spanish flu and died 14 days before the Armistice. Conan Doyle struggled to get over this double tragedy. He turned to spiritualism to seek comfort, declaring 'Christianity is dead. How else could ten million men have marched out to slaughter?'

show Kipling as the enthralling storyteller, fully in control as he depicts the world as a place of wonder before his and his children's 'fall'. The power of the drama comes partly from this use of time and also from its shifts in location, as Haig intercuts between domestic scenes in the family home, Batemans, and John's desperate trench experiences.

Poetry: *The Penguin Book of First World War Poetry*

This anthology, edited by George Walter (2004), is divided into broadly chronological sections reflecting changing attitudes to the war, complete with 'Prelude', 'Coda' and biographical notes. This arrangement and these features closely echo *Up the Line to Death*. However, Walter's selection is much larger and broader. For example, the final main section, 'Peace', contains 39 poems about the aftermath, most of which were written after the war. He also includes several lesser-known male poets and three female poets not included in *Scars Upon My Heart*.

> **Further reading**
>
> Find out more about Gurney's life and work by reading Adam Thorpe's article 'Strange Hells', available at http://www.theguardian.com/books/2007/nov/10/featuresreviews.guardianreview4

Poetry: *The Oxford Book of War Poetry*

John Stallworthy's *The Oxford Book of War Poetry* (1984) is a broad anthology of the genre in over 250 poems, arranged chronologically. There are 70 poems of direct relevance to World War I and its aftermath, from Thomas Hardy's 'Men Who March Away' (poem 99) through to Ted Hughes' 'Six Young Men' (poem 169). However, some of the earlier Victorian and Edwardian poems might help to provide an insight into the prevailing attitudes towards war in 1914, and into the poems that shaped the heroic tradition.

Poetry: *The War Poems of Wilfred Owen*

The War Poems of Wilfred Owen, edited by Jon Stallworthy (1994), selects just over 50 poems plus some fragments. Because Stallworthy was editing the work of a poet who had so few poems published during his lifetime, it is a work of meticulous research and precise scholarship, with the poems arranged strictly chronologically according to Owen's order of drafting. Whereas most readers are familiar with the frequently anthologized favourites, the full range of Owen's subject matter and methods is revealed here.

> **Activity**
>
> Discuss why you think 'Dulce et Decorum Est' has become such an iconic poem in the aftermath of World War I.

> **Did you know?**
>
> George Walter, the editor, has also written books about the poet Ivor Gurney (1890–1937) one of the writers *not* featured in *Up the Line to Death*. Gurney was the author of the much-anthologized war poem 'To His Love'.

> **Did you know?**
>
> Jon Stallworthy was the first to write a biography of Wilfred Owen, published in 1974, before going on to edit Owen's complete poems in 1983.

6 Contextualizing extracts

This chapter will:

- explore the key issues connected with World War I and its aftermath

- review the contexts of relevant texts.

This chapter consists of sample extracts from the set texts, related to the 13 key issues from the specification listed on page 83. The 13 issues have been streamlined, as follows, into six groups – each with a related extract, commentary and set of activities:

1. Different and changing attitudes to conflict

2. Imperialism and nationalism; recruitment and propaganda; heroism

3. Life on the front line; slaughter; generals and soldiers

4. Responses on the home front; pacifism

5. Peace and memorials; political and social aftermath; impact and legacies

6. Writers in action and writers looking back.

Different and changing attitudes to conflict

My Boy Jack by David Haig

> **Activity**
>
> Read and discuss Kipling's poem 'My Boy Jack', below. Why do you think Haig used this as the title of his play? In some productions, the cast recite the poem in unison at the end. What effects might be achieved by this choice?

'Have you news of my boy Jack?'
Not this tide.
'When d'you think that he'll come back?'
Not with this wind blowing, and this tide.

'Has anyone else had word of him?'
Not this tide.
For what is sunk will hardly swim,
Not with this wind blowing, and this tide.

'Oh, dear, what comfort can I find?'
None this tide,
Nor any tide,
Except he did not shame his kind –
Not even with that wind blowing, and that tide.

Then hold your head up all the more,
This tide,
And every tide;
Because he was the son you bore,
And gave to that wind blowing and that tide.

The following extract from the play is part of Act 2, Scene 3, and close to the end of the play. It takes place in 1917 at the Kipling family home, Batemans, two years after John Kipling was declared missing at the Battle of Loos. In the intervening time, Rudyard and his wife Carrie have undertaken a painstaking and systematic search for their son, which has involved interviewing a huge number of soldiers who may be able to shed light on John's fate. They have just been visited by Guardsman Bowe, who has come to confess that he could not help when John Kipling, his commanding officer, was shot and killed leading an attack on the German line. The revelation that John is dead and that he died alone, mutilated and in pain has had a devastating effect.

Carrie You said it on the day… within five minutes of hearing that Jack was missing, you told me it would be sad if he outlived the finest moment of his life.

Rudyard Did I?

Carrie That is exactly what you said.

Rudyard Well…

Carrie You believe that, yes, I know…

Rudyard Only…

Carrie So, now, nothing you say surprises me. Your cruelty doesn't surprise me. You are a cold fish, a very cold fish. But that's alright, I know that now. It doesn't hurt me, but don't pretend anymore. Jack was eighteen years and six weeks old. He died in the rain, he couldn't see a thing, he was alone, in pain, you can't persuade me there is any glory in that.

Rudyard I believe there is.

Carrie No.

Rudyard I believe there is.

Carrie You see we shouldn't talk.

Rudyard There is a glory.

Carrie No.

Rudyard Try to understand.

Carrie Oh, I understand.

Rudyard No, not in that world-weary, hurt fashion of yours…

Carrie I understand that we are very different.

Rudyard I must 'believe' in order to survive at all.

Carrie No, I can't listen to this.

Carrie tries to leave. Rudyard blocks her exit.

Rudyard We're talking.

Carrie Let me past.

Rudyard No.

Carrie tries to pass Rudyard. He grabs her.

Carrie Let go of me.

Rudyard No.

Carrie Please.

Rudyard Do you want me to go down on my knees and own up? Confess my… complicity? Admit that it's all down to me. That I… murdered my son. I will if it satisfies you.

Carrie Please let go of me.

Rudyard Is that what you'd like me to do?

Carrie Please.

Rudyard Do you think a single day passes, when I don't consider that possibility?

Activity
How does the dialogue here present differences in attitude between the two characters?

Carrie Let… go.

Rudyard releases Carrie.

Rudyard Not a single day. Many times a day. I'm not oblivious. Of course I'm not. I think about it all the time. All the time. And what truly terrifies me, is that if I am complicit, inadvertently or otherwise, if I am to blame – what have I sent him on to, if anything at all? Because, really, what possible grounds are there for assuming our lives after death are protected, in any way whatsoever. Which is why it is so important that every sacrifice we make has true value, and Jack's sacrifice is doubly glorious if there's nothing on the other side. But then I think – how dare you, how dare you, how could you, condemn your son to oblivion. To insensate nothingness. How could you, do that, to Jack?

Short silence.

I think I have been happiest of all, lying in bed, knowing that my son is asleep in the next room. And I would willingly lie down now and sleep for an eternity, if I thought it would help bring him back.

Commentary

Differences in attitude to the war are presented by the staccato conflict between Rudyard and Carrie, which has been festering since Rudyard used his influence to secure John a position as an officer in the Irish Guards – despite severe myopia. This eye condition would normally lead to failure of the mandatory medical. John's sister, Bird, is also opposed to the move, claiming that John was motivated less by patriotism and more by the desire to escape Bateman's and, by implication, his father's influence and the constraints of Edwardian Britain.

When Rudyard confesses 'I must "believe" in order to survive at all', the key word 'believe' – pre-modified by 'must' – reveals the doubt, even desperation, behind his normally robust confidence in the cause and all that underpins it. Up to this point he can only assert and repeat; after this he is more honest, more openly reflective and more philosophical, despite the personal agony this shift in position creates.

The pauses and silences are dramatically significant here. The ellipses before such loaded words as 'murder' and 'complicity' reveal the depth of his personal despair. The *Short silence* represents turning away from the most agonizing question – 'How could you, do that, to Jack?' – to find comfort in a nostalgic reverie about John and Bird as young children. Rudyard's use of the second person is partly rhetorical, but also reflects his visceral self-interrogation. When Carrie urges him to 'Let… go', the suspension marks emphasize how unlikely that is, not just for Rudyard but for all the family and perhaps for all the families of the missing.

The play begins in 1913 with Rudyard in full flow as spokesman for the Empire and for mobilization, as well as firmly in control as the family patriarch, 'Daddo'. The play ends in 1933 with Rudyard and Carrie ('*elderly and frail*') listening to the BBC news announcement of Hitler's appointment as Chancellor of Germany. Rudyard's response is 'For nothing, for nothing, for nothing'. Haig, here, is echoing the angry, critical voice of 'Epitaphs of the War' (1922):

If any question why we died
Tell them because our fathers lied.

Imperialism and nationalism; recruitment and propaganda; heroism

Oh! What a Lovely War by Theatre Workshop/Joan Littlewood

Further reading

Working individually or in groups, and to develop your grasp of the play and its impact, look at the material about the play on this BBC website: http://www.bbc.co.uk/guides/zws9xnb

The very early scene below from Act 1 establishes both the mood and the dramatic method of Theatre Workshop's improvised 'Musical Entertainment'. The whole premise – that the war can be turned into music-hall entertainment, presented by a Master of Ceremonies and performed by clowns and chorus girls – creates an instant tone of irony and satire (deliberately confusing an audience's expectations). Theatre audiences tend to want to laugh and to be entertained. On different occasions they also like to be confronted with unpleasant truths. To do both at the same time creates an unsettling effect.

M.C. Milords, ladies and gentlemen, we will now perform for you the ever-popular War Game!

Band   MARCH OF THE GLADIATORS

Circus parade: it is led by a **Pierrot***, cartwheeling.* **France** *wears an officer's cap, a sexy woman either side of him;* **Germany***, a helmet and a leather belt; beside him,* **Austria***, a girl with two yellow plaits hanging from her hat.* **Ireland** *leads the British group, wearing a green wrap-over skirt. She jigs along.* **Great Britain** *wearing a sun helmet, rides on a man's back. A character in a turban holds a square, tasselled sunshade over them. Two* **Russians***, wearing fur hats, dance along. This parade must keep moving and not stop to let the performers declaim.*

Newspanel TROOPS FIRE ON DUBLIN CROWD – AUG 1. – BRITISH CABINET VOTE AGAINST HELPING FRANCE IF WAR COMES – LIBERALS VOTE FOR NEUTRALITY UNDER ANY CIRCUMSTANCES – GERMANY SENDS 40,000 RIFLES TO ULSTER.

M.C. (as the nations pass) La Belle France – Upright, steadfast Germany – Good morning, sir – The first part of the game is called 'Find the Thief'.

Band   A PHRASE OF LAND OF HOPE AND GLORY

Britain Look here, we own 30 million square miles of colonies. The British Empire is the most magnificent example of a working democracy the world has ever seen.

Voice Hear absolutely hear.

M.C. And the lady on my right.

Band   SI LE VIN EST BON

Frenchwoman La Republique.

Frenchman The seat of reason, the centre of world civilisation – culture, and l'amour.

Activity

In what ways does this extract satirize the 'reasons' for World War 1?

M.C. They're at it again. Stop it. If they're not doing that, they're eating. How big's your acreage?

Frenchwoman Six million square kilometres.

M.C. And yours?

Band   A PHRASE OF DEUTCHSLAND UBER ALLES

Kaiser Germany – a mere three million square kilometres. But we are a new nation united only since 1871.

Frenchman When you stole Alsace-Lorraine.

Kaiser Ours, German.

M.C. Hey, we haven't started to play the game yet.

Kaiser We are a disciplined, moral, industrious people. We want more say in the world's affairs.

M.C. Have to keep an eye on you… (*To the* **Band)** Let's have the Russian Anthem.

Band   A PHRASE OF RUSSIAN ANTHEM

Russia They're all Yids.

Newspanel CHURCHILL ORDERS FLEET TO SCAPA FLOW.

M.C. (*to audience*) The second part of the War Game, The Plans.

Band   GERMAN MUSIC

Kaiser War is unthinkable. It is out of the question.

Frenchman It would upset the balance of power.

Britain It would mean the ruin of the world, undoubtedly.

Frenchman Besides, our alliances make us secure.

Kaiser But if you threaten us, then we have the supreme deterrent, which we will not hesitate to use…

M.C. Ssh.

The **M.C.** whistles. The stage darkens and the screen comes down. Everyone leaves but the **Kaise**r and **Austria**. **General Moltke** enters. **Russia, France** and **Britain** listen as if hiding.

Slide 1: Map showing the Schlieffen Plan of 1914 for an attack on Paris.

Moltke (*with a pointer to the map*) The German Army will win this battle by an envelopment with the right wing, and let the last man brush the Channel with his sleeve.

Kaiser Violate the neutrality of Belgium and the Netherlands?

Moltke World power or downfall. Liege twelve days after mobilisation M. Day, Brussels M.19, French frontier M.22 and we will enter Paris at 11.30 on the morning of M.39. I sent all the best brains in the War College into the Railway Section.

Kaiser And the Russians?

Moltke They won't be ready until 1916.

M.C. (*whistles*) Time's up!

Band   SI LE VIN EST BON

Slide 2: Map showing the French 'Plan 17' of 1914 for a French offensive.

Frenchman France admits no law but the offensive. Advance with all forces to attack the German Army. France, her bugles sounding, her soldiers armed for glory, her will to conquer. An idea and a sword. Besides, they will attack Russia first.

Slide 3: Russian infantry marching with rifles.

1st Russian The Russian steam roller. We have a million and a half bayonets. Better than bullets any day. Once in motion, we go rolling forward inex – (He hiccups.)

M.C. Inexorably! The bar's open. Go and have a vodka.

M.C. *blows bo'sun's pipe.*

Slide 4: A British battleship berthed at a pier.

Band   A PHRASE OF THE SONS OF THE SEAS

British Admiral Well done. In the event of a war, the Royal Navy will keep more than a million Germans busy. We shall disembark on a ten-mile strip of hard sand on the northern shores of Prussia and draw off more than our weight of numbers from the fighting line. The overwhelming supremacy of the British Navy is the only thing to keep the Germans out of Paris.

M.C. Hear, hear.

British General On a point of order, sir, your plans appear to have little in common with those of the Army.

British Admiral Look here, you soldiers are a pretty grotesque lot with your absurd ideas about war. Happily you are powerless. We could go right ahead and leave you to go fooling around the Vosges. Have you got a plan?

British General Of course.

Slide 5: A blank.

British Admiral Yes I thought so.

Commentary

Here the multi-modal machinery of music hall mixes verbal irony ('the ever-popular War Game!') with musical jokes (MARCH OF THE GLADIATORS) and visual humour (see the national stereotypes paraded by 'cartwheeling' Pierrots). Littlewood adds another layer of Brechtian alienation by adding the device of a Newspanel to communicate factual events and media headlines. The audience is reminded of the logistical and moral complexities of Irish support for the war due to the Home Rule question.

The play, therefore, chooses to present imperialism and nationalism in a deliberately irreverent way – but based on fact. Just as we see nations as stereotypes, so Littlewood quickly gets down to crude truths. Strip away the balance of power maintained by the Triple Alliance on the one hand and Austro-Hungary on the other, and the nations start to posture and bluster in a game of attack and defence. What really matters to them is physical size, reputation and the settling of old scores. Littlewood makes it clear that the 'thief' is Germany, but that all are to blame by subscribing to imperialism and nationalism, and ultimately to racism (see Russia's dismissal of the new Germany: 'They're all Yids'). The text's message here appears to be that all leaders turn into donkeys. The Schlieffen Plan and Plan 17 are equally reprehensible in returning to the arguments of the Franco-Prussian War. Likewise, Britain's plan – *Slide 5: A blank* – is another form of ridiculous folly.

The exchange between the British Admiral and the British General is part of a repeated motif of 'donkeys' in farcical disarray, but it is also a method of summarizing Britain's dilemma in 1914. Britain was a naval nation; its army of about 100,000 men was very small relative to the armies of its imperial allies. The British Navy was the main way by which Britain asserted its military power; the BEF was a small professional army designed to be deployed in significant but relatively small conflicts, such as the Boer and Crimean wars. Therefore, any commitment to a major conflict on mainland Europe that was commensurate with its role in the Triple Alliance was in doubt. Hence, Kitchener's recruitment campaign was born – some kind of plan, at least. The fact that the previous major conflict involving the British Army had been a hundred years before (in the Napoleonic Wars of 1799–1815) helped Kitchener enormously. War was distant (either in time, geography or both) and therefore heroic myths flourished.

Another method used by Littlewood to underline the Theatre Workshop's serious intentions is the use of historical figures such as, here, the Kaiser and General Moltke. The Kaiser's use of political propaganda and 'doublespeak' paints a caricature in simple but effective brushstrokes. One minute 'War is unthinkable' and 'out of the question', and the next he is emphatic in his threat to use 'the supreme deterrent' and he brings on Moltke to brief the assembled company and the audience on the Schlieffen Plan, complete '*with a pointer to the map*'. The satire is easily decoded, and yet there is also a higher expectation from the audience that they perhaps need a refresher course in the details of the plans that led to war.

Life on the front line; slaughter; generals and soldiers

All Quiet on the Western Front by Erich Maria Remarque

The extract below is part of an extended episode that appears in Chapter 9 of the novel. The narrator, Paul Baumer, has become stranded in a shell hole in No Man's Land during a night reconnaissance mission. A French soldier suddenly appears and, in a desperate struggle, Baumer stabs him and he dies a protracted death over several hours. During that time the man is tended by Baumer, who tries to bandage his wounds and get him water from the puddle at the bottom of the crater. The extract comes from after the Frenchman's death, when Baumer is anxious to somehow make amends.

He is silent, the front is quiet apart from the chatter of machine-guns. The bullets are close together and this is not just random firing – there is careful aiming from both sides. I can't get out.

'I'll write to your wife,' I tell the dead man breathlessly, 'I'll write to her, she ought to hear about it from me, I'll tell her everything that I'm telling you. I don't want her to suffer, I want to help her, and your parents too and your child –'

His uniform is still half open. It is easy to find his wallet. But I am reluctant to open it. Inside it will be his paybook with his name. As long as I don't know his name it's still possible that I might forget him, that time will wipe out the image of all this. But his name is a nail that will be hammered into me and can never be drawn out again. It will always have the power to bring everything back, it will return constantly and will rise up in front of me.

Extension activity

Find out more about the origins of the Schlieffen Plan and Plan 17, and present your findings to the rest of the class.

Activity

In groups, discuss what you already know about the German experience of World War I. It might be helpful to use the following historical overview as a starting point: http://www.bbc.co.uk/history/worldwars/wwone/german_experience_01.shtml

Activity

In what ways does this extract highlight the plight of the individual soldier?

I hold the wallet, unable to make up my mind. It slips out of my hand and falls open. A few pictures and letters drop out. I collect them up and go to put them back in, but the pressure that I am under, the complete uncertainty of it all, the hunger, the danger, the hours spent with the dead man, these things have all made me desperate, and I want to find out as quickly as possible, to intensify the pain so as to end it, just as you might smash an unbearably painful hand against a tree, regardless of the result.

There are photographs of a woman and a little girl, small amateur snapshots, taken in front of an ivy-covered wall. There are letters with them. I take them out and try and read them. I can't understand most of them, since they are difficult to decipher and I don't know much French. But every word I translate hits me like a bullet in the chest – or like a dagger in the chest –

My head is nearly bursting, but I am still able to grasp the fact that I can never write to these people as I thought I would earlier on. Impossible. I look at the photos again; these are not rich people. I could send them money anonymously, if I start earning later. I cling to this idea, it is at least a straw to grasp at. This dead man is bound up with my life, and therefore I have to do everything for him and promise him everything so that I can be rescued. I swear wildly that I will devote my whole existence to him and to his family. I assure him of this with wet lips, and deep within me, while I am doing so there is the hope that I can buy my own salvation that way, and maybe get out of this alive – it's a little trick of the mind, because what you promise are always things that you could only see to *afterwards*. And so I open the paybook and read slowly: Gerard Duval, compositor.

I write down the address on an envelope with the dead man's pencil, and then in a great hurry I shove everything back into his tunic again.

I have killed Gerard Duval, the printer. I think wildly that I shall have to become a printer, become a printer, a printer –

Commentary

The majority of Remarque's novel is set on the front line and depicts trench life and warfare with brutal realism. As well as portraying slaughter in hand-to-hand combat, the extract focuses on solitude and isolation, the mental as well as the physical tolls of fighting. The initial night-time setting gives the episode the unreal atmosphere of a nightmare, which then becomes extended into the following afternoon and beyond. Over the time it takes the Frenchman to die and then the further time before Baumer's rescue, Remarque presents various phases of contradictory emotions: fear of discovery (he wants to stuff earth in the dying man's mouth at one stage to stop him from revealing his position), guilt, torment and desperation. Early shock gives way to revulsion and then pity as the dying man gurgles, moves and looks at Baumer to seek help. The setting and tone, along with Remarque's use of dialogue with the dead man, calls to mind Owen's 'Strange Meeting'. Unlike in that poem, however, this narrator is alive and 'This dead man is bound up with my life'. Perhaps Baumer will not live up to relatively easy initial pledges that he will write to the man's wife and earn money to send to the man's family, but he can at least find out about this man as an individual.

Notice the ways in which Remarque implies Baumer's awareness of his own approach towards the man's corpse. In another context the man's open tunic, his paybook, then the details of his wallet might suggest an invasion of privacy, disrespect and looting. But in this context Baumer's motivation is to appreciate

Study tip

Remember that the four extracts from prose texts here can be used as practice for work on unseen texts.

the enemy he killed as a 'strange friend'. Intimate details of the photographs and the fact that they are 'small amateur snapshots' stress human vulnerability and what has been lost. The fact that Baumer can only translate occasional words in the personal letters stresses the lack of communication between all parties in war, and also gives an added poignancy to Baumer's deepening guilt. The gradual revelation of the real man behind the corpse culminates in the statement of the man's name and profession – for Baumer, this defines the man's identity. The climactic 'Gerard Duval, the printer' perhaps makes the reader think of all the sparse names and details of the missing on memorials, and the fact that they are not adequate representations of the self, but all that remains.

Remarque's style is close to the existential realism of Hemingway. His use of the first person and a simple declarative style in sentences that begin with the subject (usually 'I') followed by dynamic verbs ('I collect', 'I look', 'I write', 'I have killed', and so on) or stative verbs such as 'to be' and 'to have', create a style that is disarmingly open and honest.

Here, Remarque is able to address the horrors of warfare (as legitimized killing) for both perpetrator and victim, from the point of view of ordinary soldiers.

Responses on the home front; pacifism

The Return of the Soldier by Rebecca West

Further reading

As this text is very much concerned with the role of women in men's lives and society, it would be useful to find out more about how women had been seen up to this point. The following website provides a useful survey of how the Victorians and Edwardians viewed women:
http://www.bbc.co.uk/history/trail/victorian_britain/women_home/ideals_womanhood_09.shtml

The following extract comes from Chapter VI at the very end of the novel. The three women in Christopher's life (see page 96) collaborate with psychoanalyst Dr Gilbert Anderson to treat his amnesia, which has been precipitated by shellshock. His former lover, Margaret, uses Oliver's jersey and ball to prove his son has died and to shock Christopher back into reality.

Activity

Think about the ways in which this extract highlights aspects of the aftermath of war.

'Give me the jersey and the ball.'

The rebellion had gone from her eyes, and they were again the seat of all gentle wisdom.

'The truth's the truth,' she said, 'and he must know it.'

I looked up at her, gasping, yet not truly amazed; for I had always known she could not leave her throne of righteousness for long, and she repeated, 'The truth's the truth,' smiling sadly at the strange order of this earth.

We kissed not as women, but as lovers do; I think we each embraced that part of Chris the other had absorbed by her love. She took the jersey and the ball, and clasped them as though they were a child. When she got to the door she stopped and leaned against the lintel. Her head fell back; her eyes closed; her mouth was contorted as though she swallowed bitter drink.

I lay face downward on the ottoman and presently heard her poor boots go creaking down the corridors. Through the feeling of doom that filled the room as tangibly as a scent I stretched out to the thought of Chris. In the deep daze of devotion which followed recollection of the fair down on his cheek, the skin burned brown to the rim of his gray eyes, the harsh and diffident masculinity of him, I found comfort in remembering that there was a physical gallantry about him which would still, even when the worst had happened, leap sometimes to the joy of life. Always, to the very end, when the sun shone on his face or his horse took his fences well, he would screw up his eyes and smile that little stiff-lipped smile. I nursed a feeble glow at that. 'We must ride a lot,' I planned. And then Kitty's heels tapped on the polished floor, and her skirts swished as she sat down in the armchair, and I was distressed by the sense, more tiresome than a flickering light, of someone fretting.

She said:

'I wish she would hurry up. She's got to do it sooner or later.'

My spirit was asleep in horror. Out there Margaret was breaking his heart and hers, using words like a hammer, looking wise, doing it so well.

'Aren't they coming back?' asked Kitty. 'I wish you'd look.'

There was nothing in the garden; only a column of birds swinging across the lake of green light that lay before the sunset.

A long time after Kitty spoke once more:

'Jenny, do look again.'

There had fallen a twilight which was a wistfulness of the earth. Under the cedar-boughs I dimly saw a figure mothering something in her arms. Almost had she dissolved into the shadows; in another moment the night would have her. With his back turned on this fading unhappiness Chris walked across the lawn. He was looking up under his brows at the over-arching house as though it were a hated place to which, against all his hopes, business had forced him to return. He stepped aside to avoid a patch of brightness cast by a lighted window on the grass; lights in our house were worse than darkness, affection worse than hate elsewhere. He wore a dreadful, decent smile; I knew how his voice would resolutely lift in greeting us. He walked not loose-limbed like a boy, as he had done that very afternoon, but with the soldier's hard tread upon the heel. It recalled to me that, bad as we were, we were yet not the worst circumstance of his return. When we had lifted the yoke of our embraces from his shoulders he would go back to that flooded trench in Flanders, under that sky more full of flying death than clouds, to that No-Man's-Land where bullets fall like rain on the rotting faces of the dead.

'Jenny, aren't they there?' Kitty asked again.

'They're both there.'

'Is he coming back?'

'He's coming back.'

'Jenny! Jenny! How does he look?'

'Oh,' – how could I say it, – 'every inch a soldier.'

She crept behind me to the window, peered over my shoulder and saw.

I heard her suck in her breath with satisfaction.

'He's cured!' she whispered slowly. 'He's cured!'

Commentary

This extract shows that all three women, and Christopher himself, will pay a price for the 'cure'. Margaret must sacrifice her love for Christopher and be 'dissolved… into the night' of the past; Jenny and Kitty can only temporarily detain him in the 'yoke' of their 'embraces' before 'he would go back to that flooded trench in Flanders… where bullets fall like rain on the rotting faces of the dead', perhaps never to return again.

West's novel foreshadows Pat Barker's work in the *Regeneration Trilogy*. Like Barker, West chooses a home front setting in which to explore emerging psychoanalytical theories about conflict. Here, West's Dr Gilbert Anderson uses Freud's theories about trauma and the suppression of memory in order to 'cure' Christopher. In this way, West foregrounds memory as crucial to the individual, and perhaps also reminds us that it is also central to the way in which society makes sense of the war in the aftermath. Just as the female characters help Christopher to rediscover a coherent narrative of his past, present and future, so society uses history and literature to create a coherent narrative of the whole war experience.

The novel is also striking in its presentation of women as key to the inner life of the soldier. The returning-soldier narrative is a familiar **trope** in war literature. In some way or another it features in most of the prose and drama texts covered in the specification, and in some notable poems. The typical model, however, is that the returning-soldier narrative is set in a **patriarchal** context. The soldier returns from an almost exclusively male experience, traumatized and dislocated from a home front life that now appears meaningless and useless. West's is a radical departure from this model, and an important work of feminism.

West's narrative is subtly multi-layered with irony. The title is richly ambiguous, as are the final lines and the whole construct of his 'cure'. Similarly, the characters are presented ambivalently. Kitty is the loyal wife who wants him back safely, but perhaps his unhappiness with the emptiness of family life at Baldry Court is one reason for his amnesia. Jenny is supportive, but perhaps an unreliable narrator who desires Christopher for herself. Margaret is the lower-class, older woman predator and yet is also arguably the most intelligent, selfless contributor to Christopher's welfare. Christopher himself is the boy-man who has to come to terms with the death of his son. Notice that his smile is 'decent' but 'dreadful'; he is 'cured', but perhaps also doomed. The psychoanalyst Gilbert Anderson, too, arrives to grant a blessing but also casts a curse.

Notice the interesting way in which West uses contrasting imagery – of the natural world and the trenches, the garden and home, light and dark – to present the physical and emotional vulnerability of her characters.

THINK ABOUT IT

Find out more about Freud's work on suppressed memory and about trauma theory. More recently, some have suggested that rather than a symptom of 'sickness', the suppression of memory following trauma is a 'healthy' symptom of the will to survive. Discuss your own opinions on these theories.

Further reading

Although not exclusively about *Birdsong*, Sebastian Faulks's website provides some illuminating answers to questions about his narrative method: http://www.sebastianfaulks.com/index.php/category/faqs/

Peace and memorials; political and social aftermath; impact and legacies

Birdsong by Sebastian Faulks

The following extract is an entire chapter from the novel. It forms part of the narrative of Elizabeth Benson in the period 1978–1979, when she is researching the life and wartime experiences of her grandfather, Stephen Wraysford, the central protagonist. Most of Elizabeth's research is based in England, but here she journeys to the Somme and discovers Thiepval Memorial to the Missing near Albert in Belgium.

Through the fields to her right Elizabeth saw a peculiar, ugly arch that sat among the crops and woods. She took it for a beet refinery at first, but then saw it was too big; it was made of brick or stone on a monumental scale. It was as though the Pantheon or the Arc de Triomphe had been dumped in a meadow.

Intrigued, she turned off the road to Albert on to a smaller road that led through the gently rising fields. The curious arch stayed in view, visible from any angle, as its designers had presumably intended. She came to a cluster of buildings, too few and too scattered to be called a village or even a hamlet. She left the car and walked towards the arch.

In front of it was a lawn, lush and cropped and formal in the English style, with a gravel path between its trimmed edges. From near to, the scale of the arch became apparent: it was supported on four vast columns; it overpowered the open landscape. The size of it was compounded by its brutal modern design: although clearly a memorial, it reminded her of Albert Speer's buildings for the Third Reich.

Elizabeth walked up the stone steps that led to it. A man in a blue jacket was sweeping in the large space enclosed by the pillars.

As she came up to the arch Elizabeth saw with a start that it was written on. She went closer. She peered at the stone. There were names on it. Every grain of the surface had been carved with British names; their chiselled capitals rose from the level of her ankles to the height of the great arch itself; on every surface of every column as far as her eyes could see there were names teeming, reeling, over the surface of yards, of hundreds of yards, over furlongs of stone.

She moved through the space beneath the arch where the man was sweeping. She found the other pillars identically marked, their faces obliterated on all sides by the names carved on them.

'Who are these, these…?' She gestured with her hand.

'These?' The man with the brush sounded surprised. 'The lost.'

'Men who died in this battle?'

'No. The lost, the ones they did not find. The others are in the cemeteries.'

'These are just the… unfound?'

She looked at the vault above her head and then around in panic at the endless writing, as though the sky had been papered in footnotes.

When she could speak again, she said, 'From the whole war?'

The man shook his head. 'Just these fields.' He gestured with his arm.

Elizabeth went and sat on the steps on the other side of the monument. Beneath her was a formal garden with some rows of white headstones, each with a tended plant or flower at its base, each cleaned and beautiful in the weak winter sunlight.

'Nobody told me.' She ran her fingers with their red-painted nails back through her thick dark hair. 'My God, nobody told me.'

Consider the ways in which this chapter presents ideas about the scale of World War I, and the aftermath of loss.

113

Key term

Socratic dialogue. The form taken by many of Plato's philosophical works. Plato presents his teacher Socrates – a Greek philosopher of the fourth century BC – in dialogue with some apparently intelligent but naïve bystander. Socrates speaks as a simple man who confesses that he has little knowledge, but through the dialogue he shows the other person the way to real wisdom.

THINK ABOUT IT

By mentioning the Third Reich here, Faulks is able to juxtapose the two world wars and their respective horrors by referring to architecture. Find out more about the architecture of World War I memorials and about Speer's Third Reich buildings. Source some images to discuss with the rest of the class.

Further reading

Find out more about the memoirs of Graves's contemporaries, such as Edmund Blunden (*Undertones of War*) and Siegfried Sassoon (*Memoirs of a Fox-Hunting Man* and *Memoirs of an Infantry Officer*). How far do they agree with each other in their approach to looking back at the war as combatants? How do they compare with Vera Brittain's *A Testament of Youth*?

Commentary

Elizabeth's experience here parallels that of everyone in the aftermath of the war who discovers its truths. For most of us, this begins when we are young and is a cumulative process. For those who, like Elizabeth, take the journey of discovery further – perhaps, like her, motivated by personal reasons – there is an epiphany when something closer to a full realization dawns. So her experience here is typical. What makes it distinctive is her solitude. She is not part of a student or tourist party but virtually alone, enabling Faulks to focus on the concentrated impact of her discovery. The only other character present is the park keeper, who is peripheral yet crucial in that it is through their brief **Socratic dialogue** that she gains an understanding of what she is looking at. The sparse nature of their conversation is particularly powerful. The ways in which both Elizabeth and the park keeper refer to the dead stresses their awful anonymity: 'these', 'the lost', 'the ones they did not find', 'the unfound'.

Faulks's presentation of Thiepval itself (see page 127) is worth considering. He stresses its size and incongruity: 'a peculiar, ugly arch', 'monumental', 'dumped', 'curious', 'vast', 'brutal modern design', 'furlongs of stone'. Allusions to other monuments are poignantly ironic. Thiepval intends to create impact but perhaps also shock and reflection rather than confident assertion. It is not triumphal like the Arc de Triomphe (celebrating Napoleonic generals) or divine like the Pantheon, or aggressively assertive like Speer's Third Reich buildings. At the same time, Faulks's reference to World War II reminds us of the view that the terms of the final peace treaty, and some of the ways in which the Allies memorialized the war, humiliated Germany and sowed the seeds for revenge.

At the climactic moment of Elizabeth's realization, Faulks stresses her youth and gender in details such as her 'red-painted nails and thick dark hair', and the contrast prompts the reader to reflect on all the dualities of war and its aftermath. She sees it as an urgent responsibility of the informed to tell the naïve about the consequences of war. She also echoes a strong sense of the duty to remember, which had been instilled since the very first casualties of the war and Binyon's promise in 'For the Fallen' back in 1914 that 'we will remember them'. As an important modern writer about the aftermath of war, Faulks implies that it is *how* we remember that matters.

Writers in action and writers looking back

Goodbye to All That by Robert Graves

The following extract describes the final phase of Graves's trench combat experience, just before he was badly injured by a shell fragment to the lung. Such was the severity of the injury and the confusion of battle at the time that Graves was reported killed in a letter from his commanding officer. Although he returned to service, it was never to active combat duty. This memoir is famous as a testimonial of trench warfare by an experienced soldier and famous writer.

Activity

Consider the view that in this extract 'the horrors of war are made more significant by being under-stated'.

The next two days we spent in bivouacs outside Mametz Wood. We were in fighting kit and felt cold at night, so I went in to find German overcoats to use as blankets. It was full of dead Prussian Guards Reserve, big men, and dead Royal Welch and South Wales Borderers of the New Army battalions, little men. Not a single tree in the wood remained unbroken. I collected my overcoats, and came away as quickly as I could, climbing through the wreckage of green branches. Going and coming by the only possible route, I passed by the bloated and stinking corpse of a German with his back propped against a tree. He had a green face, spectacles, close-shaven hair; black blood was dripping from the nose and beard. I came across two other unforgettable corpses; a man of the South Wales Borderers and one of the Lehr Regiment had succeeded in bayoneting each other simultaneously. A survivor of the fighting told me later that he had seen a young soldier of the Fourteenth Royal Welch bayoneting a German in parade-ground style, automatically exclaiming: 'In, out, on guard!'

I was still superstitious about looting or collecting souvenirs. 'These greatcoats are only a loan,' I told myself. Our brigade, the Nineteenth, was the reserve brigade of the Thirty-third Division; the other brigades, the Ninety-ninth and Hundredth, had attacked Martinpuich two days previously, but had been halted with heavy losses as soon as they started. We were left to sit about in shell-holes and watch our massed artillery blazing away, almost wheel to wheel. On the 18th, we advanced to a position just north of Bazentin-le-Petit, and relieved the Tyneside Irish. I had been posted to 'D' Company. Our Irish guide was hysterical and had forgotten the way; we put him under arrest and found it ourselves. On the way through the ruins of Bazentin-le-Petit, we were shelled with gas shells. The standing order with regard to gas-shells was not to bother about respirators, but push on. Hitherto they had all been lachrymatory ones; those were the first of the deadly kind so we lost half a dozen men.

When at last 'D' company reached the trenches, scooped beside a road and not more than three feet deep, the badly shaken Tyneside Company we were relieving hurried off, without any of the usual formalities. I asked the officers where the Germans were. He said he didn't know, but pointed vaguely towards Martinpuich, a mile to our front. Then I asked him who held our left flank, and how far off they were. He said he didn't know. I damned his soul to Hell as he went away. Having got into touch with 'C' Company behind us on the right, and the Fourth Suffolks fifty yards to the left, we began deepening the trenches and presently located the Germans – in a trench system some five hundred yards to our front, keeping fairly quiet.

Commentary

This extract goes to the heart of the bitter fighting on the Somme as Graves and his company approach the front line. The blasted wood and the abandoned corpses of the battlefield are familiar, iconic images recalling the paintings of Paul Nash and Christopher Nevinson. The incidents described here were first worked into poems that same year, and then became part of Graves's memoir some 12 years later. Of most direct relevance to this episode is the description of the German corpse in Mametz Wood, which is closely echoed in Graves's poem 'A Dead Boche', which follows.

A Dead Boche

To you who'd read my songs of War
And only hear of blood and fame,
I'll say (you've heard it said before)
'War's Hell!' and if you doubt the same,
Today I found in Mametz Wood
A certain cure for lust of blood:

Where, propped against a shattered trunk,
In a great mess of things unclean,
Sat a dead Boche; he scowled and stunk
With clothes and face a sodden green,
Big-bellied, spectacled, crop-haired,
Dribbling black blood from nose and beard.

Mametz Wood had been captured on 2 July 1916, after intense fighting, and this poem describes the state of things a fortnight later, which helps to explain the green, stinking and bloated state of the corpse in the summer heat.

The poem reveals complex attitudes beneath the direct and simple prose of the memoir. Graves chooses to use the slang term 'Boche' (derived from the French slang word for 'cabbage'), a term that came to prominence after the first day of the Battle of the Somme, when attitudes towards the Germans hardened further. At the outset of the war, 'Hun' was the most common slang term for a German — reflecting a fear and ignorance about aggressors from Eastern Europe. Soon after mutual entrenchment, 'Fritz' became the common slang term, reflecting a realization that ordinary German soldiers were in much the same position as British Tommies.

In both the memoir and the poem, Graves draws our attention to physical features of the corpse that had become stereotypical of Germans — the big belly, the spectacles and the cropped hair. But arguably he is not putting this description forward as a crude piece of racism to mock and show revulsion. As the poem is framed as a warning against jingoistic 'songs of War' that tell of 'blood and fame' and as a 'cure for lust of blood', the poem is, among other things, a warning about the destructive power of xenophobia.

This episode in the memoir is notable for describing Graves's friendship with fellow Welch Fusilier Siegfried Sassoon. Although we read of Sassoon encouraging Wilfred Owen to write frankly and directly about war, he found Graves's poems such as 'A Dead Boche' too realistic and too violent. When Sassoon first arrived in France in November 1915, Graves was already an experienced trench soldier addressing the horror of war directly in his poetry. A less brutal, but no less ironic, poem is 'The Leveller' — also inspired by this episode from the memoir and fighting at nearby Martinpuich, mentioned in this extract and close to the site of Graves's own almost-fatal shell injury. Both Graves and Sassoon had their defining war experiences around this time, and both never returned to frontline action. Graves's poem 'Two Fusiliers', which follows, addresses Sassoon directly as the two look back.

Two Fusiliers

And have we done with War at last?
Well, we've been lucky devils both,
And there's no need of pledge or oath
To bind our lovely friendship fast,
By firmer stuff
Close bound enough.

By wire and wood and stake we're bound,
By Fricourt and by Festubert,
By whipping rain, by the sun's glare,
By all the misery and loud sound,
By a Spring day,
By Picard clay.

Show me the two so closely bound
As we, by the wet bond of blood,
By friendship blossoming from mud,
By Death: we faced him, and we found
Beauty in Death,
In dead men, breath.

Although it sounds as if it's describing two comrades looking back after the Armistice, it was actually written in August 1916 – looking back on their part in the Battle of the Somme, with a strong sense that this was 'the war' as far as they are concerned. Circumstances brought them into the conflict at that time, and circumstances have now taken them to a point where they can look back.

The poem, like the prose, is elliptical. To two experienced soldiers, the place names recalled are full of significance. What were once small towns and villages in an obscure part of north-eastern France, are now sites resonant with shared experience; the significance of Fricourt, Festubert and Picardy – like Mametz, Martinpuich and Bazentin – is understood by Somme veterans and does not have to be explained. The same goes for the listing of trench accoutrements ('wire and wood and stake') and natural elements ('whipping rain', 'sun's glare', 'clay', 'mud'). The poem's use of **syntactic parallelism** and **asyndetic listing** creates a simple pattern that contains the poem's message: although an abstract concept, friendship can be made up of such things.

In 1929, when Graves wrote *Goodbye to All That*, his aim was to write much more than just a war memoir, and the two soldier-poets were less close. In fact, the book's initial publication put their friendship in jeopardy, when Sassoon objected to the inclusion of a **confessional** verse letter he had written to Graves ('Letter to Robert Graves', also known as 'Dear Roberto') and intended to be private. It then had to be withdrawn.

The extract from *Goodbye to All That* and the two accompanying poems together remind us that 'looking back' can take place at any time and at multiple times along a continuum. The particular time context will, of course, determine shifting views of the past, and often of the same incident.

> **Did you know?**
>
> The Battle of the Somme lasted from 1 July 1916 through into November of that year. By the end of this battle, the British Army had suffered 420,000 casualties, including 60,000 on the first day alone. The French suffered 200,000 casualties and the Germans 500,000.

> **Key terms**
>
> **Asyndetic listing.** This involves omitting any conjunctions (such as 'and') from a list.
>
> **Syntactic parallelism.** This is where grammatical structures in one sentence are echoed in the next.

This chapter will:

- explore the literary background to the texts within this shared context

- introduce some ways of making meaning which you can apply to the texts available for study.

Overview: war literature before 1914

War literature prior to 1914 is dominated by evocations of a heroic tradition going back centuries, and permeated by ideas common to many cultures. In the Victorian and Edwardian periods, in particular, heroism in war and patriotism were held up as great virtues. Tennyson's 'The Charge of the Light Brigade' (1854) and Sir Henry Newbolt's 'Vitae Lampada' (1892) popularized the notion of stoicism in the face of defeat, so war was embedded in the national consciousness as a source of glory – almost whatever the outcome. The school curriculum and popular reading habits traced this tradition from Greek and Roman classics down through Shakespeare to these 19th-century poems and stories.

That is not to say that there was no realism or cynicism. Poems such as 'Ball's Bluff' (1866) by Herman Melville (set during the American Civil War) and 'On the Idle Hill' (1896) by A. E. Housman (perhaps reflecting on the First Boer War) both establish an ambivalent view of war as something grand and awe-inspiring but with a terrible cost. In them, we can see the precursors of moods explored in the early years of World War I in particular. A tradition of realism had begun to develop alongside the heroic tradition.

Extension activity

Find copies of the four poems mentioned above to read and study. See if you can find recordings of them to listen to. Can you link them to any World War I poems you know or have studied?

Literary context 1914–1918

Prevailing style in 1914: Edward Marsh and the Georgian poets

Edward Marsh and his collaborators published five volumes of the anthology *Georgian Poetry* between 1912 and 1922. Interestingly, those published included Siegfried Sassoon and Robert Graves, along with Rupert Brooke (1887–1915) and Edward Thomas (1878–1917). Taking their name from the accession of King George V in 1910, they sought to herald a new age of poetry by advocating the use of accessible forms and language.

However, in time the term 'Georgian poetry' came to be used pejoratively and the Georgians quickly became associated with conservatism, reaction, and failure to engage with the complexities of modern urban life. The war and the publication of *The Waste Land* in 1922 by T. S. Eliot (1888–1965) eclipsed their aims and made them appear – to some – superfluous and irrelevant. Of course, literary fashions come and go. The attitude adopted towards these movements depends on the **context of reception** and individual taste.

Realism and protest: Sassoon, Graves and Owen

This group of friends and colleagues fought and wrote in association. They were poets and letter writers – writing poems sometimes referencing one another, and writing letters to each other. They criticized one another's work. They were one another's literary advocates and apologists. They were friends who cared about each other's personal and professional lives. They reflected deeply on the progress, or otherwise, of the conflict.

To a very large extent, they came to share a viewpoint informed by the physical and emotional pains of combat. At broadly the same time, they became cynical about major aspects of the way in which the war was being conducted. In particular, they shared the experience of fighting on the Somme. In various ways, they were caught up in the repercussions following Sassoon's publication of his renouncement of the conflict – *Finished with the War: A Soldier's Declaration* (1917) – including Sassoon's time at Craiglockhart War Hospital.

Activity

Read the text below carefully: it is Siegfried Sassoon's famous declaration. Summarize *exactly* what Sassoon is saying here. Consider the *methods* he uses. Which words and phrases do you think may have caused most controversy? How can we reconcile this declaration and Sassoon's poetry with the fact that he was a decorated war hero? Is it appropriate to label such writers as 'anti-war'?

Finished with the War: A Soldier's Declaration (9 July 1917)

I am making this statement as an act of wilful defiance of military authority, because I believe that the war is being deliberately prolonged by those who have the power to end it. I am a soldier, convinced that I am acting on behalf of soldiers. I believe that this war, on which I entered as a war of defence and liberation, has now become a war of aggression and conquest. I believe that the purposes for which I and my fellow soldiers entered upon this war should have been so clearly stated as to have made it impossible to change them, and that, had this been done, the objects which actuated us would now be attainable by negotiation. I have seen and endured the sufferings of the troops, and I can no longer be a party to prolong these sufferings for ends which I believe to be evil and unjust. I am not protesting against the conduct of the war, but against the political errors and insincerities for which the fighting men are being sacrificed. On behalf of those who are suffering now I make this protest against the deception which is being practised on them; also I believe that I may help to destroy the callous complacency with which the majority of those at home regard the contrivance of agonies which they do not, and which they have not sufficient imagination to realize.

In a short space of time, Graves and Owen became associated with these sentiments and the need to inform their fellow soldiers and the Home Front of the realities behind the official propaganda.

Given that so many educated, literate men either volunteered or were later conscripted, the network of connections between writers went way beyond this group of three. As well as various friendships, meetings and associations of different types, many writers were connected by shared literary mentors and publishers. Two of the most influential were Edward Marsh (1858–1927) – who with his circle published the anthology *Georgian Poetry* – and Edith Sitwell (1887–1964), who published *Wheels*.

New forms of modernism: the Sitwells and *Wheels*

Seen as a counterpoint to Marsh's *Georgian Poetry*, *Wheels* was a modern verse anthology published between 1916 and 1921, and was the first to publish Wilfred Owen's work posthumously in 1919. The Sitwells – in particular Edith, her brother Osbert and their circle – were closely linked to experimental aspects of **modernism**. Along with the Bloomsbury Group and the artist/writers of the Vorticist and Imagist movements, they sought innovations to reflect a rapidly changing and destructive world.

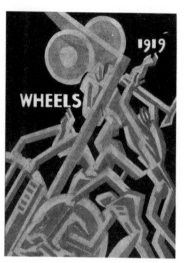

These two front covers of Edith Sitwell's anthology *Wheels*, from 1916 and 1919, could not be more different: poetry is suddenly transformed from a sedate Home Front activity into a potent, loud and angry voice – reflecting a world plunged into turmoil through war.

Extension activity

Find out more about the anthologies *Georgian Poetry* and *Wheels*. You could also research the artists and writers who made up the Vorticists, led by Wyndham Lewis, including their anthology *Blast*, and the Imagists, led by Richard Aldington and Ezra Pound, including their anthology *The Egoist*.

Female voices

Women poets

Women writers of the time, mostly writing on the Home Front and separately rather than as part of a group, have become central to the canon of World War I literature, despite being relatively unknown in their lifetimes. Writers such as Jessie Pope (1868–1941) became an unofficial part of the war machine, writing propaganda poetry for newspapers such as *The Daily Mail*. Working-class and some middle-class women relished the opportunity to move into jobs normally undertaken by men, and wrote about these experiences. Sylvia Pankhurst (1882–1960), for example, wrote from a suffragette's perspective but also with an awareness that opportunities for women were often at the cost of men's lives in the trenches.

Many educated, middle-class women reflected on their role as sisters, girlfriends, wives, mothers and homemakers in writing from a personal perspective about worry and grief for their own menfolk, or for menfolk en masse. Poets such as May Wedderburn Cannan (1893–1973) and Eleanor Farjeon (1881–1965) wrote about their own experiences and explored their own grief. They often took comfort from the natural world and its cycles of life, death and rebirth, or wrote about the contrast between the living, natural world and the slaughter of the war. Sometimes they attempted to write empathetically from male combatants' perspectives. A number of women who were in service overseas in various capacities (such Voluntary Aid Detachment (VAD) nurses, ambulance drivers and signal operators) also provided significant testimonies of their war experiences.

Vera Brittain and her circle

Another distinct and easily identifiable group is Vera Brittain's circle. Brittain (1893–1970) was a VAD nurse and poet who is perhaps best known for her memoirs *Testament of Youth* (1933) and *Testament of Experience* (1957). Her brother Edward attended Uppingham School, where Vera met and became engaged to Roland Leighton. Both Roland and Edward were killed in action – Roland in France in 1915 and Edward on the Italian Front in 1918. Vera Brittain's writings chronicle their early hopes and fears and, later, her own grief. Her concern for her brother Edward, following injuries sustained on the first day of the Battle of the Somme, and her accounts of the deaths of mutual friends such as Victor Richardson (who died after being blinded at the Battle of Vimy Ridge) convey a strong sense of a group of literary friends desperately seeking to support one another through the devastating events of the war.

Writers, publishers and mentors: the literary milieu

Given that homosexuality had been illegal in English law since 1533 – and punishable by hanging until 1861 – those writers who were gay, hid or suppressed their sexuality and often lived in fear of exposure, condemnation and punishment. Many lied to their families and some to themselves in the desire to live a 'normal' life. The law was not reformed until the Sexual Offences Act of 1967. Edward Marsh was a homosexual who, because of his profession, mixed with a large network of other writers, many of whom were also gay.

Marsh was part of a network of mentors that included Siegfried Sassoon, who had discovered that he was gay while at Cambridge and had an intense relationship there. Sassoon's relationship with Wilfred Owen was primarily artistic, but their shared sexuality perhaps gave them a particular understanding of one another's sensibilities. Sassoon introduced Owen to his friend, the editor Robert 'Robbie' Ross (1869–1918), who was, unlike the equally well-connected Marsh, openly gay and had achieved some notoriety as the friend and literary executor of Oscar Wilde. To an extent, Ross's position as a pivotal figure in the literary scene at the time was due to his professional life and his sexual orientation, being both at the heart of and on the edge of society. Ross, in turn, introduced Owen to the Sitwells and so brought him closer to the heart of modernist and liberal thinking, which embraced unconventional approaches towards sexuality as well as to literature and art.

Many writers, therefore, were linked directly. They can be grouped in a range of other ways too, such as by education. A large number of the most famous writers were from the privileged classes and attended public school. Few of the World War I writers were direct contemporaries, but the education they received at schools such as Charterhouse, Clifton, Eton, Marlborough, Rugby, St Paul's, Uppingham, Westminster and Winchester gave them a shared

> **Did you know?**
>
> When Vera Brittain died in 1970, her ashes were scattered on the grave of her brother, Edward, in northern Italy. He is the subject of her poem 'To My Brother'. Her wish was carried out by her daughter, Shirley Williams, now a Liberal Democrat peer. Brittain wrote: 'for nearly 50 years much of my heart has been in that Italian village cemetery'.

> **Did you know?**
>
> In his career as a senior civil servant, Marsh worked as private secretary to a succession of Britain's most powerful politicians, including Winston Churchill.

THINK ABOUT IT

Find out more about the role of public schools in World War I. As a starting point, you could read and discuss this article: http://www.newstatesman.com/2013/12/real-eton-rifles

experienced of a broadly common curriculum – both academic and sporting – and immersion in a culture where patriotism and religious faith were largely unquestioned. Such schools cultivated reading that celebrated the heroic tradition of Homer, Virgil, Shakespeare and Tennyson.

Some, such as Brooke, Julian Grenfell (1888–1915) and Herbert Asquith (1881–1947) went on to seek and find a heroic aesthetic in their response to the war, but the majority chose to spend their writing career exploring the gap between heroic expectation and the appalling reality of trench warfare. Cynicism tended to involve finding new forms and a new language to express strongly anti-war thoughts and feelings. Never had a war involved such literate and intellectual combatants.

Beyond the war, writers such as Graves, Edmund Blunden (1896–1974) and A. E. Housman (1859–1936) continued as academics, writers and journalists – further evidence, perhaps, of the level of education and literary talent among those involved in the war, either actively in the case of Graves and Blunden, or as commentators such as Housman.

Writing and publishing during the war

Sassoon's *Finished with the War: A Soldier's Declaration* caused a scandal at the time, because he was a well-known and well-connected war hero who had won the Military Cross for 'conspicuous gallantry' following a raid on an enemy trench early in 1916. It was very difficult to publish views other than the heroic at the time. Two playwrights are relevant here: Miles Malleson (1888–1969), who had briefly seen action before writing *Black 'Ell* (1917), and John Drinkwater (1882–1937) who wrote *x = o: A Night of the Trojan War* (1917) following a time in France entertaining the troops.

Malleson's play was confiscated on publication under the Defence of the Realm Act. Drinkwater's one-act play had to be sandwiched between two comedies performed in the same evening and deliberately set in the distant past to avoid the censor's disapproval. Meanwhile, in France in 1916, Henri Barbusse (1873–1935) published *Le Feu (Under Fire)* to controversy, but also to great acclaim.

Did you know?

The Defence of the Realm Act was passed on 8 August 1914, and gave the government an extensive range of powers to protect national security, including censorship: 'No person shall by word of mouth or in writing spread reports likely to cause disaffection or alarm among any of His Majesty's forces or among the civilian population.'

Further reading

Find out which writers might be included in the following sub-group headings, and why they are significant. Gather dates, major works and an overview of their attitude to the war.

- Combatants
- Women writers who were VADs, ambulance drivers, signals operators, and so on
- Non-combatants
- Those who died in action
- Those who won military honours
- Those who chronicled their experiences at the time in diaries and journals
- Those who went on to write memoirs and autobiographies featuring their war experiences
- English-speaking writers of other nationalities, including those from the Commonwealth, and those who were translated into English
- Visual artists

Commentary

There is a sharp authenticity in the writing of combatants and those who experienced other kinds of active service, particularly in Belgium and France. Such writing is often informed, rather than naïve, and cynical rather than accepting the myths of propaganda and the heroic tradition.

There is perhaps a particular poignancy to the writing of those who died in the war. Such writings can often appear prescient and full of sad irony. Biographical details, such the age of writers when the war broke out and at their deaths, can also be illuminating, as can their service records.

It is worth exploring the most popular genres that writers used to respond to the war, particularly those chosen by combatants. Most were regular letter writers, and these letters are often crafted in a literary style. Wilfred Owen's are a well-known example. The same can be said of diaries and journals; the intensity of such writing, composed on the same day as events or very soon afterwards, is intriguing. Sassoon's diaries are a good example.

It is interesting to consider the effects of time on memoirs and autobiography. Have the intervening years made the account less authentic and less comprehensively realistic? Or have thoughts and feelings matured into wisdom informed by a sense of perspective?

The Commonwealth made a huge contribution to the war effort on the Allies' behalf, and the writings of those involved either directly or as commentators – at the time and since – should be recognized.

Just as writers looked to new methods to make art reflect the extraordinary destruction of war, visual artists also experimented to convey brutal truths in styles that were initially shocking. Paul Nash was appointed as on official war artist but the shock and impact of his experiences at the front, recorded in his war diary, led him to record the war as it was, not as some idealized myth.

'The Menin Road' by Paul Nash, painted in 1919 ▶

Post-war literary contexts

Consider possible groupings for texts written in the aftermath of World War I. The commentary above provides one such group.

Combatants and service personnel as post-war writers

The post-war literary scene was dominated by memoirs that were of different kinds and fictionalized to different degrees. The most famous of these include

Undertones of War (1928) by Edmund Blunden, *Goodbye to All That* (1929) by Robert Graves, and *Memoirs of an Infantry Officer* (1930) by Siegfried Sassoon. There were numerous others by writers notable at the time, such as A. P. Herbert (1890–1971) and Henry Williamson (1895–1977). Vera Brittain also published *Testament of Youth*. In terms of fiction, Ford Madox Ford (1873–1939) published the tetralogy *Parade's End* (1924–1928), partly inspired by his posting to France in 1915. A veteran of the German campaign, Erich Maria Remarque (1898–1970) published *Im Westen nichts Neues* (*All Quiet on the Western Front*) in 1929.

R. C. Sherriff (1896–1975) drew on his experiences as a captain during the war when he wrote *Journey's End* (1928). Sherriff's was the first developed and direct representation of trench life on the stage since the war. Given the immediacy of drama and its impact on a live audience, it became perhaps the most 'difficult' genre, because audiences were made to witness harrowing scenes in public. The discourse of live theatre – particularly when suffering, death and grief are being presented – can have a particularly potent effect. Even ten years on from the end of the war, the publication of Sherriff's play stirred strong and difficult emotions, because veterans and the families of casualties experienced an uncomfortably realistic presentation of the war along with young, naïve members of the public.

Wilfred Owen: a keynote voice emerges

As well as memoirs and some dramatic fiction, the years between the wars and beyond World War II were notable for the issues surrounding the publishing, editing and presenting of Owen's poems.

Very soon after the war, the view emerged that Owen's was the most authentic voice of the experience, and that his poems must be saved through publication. The three earliest editions were produced by Siegfried Sassoon and Edith Sitwell (1920), Edmund Blunden (1931) and Cecil Day-Lewis (1963). Underpinning the first two editions was a struggle for intellectual ownership; Sassoon felt that, although Sitwell was the first to publish Owen's poems, a fellow veteran such as himself was best placed to supervise Owen's legacy. Sassoon approved of the younger Blunden carrying on with the task for the same reason.

Owen's legacy was jeopardized by the approach of the poet W. B. Yeats (1865–1939) to editing *The Oxford Book of Modern Verse* in 1936. Yeats decided to exclude war poetry on the grounds that 'passive suffering is not a subject for poetry'. Then the debate about Owen was eclipsed by the events of World War II. No one voice seemed to emerge as dominant following that conflict, so Day-Lewis's edition argued that Owen remains the definitive commentator on war into the second half of the 20th century.

The 1960s: the turning point

Day-Lewis's work played a key role in creating a powerful reading of World War I as a futile waste of life and talent. The publication of *The Donkeys* (1961) by military historian and politician Alan Clark (1928–1990) was one of the inspirations for the Theatre Workshop's satirical drama *Oh! What a Lovely War* (1964). These works were part of a wider revival in interest prompted by the 50th anniversary of the outbreak of the war and a mid-century, post-World War II reflection on the direction of Western civilization. The BBC also produced the documentary series *The Great War* in 1964.

Did you know?

Yeats wrote to a friend: 'When I excluded Wilfred Owen, whom I consider unworthy of the poets' corner of a country newspaper, I did not know I was excluding a revered sandwich-board Man of the revolution & that somebody has put his worst & most famous poem in a glass-case in the British Museum – however if I had known it I would have excluded him just the same. He is all blood, dirt & sucked sugar stick (look at the selection in Faber's Anthology – he calls poets 'bards', a girl a 'maid', & talks about 'Titanic wars'). There is every excuse for him but none for those who like him.'

Activity

The Great War is available on YouTube, and an accompanying book by Corelli Barnett is still available. Look at these sources and discuss the ways in which the 1960s context is reflected. What similarities and differences between then and now can be observed?

THINK ABOUT IT

Clark's title *The Donkeys* is a reference to the expression 'lions led by donkeys'. Find out about the various theories surrounding the origin of this phrase.

These literary activities can be seen as part of the evolution of a new consciousness about the way in which individual lives can be compromised by war. This mood was also precipitated by the Cold War and the growing fear that World War III would be nuclear. The Campaign for Nuclear Disarmament (CND) had been founded in 1958 and was a growing force. In 1964, a new Labour government came to power and represented a wide spectrum of voices from socialist to social democrat. In America in the same year, the Civil Rights Act was published and there was an escalation in the American anti-war movement, when draft cards were burned in various demonstrations prior to the American intervention in Vietnam from 1965 to 1973.

The prevailing political climate in the UK, and broader political movements such as the Civil Rights and Peace Movements, gave added impetus to the view that both world wars represented an unacceptable loss of life and must not happen again. Most people recognized that wars of the future would be different. They could see that Hitler had had to be stopped, but the necessity of World War I was less clear and its futility more apparent. It seemed that World War III might be a return to mass conflict and futility on an even grander scale.

Late 20th to early 21st centuries: more reflections on futility

An orthodox view emerged from the 1960s onwards that World War I had been a futile waste of life and talent, that the ruling class had been to blame, and that the truth could be accessed by exploring the thoughts and feelings of those who were dispossessed at the time and therefore not heard or fully appreciated. Following the 1960s, there appeared a succession of clusters, particularly of prose fiction and drama, which explored and consolidated that orthodoxy.

Susan Hill's novel *Strange Meeting* (1971) extrapolated the interest in Owen into fiction. Then, in the wake of Vietnam and the Falklands War of 1982, there was a further spate of publications exploring the futility viewpoint. These included *War Horse* (1982) a novel for children by Michael Morpurgo; *Not About Heroes* (1982), a play about Sassoon and Owen by Stephen Macdonald; *The Accrington Pals* (1982), a play about the devastation of a Lancashire mill town by Peter Whelan; and *Observe the Sons of Ulster Marching Towards the Somme* (1985), a play about the fates of eight Unionist soldiers by Frank McGuinness. As the end of the century approached and the last surviving World War I combatants reached the ends of their lives, there was a further examination of futility with the publication of texts such as *The Regeneration Trilogy* (1991–1995) by Pat Barker, *Birdsong* (1993) by Sebastian Faulks, *To the Green Fields Beyond* (2000) by Nick Whitby, and *A Long, Long Way* (2005) by Sebastian Barry.

THINK ABOUT IT

Find out about your own family history during World War I. What, if any, records, documents and artefacts survive? What oral history is there within the family? If you have some rudimentary information about those involved, you can try the various websites offering to help you to research their stories.

The centenary shifts the mood

In the first part of the 21st century, leading up to the centenary of the outbreak of World War I, so-called revisionist historians challenged the orthodox view of 'lions led by donkeys'. They questioned the accepted view of events, tactics and military commanders. They pointed to the relative success of trench warfare, the Battle of the Somme and the record of Haig – stressing that the war was an Allied victory. Similarly, some politicians and commentators began to worry that the orthodox view created a myth that was disrespectful to those who had fought and died in World War I, and that it was out of tune with the mood of the nation as the centenary of the outbreak of the war approached.

The aftermath: memorialization and remembrance

The process of memorialization began very early in World War I, in the sense that from the first casualties onwards there was a desire to create memorials and remember. A text that is often regarded as prominent in this process – Laurence Binyon's 'For the Fallen' – was first published in *The Times* on 21 September 1914. Similar elegies were written throughout the war, both by non-combatants like Binyon and by combatants. Because of the frequency and number of deaths, ideas about looking back, reflecting and thinking about the war's aftermath are concepts that were current almost from the outset.

Similarly, visiting the battlefields as a tourist destination began almost immediately. It was envisaged as early as February 1918, when Phillip Johnstone wrote his poem 'High Wood' (in both the Gardner and Walter anthologies) in the voice of a tour guide appalled at the lack of real respect shown by the tourists.

Perhaps inspired by his son's death, Rudyard Kipling joined the Imperial War Graves Commission – later the Commonwealth War Graves Commission – the organization responsible for the beautifully ordered and tended graveyards and memorials that visitors see today. It was Kipling who originally suggested forms of words that have now become iconic for memorials. 'Their Name Liveth For Evermore', a quotation from the Book of Ecclesiasticus, is often found on larger memorials to the dead. 'The Glorious Dead' is a phrase that features on the Cenotaph in Whitehall; the permanent stone structure to replace the earlier version in wood and plaster was designed by Sir Edward Lutyens and unveiled in 1920. Perhaps most poignantly for Kipling himself, 'Known Unto God' was the phrase used on the many thousands of individual headstones on graves of unidentified soldiers.

The most obvious memorials were initially the graveyards themselves. One example is Tyne Cot near Ypres in Belgium. Originally, this contained 343 graves, but that number was soon expanded by the Commission's burial work across the area to include 11,954 individual graves, 8,367 of which are unnamed. In 1927, an inscribed stone wall was added as a memorial to the missing, and contains the names of 34,959 British and Commonwealth soldiers.

Indeed, suitably large and respectful memorials to the missing became integral to the process of memorialization. For example, the restoration and rebuilding of Ypres included a new version of the medieval Menin Gate entrance to the city. The New Menin Gate was unveiled in 1927 and recorded the names of 54,896 missing soldiers. The Tyne Cot Memorial to the Missing was used for the names that could not be fitted into Sir Reginald Blomfield's design.

Did you know?

In Greek, 'cenotaph' means 'empty tomb'.

On the Somme, the iconic Thiepval Memorial to the Missing was an Anglo-French initiative, designed by Sir Edward Lutyens and inaugurated in 1932. It contains inscriptions for 72,194 servicemen, 90 per cent of whom were lost in the Somme conflict of 1916. This monument forms the setting for the extract from *Birdsong* on page 113.

The plainness of the design that characterized this and other monumental arches, such as the New Menin Gate, is an appropriate way of evoking death in general and the missing in particular. Arches had often been associated with triumph in the past. However, these arches can be read as less triumphalist and more reflective in their style.

Elsewhere, the process of creating an appropriate mood of reflection was being elaborated by other kinds of monuments and statuary. For example, The Royal Artillery Memorial at Hyde Park Corner in London, unveiled in 1925, bears the hallmarks of Charles Jagger (1885–1934) a sculptor and designer who served at Gallipoli and on the Western Front and was seriously injured three times.

> **Activity**
>
> Carefully study the two images below of the Royal Artillery Memorial in Hyde Park, London, and consider what significance you can find in these symbolic memorial images.

Thiepval Memorial to the Missing of the Somme.

Details from the Royal Artillery Memorial, Hyde Park.

THINK ABOUT IT

Consider the war memorials that exist in your area. Perhaps there are memorials in your local park, at the church or perhaps even in your school or college. Study and discuss the styles and texts used.

 Extension activity

Find out about Jagger's Great Western Railway Memorial, situated on Platform 1 of Paddington Station in London. It inspired Ted Hughes's poem 'Platform One'. You can read more about this poem at:

http://www.theguardian.com/books/2014/jul/30/top-10-war-poems-first-world-war-jon-stallworthy

Critical approaches

Critical approaches to the literature of World War I and its aftermath are, to a large degree, tied up with changing attitudes to the conflict during the war and in the post-war period up to the present day. As with all literature, a range of perspectives can be adopted. The section of this book that deals with Modern Times looks at the proliferation of 20th- and 21st-century critical ideas that can be applied to the study of literature from 1945 to the present day. Many of these ideas were emerging at the time of World War I, so in many ways they apply equally to this topic. These approaches can inform your study of the literature of the war.

 Activity

Based on your work so far on the set texts and their contexts in Chapters 6 and 7, consider which set texts might lend themselves most readily to the following approaches, and why. Read Chapter 11 (pages 180–184) to find out more about these approaches:

- Marxist and new historicist
- psychoanalytical
- feminist

- queer theory
- theatre and performance criticism.

Given the focus on historicism in this AQA specification in general, and this topic in particular, it is important to consider how time can affect and alter critical responses to a World War I text. The next section of this chapter will look briefly at two set texts written close in time to the war itself – by those with direct experience of the war and its immediate effects. These are *Journey's End* and *A Farewell to Arms*.

Journey's End

When this play was first performed, late in 1928, it was almost universally admired as an authentic account of trench warfare; the play's commitment to realism and pessimism were seen as radical and necessary in bringing the war to the stage. The first audiences remembered the war and many had fought in it.

 Activity

Read the following extract from a review of the first production of *Journey's End* in 1928. It was written by W. A. Darlington, who was a former combatant and a playwright as well as a critic. Discuss the ways in which the play makes an impact on the reviewer. Also consider how he expresses his response.

The curtain rose – and instantly I was taken back into the very atmosphere of the trenches; and as luck had it, into the very same sector of the trenches in which I had my own experience of the front line, and which had supplied me with a setting for my own very different war story, *Alf's Button*. I had not conceived it possible that any play could so exactly recall those old memories. As the first act developed, I suddenly found myself fighting for self-control, and knew that unless I could summon reserves of restraint from somewhere, the first interval would display to the light the shocking spectacle of a hard-boiled dramatic critic in tears. I reached the end of the act safely, and my wife, turning to me, asked 'Was it like that?' I gave a couple of horrid gulps and said, 'Exactly like that.' She nodded and said almost to herself, 'I've never really known till now.'

Commentary

- Notice how Darlington is struck by the verisimilitude but also by the setting. He survived the onslaught around St Quentin in the final months of the war but Sherriff's characters do not.

- The stiff upper lip that prevails in the play also affects him as he struggles for self-control. Ironically, this attitude links the reviewer and the characters on stage. Together they share a horror of giving in to emotion and trauma.

- His wife's reaction foreshadows that of Elizabeth Benson at Thiepval in the *Birdsong* extract.

- The reference to himself as a storyteller of the trenches is full of irony. *Alf's Button* is a whimsical fantasy about a soldier with a magic lucky button to summon a genie as his saviour. It also begins with a trench handover and a portrayal of prosaic routines. There is no magic button, though, for Stanhope and his company.

The following review of the 2004 London revival of *Journey's End* is from the American drama magazine *Variety*. This production owed its success partly to the lighting design, the explosive ending where hydraulics and darkness created the illusion that the theatre had been hit by a shell, and the final tableau of the dead resurrected and standing statue-like in front of a wall of carved names, like those found on memorials to the missing.

> ### Activity
> Discuss the ways in which the following review reflects changing attitudes to the war and to the play in performance. How far does the way in which the article is written make it a product of its time?

A lot of stiff upper lips are sure to soften with honestly earned remorse in the new West End revival of 'Journey's End', a play of enormous savagery and delicacy that has at last found the production to match. Often written off as a period warhorse, R. C. Sherriff's play – Laurence Olivier starred in a single Sunday performance of the show late in 1928 – has an abiding and abundant power, especially as acted by a well-nigh flawless cast on a set by Jonathan Fensom that places us, in March 1918, in an earwig-ridden dugout on the Western front, three days before the major German offensive of World War I. Without distorting the play in any way, director David Grindley takes the text slowly and seriously, pushing every pause to the wrenching limit. The result is the most startling reappraisal of a potentially shopworn British play since Stephen Daldry revived J. B. Priestley's 'An Inspector Calls' for keeps more than a decade ago.

This is actually the third 'Journey's End' in London in the last 15 or so years (Jason Connery, Sean's son, led a previous West End outing), and it's virtually impossible to imagine a more sympathetic production. With the front a scant 50 yards away, Sherriff animates a life in and around the trenches that is terrible, to be sure, but also marches to the beat of a gallantry all its own. At once an acknowledgment of the supposed romance of war, the play doubles as a compassionate corrective to the perceived glamour of any activity that leads senselessly to death.

For its part, the production's ability to pay homage while pointing the finger at the futility of combat extends right through the curtain call. Anyone not moved beforehand surely will be done in by the final tableau, here accompanying the final and somewhat stunned applause.

This revival opened 75 years to the day after its first London run, and maybe — as, to some extent, with the Priestley — it takes that amount of time for a play presumably tethered to a particular place and era to reveal its true colors as a classic.

Whatever the reason, director Grindley leads a spectator to make connections all over the place, from Beckett (one person's decision that 'nothing matters') to Milos Forman's film of 'Hair' (that closing image) while fully conveying 'Journey's End's' qualities as dramatic template. Nick Whitby's recent Donmar entry, 'To the Green Fields Beyond', is just one recent English play that owes a debt to Sherriff, whose depiction of a societal cross-section of soldiers individually and collectively staving off madness is rooted both in the utmost realism and in a nearly surreal awareness of wartime's awful risks. Not for nothing is Osborne (David Haig), the wise, kindly lieutenant, seen to be re-reading 'Alice in Wonderland'. Osborne, the second-in-command, is the tremulous heart of the piece, incomparably so in a performance from Haig (late of 'Hitchcock Blonde' and 'Art') that raises English understatement to a high art. The veteran thesp further stills an already hushed house as this onetime schoolmaster recounts an anecdote during leave when he and his wife couldn't bring themselves to discuss the war, even as their children innocently — if that could ever be the word — played their own war games, oblivious to their father's acquaintance with the real thing.

A figure of calm who is beginning to crack, Osborne in his composure is the exact opposite of the desperate, neuralgia-stricken Hibbert (Ben Meyjes) and, even more so, of the whiskey-sodden Stanhope (Geoffrey Streatfeild, inheriting the Olivier role), the company's bully-boy captain: a 21-year-old vicar's son who is weary and scared beyond his years.

Stanhope, eyes ablaze, doesn't take kindly to the arrival in his dugout of the worshipful younger second lieutenant Raleigh (an open-faced Christian Coulson), not least because Stanhope doesn't want former schoolmate Raleigh reporting on the older man's emotional decline to Raleigh's sister, with whom Stanhope has had a fling. 'Men are different out here,' notes Osborne, almost without inflection, and Raleigh will come to recognize as much as he witnesses the collapse of the man, Stanhope, whom he once adored — a superior, by the way, not so hardened that he can't still request a kiss.

The retinue also includes Private Mason (Phil Cornwell), the resident chef with an avidity for cutlets, and Trotter (Paul Bradley), the second lieutenant who has his own obsessive mathematical method for making it through each day, even if the events of the play prove the only numerical laws by which war ever works is that people in some number will pay with their lives.

Grindley catches the dusky environs required by the setting with unerring skill, abetted no end by Jason Taylor's low-level lighting that gradually moves the stage in and out of darkness.

That's pretty much the same path travelled by a text that could seem encrusted in period speech ('keen' and 'topping' are the adjectives of choice) and outmoded social distinctions, only to catch one up in an immediacy that is reinforced by the reported casualties that fill our own newspapers daily.

'You think there's no limit to what a man can bear?' Stanhope asks near the end, and the question hangs in the air to haunt audiences in a new century facing civilization's centuries-old and lasting blight.

> **Did you know?**
>
> There have been three film adaptations of *Journey's End*. A British-American production was made in 1930. A German version *Die andere Seite* was banned when the Nazis came to power in 1933. The 1976 film *Aces High* transposed the story to the Royal Flying Corps.

Commentary

- The review alludes to familiarity dulling the impact of the play on the intervening generations – 'period warhorse', 'shopworn', and so on – and implies an ongoing obligation to ensure that audiences and readers of World War I texts are reconnected to the realities of the conflict.

- The author's use of phrases such as 'corrective to the perceived glamour', 'leads senselessly to death' and 'the futility of combat' place the review clearly in the context of how the war has been viewed for much of the 20th and 21st centuries.

- At the same time, the author is aware of the precise theatrical chronology, referring to Nick Whitby's *To the Green Fields Beyond* as being in the sub-genre presenting the fortunes of doomed soldiers established by *Journey's End*. Similarly, a review of an American production of the play in 2005 in *Variety* referred to the play as 'warfare without an exit strategy', an explicit reference to how the play can resonate by reminding audiences of recent wars such as Iraq.

- The critical reaction has remained constant; again, in 2004, the unbearable, claustrophobic intensity and authenticity of the play are hailed as its distinctive achievements. But some responses to some aspects of the play change over time. For example, presumably there was always a tendency for vogue words such as 'keen' and 'topping' (both referred to here) to sound effectively inappropriate, but to modern audiences they intensify Sherriff's presentation of Edwardian understatement and stiff upper lip. At the same time the review's use of language reflects its time too – contractions such as 'can't', ironic clippings such as 'thesp' and colloquialisms such as 'pretty much' all demonstrate the process of informalization in such texts.

A Farewell to Arms

When Hemingway's novel first appeared, it was applauded in much the same way as *Journey's End* and for similar reasons. The review from *The Guardian* below is typical:

Activity

What do you notice about aspects of gender in this review?

Goodbye to all that?

There is something so complete in Mr Hemingway's achievement in *A Farewell to Arms* that one is left speculating as to whether another novel will follow in this manner, and whether it does not complete both a period and a phase.

The story starts brilliantly with the love-making between the young American hero, Henry, a volunteer in the Italian Ambulance Service, and Catherine Barkley, an English nurse in the British hospital at Goritzia. There is subtle feminine charm in the Englishwoman's response to the man, who, at first, is just amusing himself, but the affair soon develops into real passion.

Henry, whose good relations with the Italian officers in his mess are drawn with delightful freshness, is wounded, with a smashed knee in a night assault near Plava, and is sent down from the field hospital to the American hospital at Milan, where he is the first case, and here Miss Barkley gets a transfer to nurse him.

All the descriptions of life at the front and in the hospitals, the talk of the officers, privates, and doctors, are crisply natural and make a convincing narrative, though the hero is perhaps already a little too mature and experienced. Catherine (who might be a younger sister of the heroine of *Fiesta*) is most skilfully modelled as the eternal feminine in nursing dress.

In the scenes in the Milan hospital, where love laughs at matrons and maids, the author increases his hold over us. And the story deepens in force when Henry, patched up, returns to the Isonzo front. The year has been a serious one for the Italian army, and the breakthrough of the Germans at Caporetto brings disaster.

The last 50 pages of book three describe the Italian army in retreat, the block of transport on the main roads, the bogging and abandonment of Henry's cars on a side road, the Italian privates' behaviour and their hatred of the war, and finally the shooting of the elderly officers in retreat by the Italian battle police at the Tagliamento – these pages are masterly.

The American hero escapes death by diving into the river and, later, arrest by concealing himself in a gun truck till it reaches Milan. Thence in mufti he gets to Stiesa and meets Catherine, and the lovers escape to Switzerland by a long night row up the lake. The scenes on the Italian plains hold more atmospheric truth than those of the mountain roads, but all are admirably wrought.

The impartiality of the presentation of war is as remarkable as the sincerity of the record of love passion. With remorseless artistic instinct Mr Hemingway proceeds to match the horrors of human slaughter by his final chapter of Catherine's agony and death as, 'a maternity case'.

Here he rises to his highest pitch, for Catherine's blotting-out is but complementary to the massacre of the millions on the fronts. Henry's coolness of observation in its detailed actuality is perhaps too stressed in the last pages, for in hours of great emotional strain material fact seems to detach itself as a separate phenomenon, and Henry remains too set; but the author's method prevails and triumphs in the last line.

Commentary

Hemingway was a more established writer in 1929 than West or Sherriff in their day, having published *The Sun Also Rises* and the short-story collection *Men Without Women*. Even so, reviews such as this are keen to hail the novel without any reservations. Since then the critical context has changed in various ways:

- Hemingway is not read as widely now by the public or in schools. For much of the 20th century, however, he was a best-selling author of enormous critical reputation, and his work was read in this light.

- The early representation of the 'love-making' is seen very much from a male point of view. 'Feminine charm' is 'subtle' and the future of the relationship depends upon what Henry wants. Catherine has archetypal qualities as 'the eternal feminine in nursing dress'. There are several other points you can find about both masculinity (the 'patched-up' soldier) and femininity (the matron to be laughed at), but the key thing to do is to take the views found in this review and see if they are endorsed by your reading of the novel itself.

- Some have seen his sparse style as an extension of his machismo, and his presentation of Catherine has been hotly debated in the light of feminist readings.

- More serious biographical criticism has revealed much about his painstaking writing method, and this is another critical context worthy of study. For example, he claimed to have re-written the ending 39 times, and research has posited that there is evidence of 47 re-draftings.

> **THINK ABOUT IT**
>
> Find out more about Hemingway's war experiences and war writing. Use this article as a useful starting point: http://www.archives.gov/publications/prologue/2006/spring/hemingway.html

Working with unseen extracts and comparative approaches

This chapter will:

- introduce the idea of contextual linking

- investigate ways of responding to an unseen prose extract

- look at ways of comparing two texts from different genres

- help you to start your further research into your chosen texts and contexts.

The contextual linking question

So far, the chapters in this option have introduced you to the texts available for study within the shared context of World War I, and have looked at some of the ways in which you might explore them. Now you will extend the literary and contextual knowledge and understanding you have built up, so that in the examination you can apply your skills to a prose extract you have never seen before.

The wording for this task on the examination paper has a very clear framework:

By exploring the methods [WRITER X] uses, write about the significance of [THEME Y] in this extract.

Following on from this test of your close-reading skills is a linked task which tests your wider reading by asking you to explore the same theme as it is represented in two of your World War I texts:

By exploring the methods used, compare the significance of [THEME Y] in two other texts you have studied.

The fact that the given theme appears in both questions is important. Because everyone answers the same contextual linking questions, the tasks must be accessible to all, regardless of which texts you have studied. Knowing that the given theme has to be broad enough to work with every possible grouping of three texts makes it quite possible to design questions of your own. Thinking like an examiner can help you to work on the close-reading skills you need in order to respond with confidence to unseen prose in your exam. In this chapter you will explore some ways of responding to both *prose fiction* and *prose non-fiction* that you have not read before.

Analysing unseen prose fiction: 'A Very Short Story' (1924) by Ernest Hemingway

Activity

Working either on your own or with other students, plan a response to this typical AQA-style sample question:

By exploring the methods that Ernest Hemingway uses, write about the significance of love in wartime in this extract.

Read the following extract carefully. It is a **modernist** short story in the style of a vignette, first published in Paris in 1924 as part of a collection of short fiction called *In Our Time*. It was expanded to include some of Hemingway's best-known short stories in a New York edition in 1925, where the shorter pieces such as this appear as 'interchapters'. The collection made an immediate impression, because of its spare style and unadorned directness. The disarming title gives little away but establishes the tone for a wartime love affair cut brutally short. It is based on Hemingway's own wartime experiences. The relationship depicted here was also the inspiration for *A Farewell to Arms*.

One hot evening in Padua they carried him up onto the roof and he could look out over the top of the town. There were chimney swifts in the sky.

After a while it got dark and the searchlights came out. The others went down and took the bottles with them. He and Luz could hear them below on the balcony. Luz sat on the bed. She was cool and fresh in the hot night.

Luz stayed on night duty for three months. They were glad to let her. When they operated on him she prepared him for the operating table; and they had a joke about friend or enema. He went under the anaesthetic holding tight on to himself so he would not blab about anything during the silly, talky time. After he got on crutches he used to take the temperatures so Luz would not have to get up from the bed. There were only a few patients, and they all knew about it. They all liked Luz. As he walked back along the halls he thought of Luz in his bed.

Before he went back to the front they went into the Duomo and prayed. It was dim and quiet, and there were other people praying. They wanted to get married, but there was not enough time for the banns, and neither of them had birth certificates. They felt as though they were married, but they wanted everyone to know about it, and to make it so they could not lose it.

Luz wrote him many letters that he never got until after the armistice. Fifteen came in a bunch to the front and he sorted them by the dates and read them all straight through. They were all about the hospital, and how much she loved him and how it was impossible to get along without him and how terrible it was missing him at night.

After the armistice they agreed he should go home to get a job so they might be married. Luz would not come home until he had a good job and could come to New York to meet her. It was understood he would not drink, and he did not want to see his friends or anyone in the States. Only to get a job and be married. On the train from Padua to Milan they quarreled about her not being willing to come home at once. When they had to say good-bye, in the station at Milan, they kissed good-bye, but were not finished with the quarrel. He felt sick about saying good-bye like that.

He went to America on a boat from Genoa. Luz went back to Pordonone to open a hospital. It was lonely and rainy there, and there was a battalion of arditi quartered in the town. Living in the muddy, rainy town in the winter, the major of the battalion made love to Luz, and she had never known Italians before, and finally wrote to the States that theirs had only been a boy and girl affair. She was sorry, and she knew he would probably not be able to understand, but might some day forgive her, and be grateful to her, and she expected, absolutely unexpectedly, to be married in the spring. She loved him as always, but she realized now it was only a boy and girl love. She hoped he would have a great career, and believed in him absolutely. She knew it was for the best.

The major did not marry her in the spring, or any other time. Luz never got an answer to the letter to Chicago about it. A short time after he contracted gonorrhea from a sales girl in a loop department store while riding in a taxicab through Lincoln Park.

> **THINK ABOUT IT**
>
> Discuss the possible effects of the central character remaining anonymous in this short story. What questions are posed but never definitively answered in such a sparse telling of the story?

Commentary

The initial hospital setting, with a patient falling for an attractive nurse and the whirlwind romance that follows, is a familiar romantic trope. However, Hemingway uses the Italian warfront setting to expose the hollowness of the relationship while at the same time creating pathos for the naivety of those involved. In an extremely concise form, he builds and then destroys the relationship with credible detail and deft, yet devastating irony. There is considerably more to this than the assumption often made about Hemingway that he is interested only in machismo. There is something beautifully delicate in his presentation of the two protagonists and the succinctness with which he presents their complexities and the complexities of their situation.

When presenting places and characters, Hemingway uses apparently simple methods. The Italian place names instantly create authenticity. His choice of adjectives is restrained and disarmingly simple ('cool', 'fresh', 'hot', and so on). Yet the structure of their placing conveys more than the sum of the parts. His choice of detail is similarly elliptical. For example, look at the impressionistic way in which he paints the picture of the rooftop of the hospital with chimney swifts, searchlights and bottles. The relationship with Luz is evoked in snapshots: their jokey, punning exchange before the anaesthetic; their emphatic belief in their future; their argument on the train; their farewell; the break-up.

Hemingway suggests that, almost inevitably, war undermines and destroys young love. Was it ever more than romantic delusion and infatuation? The war setting is not just a backdrop for romance; it is a haunting and brutal threat. The soldier is emasculated by his injuries and too desperate perhaps to find fun, self-worth, a future to which he can 'return'.

Even after the armistice, Luz's decision to stay on spells their end. It is, after all, a 'major' with a 'battalion' who 'conquers' Luz and destroys their dream when he has fled the field for New York. When he learns his fate, it is revealed through Hemingway's use of point of view in the series of letters he receives. Hemingway does not have to do any more than select and report extracts from these letters to convey the pain of rejection and Luz's belief that she has now found true love.

The ending of the story is the final and most brutal irony. His 'revenge' sex is sordid and this is conveyed in a simple statement of fact. The final sentence is strikingly prosaic and **dysphemistic**. Setting is crucially **significant** here. It is a long way from the Italian Front and the war hospital. Hemingway wants us to know exactly where, how and with whom – to demonstrate the extent of the fall. The reader might not be aware that 'the loop' is an area of downtown Chicago, but the other details are unmissable and shocking. Perhaps there is a further irony in evoking the name of Abraham Lincoln and the moral aspirations that have become almost synonymous with him.

Analysing unseen prose non-fiction: *World Without End* (1931) by Helen Thomas

> **Key term**
>
> **Dysphemism.** The opposite of euphemism – where the grim reality is foregrounded, or exaggerated, rather than politely avoided. Heroic war literature and propaganda often use euphemism; writers try to shock readers about the brutal truth.

> **Activity**
>
> In the previous activity, you worked through a sample contextual linking question. Now you are going to design your own. Read the following extract from Helen Thomas's memoirs and explore with the other students in your class the themes connected with World War I and its aftermath that you feel she deals with. It is an extract from the second volume of autobiography by Helen Thomas, the first volume being *As It Was* (1926). Helen Thomas (1877–1967) was the wife of Edward Thomas, the writer and poet who was killed at the Battle of Arras soon

after arriving in France. To create your question, drop the name 'Helen Thomas' into the standard question template as (**WRITER X**) and any one of the big issues you have identified as **THEME Y**. It would be possible to re-use 'love in wartime', but it would be more useful perhaps to consider a theme that enables you to explore other possibilities. Then, prepare and write up your answer to practise your technique.

And I knew Edward's agony and he knew mine, and all we could do was to speak sharply to each other: 'Now do, for goodness sake, remember, Helen, that these are the important manuscripts, and that I'm putting them here, and that this key is for the box that holds all important papers like our marriage certificate and the children's birth certificates, and my life-insurance policy. You may want them at some time, so don't go leaving the key about.'

And I, after a while: 'Can't you leave all this unnecessary tidying business, and put up that shelf you promised me? I hate this room but a few books on a shelf might make it look a bit more human.'

'Nothing will improve this room, so you had better resign yourself to it. Besides, the wall is too rotten for a shelf.'

'Oh, but you promised.'

'Well, it won't be the first time I've broken a promise to you, will it! Nor the last, perhaps.'

Oh, God! melt the snow and let the sky be blue.

The last evening comes. The children have taken down the holly and mistletoe and ivy, and chopped up the little Christmas tree to burn. And for a treat Bronwen and Myfanwy are to have their bath in front of the blazing fire. The big zinc bath is dragged in, and the children undress in high glee, and skip about naked in the warm room, which is soon filled with the sweet smell of the burning greenery.

The berries pop and the fir tree makes fairy lace, and the holly crackles and roars. The two children get in the bath together, and Edward scrubs them in turn – they laughing, making the fire hiss with their splashing. The drawn curtains shut out the snow and the starless sky, and the deathly silence out there in the biting cold is forgotten in the noise and warmth of our little room.

After the bath Edward reads [to] them. First of all he reads Shelley's 'The Question' and 'Chevy Chase', and for Myfanwy a favourite Norse tale. They sit in their nightgowns listening gravely, and then, just before they kiss him good night, while I stand with the candle in my hand, he says: 'Remember while I am away to be kind. Be kind, first of all, to Mummy, and after that be kind to everyone and everything.'

And they all assent together, and joyfully hug and kiss him, and he carries the two girls up, and drops each in her bed.

And we are left alone, unable to hide our agony, afraid to show it. Over supper, we talk of the probable front he'll arrive at, of his fellow officers, and of the unfinished portrait-etching that one of them has done of him and given to me. And we speak of the garden, and where this year he wants the potatoes to be, and he reminds me to put the beans in directly the snow disappears…

He reads me some of the poems he has written that I have not heard – the last one of all called 'Out in the Dark'. And I venture to question one line, and he says: 'Oh, no, it's right, Helen, I'm sure it's right.'

And I nod because I can't speak, and I try to smile at his assurance.

I sit and stare stupidly at his luggage by the wall, and his roll of bedding, kit bag, and suitcase. He takes out his prismatic compass and explains it to me, but I cannot see, and when a tear drops onto it, he just shuts it up and puts it away.

Then he says, as he takes a book out of his pocket: 'You see, your Shakespeare's *Sonnets* is already where it will always be. Shall I read you some?'

He reads one or two to me. His face is grey and his mouth trembles, but his voice is quiet and steady. And soon I slip to the floor and sit between his knees, and while he reads his hand falls over my shoulder and I hold it with mine.

'Shall I undress you by this lovely fire and carry you upstairs in my khaki greatcoat?' So he undoes my things, and I slip out of them; then he takes the pins out of my hair, and we laugh at ourselves for behaving as we so often do, like young lovers.

'We have never become a proper Darby and Joan, have we?'

'I'll read to you till the fire burns low, and then we'll go to bed.'

Holding the book in one hand, and bending over me to get the light of the fire on the book, he puts his other hand over my breast, and I cover his hand with mine, and he reads from *Antony and Cleopatra*. He cannot see my face, nor I his, but his low, tender voice trembles as he speaks the words so full for us of poignant meaning. That tremor is my undoing.

'Don't read any more. I can't bear it.'

All my strength gives way. I hide my face on his knee, and all my tears so long kept back come convulsively. He raises my head and wipes my eyes and kisses them, and wrapping his greatcoat round me carries me to our bed in the great, bare ice-cold room.

Further reading

Find out more about Thomas's war experiences and war poems by using the University of Oxford's First World War Poetry Digital Archive. There are facsimiles of letters, his war diary and some of the poems themselves.

Commentary

The aspects of the text that you will wish to explore in depth will depend upon the theme you have chosen for your question. However, you may like to incorporate some of the ideas below as starting points:

- Helen Thomas uses a first-person narrative to convey the subtext of the exchange between husband and wife here. On the surface they fuss and bicker about domestic issues as a way of expressing their anxiety about Edward's imminent departure for the Front. Early on in the extract, Thomas establishes this as the prevailing mood: 'I knew Edward's agony and he knew mine.'

- A series of tone shifts contribute to the compelling nature of this exchange. When Edward admits that 'it won't be the first time I've broken a promise to you, will it! Nor the last perhaps', the confidence underlying 'last' evaporates almost as the words are spoken, revealing the fear that all these words and actions will be, for her, Edward's last. The intimacy evoked at this point leads to the scene with the children and its safe, cosy, post-Christmas excitement and contentment. The bedtime readings and fatherly advice to children too young perhaps to realize the peril he is about to face are particularly touching. After the children have gone to bed, the mood changes again and the 'agony' Thomas described is laid bare. At first, there is the writer sharing his latest work with his wife, and the sharing of literature is, it is implied, a consoling interest. Then, she becomes increasingly distracted by the evidence that he is about to leave for the Front – bedding, kitbag and suitcase. However, there is an erotic charge to their sadness, reminding the reader that this relationship is real and alive. Briefly, they escape into their lovemaking. Even his khaki greatcoat becomes a romantic way to spirit her to bed.

- Their various ways of avoiding talking about their naked fear that he will be killed become dysfunctional displacement activities echoing scenes from other literature, such as the conversation between Osborne and Raleigh before the raid in *Journey's End*. The most revealing point perhaps is when Edward tries to interest Helen in the prismatic compass, but the teardrop inadvertently betrays their real feelings.

- Thomas uses the **pathetic fallacy** to emphasize the underlying sadness and loneliness the two feel. Thomas reminds us that outside it there is 'deathly silence' and 'biting cold'. Similarly, the final detail with its succession of monosyllables implies what is to come: 'great bare ice-cold room'.

> **Key term**
>
> **Pathetic fallacy.** A form of personification, whereby things in the natural world are given human attributes. The term was coined by John Ruskin, with the 'fallacy' part suggesting that over-use of the device leads to poor writing.

Comparing writers' ideas and attitudes

The last section of this chapter focuses on *comparing* texts within the shared context of World War I and its aftermath. In your examination you must explore the *same theme* as it is represented in *two texts from different genres*, and in order to do this you need to think about the reasons a writer might have for choosing to express his or her ideas in the form of poetry, prose or drama.

Texts can be compared in a variety of ways. One obvious way is to use the list of key themes that underpin the texts within this shared context:

1. Different and changing attitudes to conflict
2. Imperialism and nationalism; recruitment and propaganda; heroism
3. Life on the front line; slaughter; generals and soldiers
4. Responses on the home front; pacifism
5. Peace and memorials; political and social aftermath; impact and legacies
6. Writers in action and writers looking back.

When comparing the ways in which different writers have approached these issues, you need to think about why they are so different. Important variables here are as follows.

Key term

Intentional fallacy. The error of basing an interpretation on assumptions about the author's intentions, rather than one's own response.

Study tip

The remaining activities in this chapter would perhaps work best as group activities, with each group assigned to one of the six themes. There would then be many possibilities for sharing ideas with the whole class.

- Contexts: It might be worth reminding yourself about the **contexts of production and reception**. Also remember the framework used when considering the contexts of the core set texts in Chapter 5: time, genre, gender and location.

- Purposes: Without being drawn into the **intentional fallacy**, it is useful to consider what the reader perceives as the intentions of the text and its messages. Rather than being a crude and simplistic reduction of a text, it is often useful to think about the key message or messages of the text and what kind of broad statement or statements it is making. It is also worth bearing in mind the philosopher Marshall McLuhan's observation that 'the medium is the message'. In other words, the genre (and the ways in which a writer's methods operate within the genre) is inextricably a part of the message, and the way it is perceived and understood.

- Writer's lives: Finding out as much as you can that is relevant about the lives of the writers you are studying is often illuminating. It is a crucial part of extending your consideration of the contexts of production.

Activity

Review the three texts you have studied and how they might be compared in their approach to the six themes above, using the three variables also described above. Remember that to 'compare' involves considering the extent to which approaches might be similar or different. It might be that you need to evaluate here. In other words, what appears to be a similarity might, on further exploration, reveal interesting differences – and vice versa.

Comparing pairs of texts: prose and drama

Activity

For one, more or all of the themes below, look across the table and choose two texts, one prose and one drama, and discuss ways in which you might compare their approach to the theme.

	Theme	Prose	Drama
1.	Different and changing attitudes to conflict	A Farewell to Arms The Return of the Soldier Strange Meeting	My Boy Jack The Accrington Pals
2.	Imperialism and nationalism; recruitment and propaganda; heroism	The First Casualty All Quiet on the Western Front	Oh! What a Lovely War My Boy Jack
3.	Life on the front line; slaughter; generals and soldiers	All Quiet on the Western Front Birdsong A Long, Long Way	Journey's End Blackadder Goes Forth
4.	Responses on the home front; pacifism	The Return of the Soldier Life Class	The Accrington Pals Oh! What a Lovely War

	Theme	Prose	Drama
5.	Peace and memorials; political and social aftermath; impact and legacies	*Birdsong* *Regeneration*	*Blackadder Goes Forth* *Oh! What a Lovely War*
6.	Writers in action and writers looking back	*Goodbye to All That* *A Farewell to Arms*	*Journey's End*

Comparing pairs of texts: poems

> **Activity**
>
> Because it is harder to generalize about anthologies of multiple poems, let's consider comparing individual poems first. Looking at one or more of the anthologies, think of some individual poems that might fit the themes listed. Then, take one theme at a time and **compare** two chosen poems within that theme. Whichever anthology you choose, there should be enormous scope here.

	Theme	Poetry
1.	Different and changing attitudes to conflict	Perhaps look for early, 'naïve' poems and then compare them with later, more cynical and disillusioned poems.
2.	Imperialism and nationalism; recruitment and propaganda; heroism	Again, early, 'naïve' poems may be relevant here, but also look for those concerned with leadership or the attitudes of the countries involved.
3.	Life on the front line; slaughter; generals and soldiers	Categorizing poems by their combat zone (e.g. Ypres, Somme, other fronts or locations) and by the kinds of activities/scenarios involved is often illuminating.
4.	Responses on the home front; pacifism	Use gender and attitude to distinguish between poems.
5.	Peace and memorials; political and social aftermath; impact and legacies	Precise time settings and attitudes will help refine your responses.
6.	Writers in action and writers looking back	Find out which poets died and how; make sure you know what happened to survivors and how and when they came to look back.

Further comparison between texts and across genres

There are many linking threads to be explored between texts and across genres. This is a way of comparing that can provide precise focus. One example would be the presentation of trench gas attacks and the ways in which these scenes can illuminate 'Life on the front line; slaughter; generals and soldiers'. 'Dulce et Decorum Est' by Wilfred Owen is very well known. It would be interesting to put this alongside the gas attack scenes in *A Long, Long Way* (Penguin, Chapter 4, pages 42–43) and *All Quiet on the Western Front* (towards the end of Chapter 4).

Activity

To complete the comparative process so that you can practise comparing across three genres (for one, more or all of the themes), choose one set of a novel, play and poem that you can fit together and discuss the ways in which the three texts can be compared.

- Identify extracts for close reading and analysis.
- Discuss the links that could be made in a particular thread.
- Identify and research your own suggestions for threads.

	Theme	Thread
1.	Different and changing attitudes to conflict	Confrontations between pro- and anti-war parties
		Soldiers' parents, mentors and lovers
		Letters home
		Pre-Somme attitudes
		Post-Somme attitudes
2.	Imperialism and nationalism; recruitment and propaganda; heroism	Volunteering/being conscripted
		Accounts of 1914
		Leaders of countries/forces
		Propagandists at work
3.	Life on the front line; slaughter; generals and soldiers	Gas attacks
		Going over the top
		Critiques of commanding officers
		Routines
		Dealing with the dead and injured
		Incidents responsible for post-traumatic stress disorder
		Letter/diary writing
4.	Responses on the Home Front; pacifism	Soldiers' parents, mentors and lovers
		Soldiers' communications with home
		Treatment of conscientious objectors/non-volunteers
		Confrontations between pro- and anti-war parties
5.	Peace and memorials; political and social aftermath; impact and legacies	Accounts of and responses to the Armistice
		Responding to memorials
		Subsequent generations looking back
		Making links with subsequent wars
6.	Writers in action and writers looking back	First-hand accounts, particularly with reference to themes 3–5
		Portrayals of writers in fiction and non-fiction

Further reading

Barlow, Adrian. (2000). *The Great War in British literature*. Cambridge: Cambridge University Press.

Fussell, P. (1975). *The Great War and modern memory*. New York: Oxford University Press.

Hibberd, Dominic. (2003). *Wilfred Owen: a new biography*. Chicago, Ivan R. Dee.

Hynes, S. (1991). *A war imagined: the First World War and English culture*. New York: Atheneum.

Hynes, S. (1968). *The Edwardian turn of mind: the First World War and English culture*. Princeton N.J.: Princeton University Press.

MacArthur, B. (2008). *For king and country: voices from the First World War*. London: Little, Brown.

Marlow, Joyce. (2008). *The Virago book of women and the Great War, 1914-18*. London: Virago Press.

Reynolds, D. (2013). *The long shadow: the Great War and the Twentieth Century*. London: Simon & Schuster.

Roberts, D. (1996). *Minds at war: the poetry and experience of the First World War*. Burgess Hill: Saxon Books.

Sheffield, G.D (2014). *The First World War remembered*. London; Andre Deutsch.

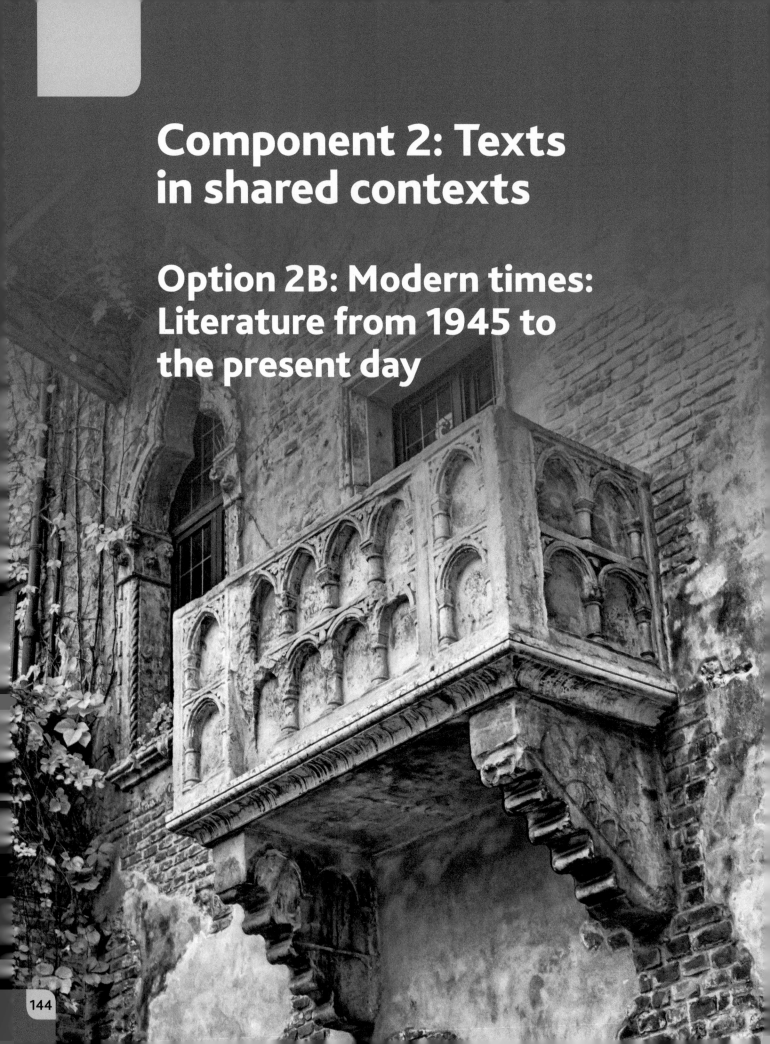

Component 2: Texts in shared contexts

Option 2B: Modern times: Literature from 1945 to the present day

The contextual framework

The poetry, prose and drama that you will study for the 'Modern times' option was published in the second half of the 20th century and the early years of the 21st – with a historical starting-point of 1945 (the end of World War II). The horrors of the Nazi Holocaust and the atomic bomb attacks on the Japanese cities of Hiroshima and Nagasaki profoundly affected many writers, as did the momentous historical events of the second half of the 20th century (from the Cold War through the Civil Rights Movement, the rise of feminism, decolonization, the fall of the Berlin Wall, the advent of communications technology such as the Internet and the 9/11 Al-Qaeda attack on the Twin Towers in New York). As you read within this shared context, therefore, you will be exploring the ways in which modern and contemporary literature has engaged with some of the climactic social, cultural, political and personal issues that have shaped the lives of everybody who has lived through the latter half of the 20th century and the early years of the 21st.

> This chapter will:
> - explore the idea of studying texts in a shared context
> - review the texts available for study within this shared context.

Activity

American singer-songwriter Billy Joel's song *We Didn't Start the Fire* memorably synthesizes some of the most iconic historical events and characters of the years 1949 (when Joel was born) to 1989 (when the song was written). Working as a group, do an Internet search for both the lyrics of the song and the original video, in which the changing lives of a typical young couple trying to achieve the American Dream are offset with images of tumultuous social, cultural and political events. As you analyse this rapid-fire pop-cultural overview of the 'Modern times' context, discuss as a class any patterns that you may find in the allusions Billy Joel – a self-confessed 'history nut' – has chosen to define and summarize the latter half of the twentieth century.

Modern times: key issues

Key issues that might be covered within the context of 'Modern times' include:

1. Wars and the legacy of wars
2. Personal and social identity
3. Changing morality and social structures
4. Gender, class, race and ethnicity
5. Political upheaval and change
6. Resistance and rebellion
7. Imperialism, post-imperialism and nationalism

Before you begin to explore the ways in which some of these key issues have been represented in *your* poetry, prose and drama texts, however, it is important to review *all* of the texts that have been grouped together within this shared context. Although you will only study *three* texts in depth, finding out about the others will give you a very useful overview of the whole 'Modern times' context.

Activity

Read the following text summaries and discuss with your fellow students why you think each text has been chosen as representative of this shared context. Think about how these texts might be seen as dealing with the key issues listed overleaf and thus how they reflect the time period in which they were produced.

Modern times: requirements

Six core set texts and 15 chosen comparative set texts can be studied in this option. You will focus on *one prose text*, *one drama text* and *one poetry text*, one of which must have been published after 2000. The texts are all introduced below.

- **Core set texts:** You must study *at least one* of these in order to answer a question in Section A of your Paper 2 exam.
- **Chosen comparative set texts:** You must study *two* texts in order to answer the comparative context question in Section B of your Paper 2 exam. (*One* of the texts can be from the core set text list, if you *do not* use it in your Section A answer.)

Core set texts

Prose: *The Handmaid's Tale* by Margaret Atwood (1985)

The Handmaid's Tale is a **dystopian** novel set in the near future, after the **totalitarian** Republic of Gilead has overthrown the government of the USA. Women's rights have been quickly eroded as society has restructured itself along ultra-conservative social and religious lines. The central character, Offred, a concubine or 'handmaid' used for sexual reproduction by the members of Gilead's elite, tells the story of her life as the handmaid of 'the Commander' and his wife, Serena Joy.

Prose: *Waterland* by Graham Swift (1983)

Waterland looks at why people tell stories and how narratives work. Past, present and future collide for history teacher Tom Crick, as he discloses a personal tragedy of sexual jealousy, kidnap and murder to his unimpressed school students – themselves haunted by the threat of nuclear war. The narrative unfolds in a compelling and apparently haphazard manner, as Crick interweaves world events (history) with gothic tales about his own family, the landscape of the East Anglian Fens and even the life cycle of the eel ('his/story').

Drama: *Top Girls* by Caryl Churchill (1982)

Set in the early 1980s, *Top Girls* is the story of Marlene, who makes many personal sacrifices in order to pursue a successful career. Ideas about what it means to be a woman are explored – partly through a fantastical dinner party sequence in which famous characters from history discuss their lives. The play asks searching questions about the extent to which women can really ever 'have it all' in the sense of juggling a fulfilling career and a happy family.

Key terms

Dystopian. The opposite of Utopian – a (usually invented) society in which people are disjointed and unhappy.

Totalitarian. A system of government which has complete State control and no democratic structures.

Did you know?

To a 21st-century audience, the office scenes in *Top Girls* can seem almost as historic as the dinner party guests, given that no one in the play uses everyday technology such as a smart phone, email or the Internet.

Drama: *A Streetcar Named Desire* by Tennessee Williams (1947)

English teacher Blanche DuBois arrives to stay with her sister and brother-in-law, Stella and Stanley Kowalski, in working-class New Orleans just after World War II. Stanley and Blanche's mutual loathing simmers throughout a long hot summer as the pregnant Stella tries to keep the peace. On the night Stella goes into hospital to have her baby, the tension explodes in an orgy of frantic violence.

Poetry: *Feminine Gospels* by Carol Ann Duffy (2002)

In the first part of this poetry collection, queens, movie stars, mothers, wives, witches, femmes fatales, dieters, shopaholics and schoolgirls all tell their tragic, startling, surprising and often very funny stories. The title of this text reflects Duffy's aim to rewrite the 'gospel truth' of scripture from a female point of view, and she refers to the grim reality of modern life and the cheap brutality of popular culture as often as she evokes literature, myth and fairytale. A long narrative poem, 'The Laughter of Stafford Girls' High', dominates the middle section of the book; it tells the surreal story of an unstoppable wave of joy that bubbles up among a group of schoolgirls and transforms their teachers' lives. The collection ends with a wistful group of lyrical love poems and personal meditations.

Poetry: *Skirrid Hill* by Owen Sheers (2005)

The title of this poetry collection is very important, as the word 'Skirrid' is derived from the Welsh 'Ysgyrid' meaning 'divorce' or 'separation'. Sheers is very concerned with exploring the geography and history of the Welsh border country – its location in time and place – as well as humanity's relationship with the natural world. Yet he is equally interested in writing about war, conflict and death, as well as love, life, growing up and the family.

Further reading

Sheer Poetry (http://www.sheerpoetry.co.uk/) is a subscription-only website that currently costs £12 a year to join. It contains an excellent range of exclusive resources by Carol Ann Duffy, Gillian Clarke, Seamus Heaney, Simon Armitage, Owen Sheers and others. Your teacher may wish to consider subscribing to the site.

Luke McBratney's *Skirrid Hill A-level English Literature Study Guide* (Philip Allan, 2011) gives a rich interpretation of each individual poem, as well as the themes and ideas of the collection as a whole. The book was written with the cooperation of Owen Sheers.

Did you know?

Owen Sheers has said looking over the Black Mountains makes him think about 'the relationship between humans and nature in this half-farmed part of the world; about Wales's defensive history; about the sweep of geographical time in the glacier-carved valleys, and the shorter arc of historical time in the concentric rings of a hill-fort on the opposite ridge'. He went on: 'In both landscape and poetry, therefore, a vast array of abstract associations are delivered in concrete form and presented as a coherent whole.'

Did you know?

The best-known play of Michael Frayn – a playwright as well as a novelist – is the ingenious comic farce *Noises Off* (1982). The play's title, which refers to a stage direction indicating sounds coming from offstage, hints at its inventive 'play-within-a-play' structure; a ramshackle theatre company implodes while rehearsing a dated sex comedy called *Nothing On*.

Did you know?

The God of Small Things is Arundhati Roy's only published novel. Since 1997 she has focused on campaigning for political, human rights and environmental causes.

Did you know?

Asked about being a white woman who has chosen to write the stories of black women, Kathryn Stockett has said: 'At first, I wasn't nervous writing in the voice of Aibileen and Minny because I didn't think anybody would ever read the story except me.' She went on: 'But when other people started reading it, I was very worried about what I'd written and the line I'd crossed. And the truth is, I'm still nervous. I'll never know what it really felt like to be in the shoes of those black women who worked in the white homes of the South during the 1960s and I hope that no one thinks I presume to know that. But I had to try. I wanted the story to be told. I hope I got some of it right.'

Chosen comparative set texts

Prose: *Spies* by Michael Frayn (2002)

Stephen Wheatley looks back half a century to his World War II childhood, to remember when he and his friend Keith Hayward spied on Keith's mother – convinced that she was a Nazi secret agent. The mature Stephen describes the troubling process through which he patches together fragments of history, and his own mysteriously conflicted personal identity, to reveal that the 'real' spy in the neighbourhood was unsuspected all along.

Further reading

The *Guardian* newspaper's Book Club has produced a podcast of Professor John Mullan interviewing Michael Frayn about *Spies* in front of a live audience.

Equally useful is Professor Mullan's linked series of four mini-essays on the novel, each of which examines a key aspect of narrative in a brief but illuminating way. You can access this at: http://www.theguardian.com/books/audio/2012/jun/14/michael-frayn-spies-book-club. John Mullan's critical analysis of *Spies* is available at: http://www.theguardian.com/books/2012/may/25/book-club-spies-michael-frayn

Prose: *One Flew Over the Cuckoo's Nest* by Ken Kesey (1962)

Set in an American psychiatric hospital, this cult 1960s novel dramatizes the sinister ways in which an authoritarian regime characterized as 'The Combine' can overpower the individual. The power of 'The Combine' is symbolized by Nurse Ratched, who exerts a sinister form of covert control over the patients on her psychiatric ward. The narrator, Chief Bromden, describes the behaviour of the rebellious anti-hero Randle Patrick McMurphy, who is only faking madness in order to serve his sentence in hospital rather than jail. As McMurphy's anarchic resistance to Nurse Ratched's authority encourages the other patients to defy 'The Combine', the stage is set for an appalling and tragic finale.

Prose: *The God of Small Things* by Arundhati Roy (1997)

This novel tells the tragic and turbulent story of Indian twins Rahel and Estha, their mother Ammu, and her doomed love affair with the 'Untouchable' Velutha. Set in the fragmented and complex surroundings of multicultural Kerala in the late 1960s, the novel is told largely from Rahel's point of view and reveals why and how she and Estha have been left trapped within their traumatic shared past. When they meet again after years of estrangement, the twins' complex history leads them to comfort each other through embarking on a sexual relationship.

Prose: *The Help* by Kathryn Stockett (2009)

This novel tells the hidden stories of the African-American maids – 'the help' – who work for the wealthy white families of Jackson, Mississippi, in the early 1960s. The narrative switches between the first-person viewpoints of two mature black women, Aibileen and Minny, and the young daughter of an affluent white family, Skeeter, who all work together in order to tell the ugly and dangerous truth about the secret lives of 'the help'.

Prose: *The Color Purple* by Alice Walker (1982)

Raped by her stepfather at the age of 14, deprived of her two children and forced to marry a man who cares nothing for her, the heroine of this novel seems doomed to a tragic existence. Yet by the end of *The Color Purple*, which is set in rural Georgia in the early years of the 20th century, Celie is a successful business entrepreneur, whose clothing collective 'Folkspants Unlimited' is a touchstone of economic, political, social and cultural progress, and represents the heart of a vibrant and lively extended family.

Prose: *Oranges are not the Only Fruit* by Jeanette Winterson (1985)

This novel is the story of Jeanette, who grows up in an extremely strict Christian community in the north of England, and her love affair with a young woman called Melanie. The central character bears the name of the writer and the narrative has clear links with Jeanette Winterson's own difficult personal relationship with her adoptive mother. The novel asks big questions about family, identity, society and sexuality as the heroine finds the courage to challenge her mother's authoritarian regime.

> ### Did you know?
> *Oranges are not the Only Fruit* has been described as a *roman à clef* (a French term meaning 'novel with a key') because it has such a strong connection with aspects of the writer's own past. The term suggests that a 'code' within a fictional text can be used to decipher real-life events.

> ### Further reading
> The *Guardian* newspaper's Book Club has produced a podcast of Professor John Mullan interviewing Jeanette Winterson about *Oranges are not the Only Fruit* in front of a live audience.
>
> Equally useful is Professor Mullan's linked series of four mini-essays on the novel, each of which examines a key aspect of narrative in a brief but illuminating way. You can access this at: http://www.theguardian.com/books/audio/2007/nov/02/books1222
>
> John Mullan's critical analysis of *Oranges are not the Only Fruit* is available at: http://www.theguardian.com/books/2007/oct/20/jeanettewinterson

Prose: *Revolutionary Road* by Richard Yates (1961)

Computer salesman Frank Wheeler and his wife April deliberately set themselves apart from their conformist neighbours living in a suburban Connecticut housing estate in 1955. They plan a daring move to cosmopolitan France, to escape the conventionality of their dead-end existence, but when April becomes pregnant for the third time, the escape plan founders and their marriage begins to fall apart. The novel's tragic and shocking denouement leaves Frank contemplating a bleak and empty future.

> ### Did you know?
> Described by Kurt Vonnegut as 'The Great Gatsby of my time' and by Tennessee Williams as 'a masterpiece in modern American fiction', *Revolutionary Road* was for years considered a hidden cult classic as opposed to a bestseller, with Yates himself characterized as a 'writer's writer' whose literary skill was too subtle to earn mass popular approval.

> ### Further reading
> Julia Millhouse has written two very useful articles about *Revolutionary Road*:
> - 'Can't Act, Won't Act' (*English Review* 21:1, pages 18–21, September 2010) looks at April's stage career as a metaphor for the Wheelers' failed lives.
> - 'Baby, Baby, Where Did Our Love Go? Love, Children and Parenting' (*English Review* 23:4, pages 38–41, April 2013) focuses on the narrative importance of the Wheelers' children, Jennifer and Mike.

Drama: *Translations* by Brian Friel (1980)

It is 1833. Two Englishmen, Lancey and Yolland, arrive in Baile Beag (Ballybeg) to map the Irish countryside for the Ordnance Survey. As he translates local place names into English for the map, Yolland, who has fallen in love with a local girl, becomes increasingly uneasy at the part he is playing in destroying Irish history, language and culture. The play's downbeat and uneasy ending reflects the longstanding inability of the Irish and English to overcome the barriers that divide them and to understand each other.

Drama: *All My Sons* by Arthur Miller (1947)

All My Sons dramatizes the consequences of Joe Keller's wartime past, as his guilty secret re-emerges to destroy him. During World War II, he knowingly allowed his factory to supply faulty aeroplane parts that led to the deaths of 21 American pilots, and whereas his business partner took all the blame and went to jail, Keller was cleared. Both of Keller's sons served in the war, but while Chris returns home, Larry is still listed as Missing in Action after a plane crash in China. The tragic postwar aftermath shows how the past casts a looming shadow over the future.

Drama: *Our Country's Good* by Timberlake Wertenbaker (1988)

It is the 1780s. A group of convicted criminals and Royal Marines travel to found the first penal colony in Australia on board the ship *Sirius*. Both the transported convicts and the sailors in charge are fearful of the future. When the authorities decide to let the convicts put on a play, George Farquhar's 1706 comedy *The Recruiting Officer* is chosen. Auditions are held and, as the convicts stage their first performance, issues of class, gender and justice are opened up as we are invited to debate how far art can 'civilize' the underclass.

Drama: *Cat on a Hot Tin Roof* by Tennessee Williams (1955)

The wealthy Pollitt family is in crisis – trapped in a web of lies, secrets and silences of its own making. The three main characters – Brick, his wife Maggie, and his father Big Daddy, who owns an enormous Mississippi cotton plantation – all face up to their deepest psychological fears during the course of one hot, sultry summer night. Big Daddy challenges Brick about his alcoholism, Brick tells Big Daddy the truth about his diagnosis of terminal cancer, and Maggie determines that Brick will get her pregnant. The play ends on an uncertain note, poised between the extremes of life and death.

Further reading

Nicola Onyett's article 'The Many Lives of Cat on a Hot Tin Roof' (*English Review* 18:2, pages 21–24, November 2007) looks at Williams' blurring of literary genres as well as reviewing the cultural contexts of the play.

Poetry: *Selected Poems* by Tony Harrison (2013)

This revised selection includes the long narrative poem 'v', written during the bitter 1984–85 miners' strike and set in the ruined cemetery (vandalized by graffiti) where Tony Harrison's parents are buried. The poet sees the

---

Did you know?

All My Sons is based on the true story of an Ohio firm which was investigated by the US government after several workers blew the whistle on the company's corrupt practices. Arthur Miller's mother-in-law told him about the case after reading a newspaper report.

Did you know?

Timberlake Wertenbaker based her play on the Australian writer Thomas Keneally's 1987 novel *The Playmaker*. Another of Keneally's novels has been adapted into a dramatic form, with *Schindler's Ark* forming the basis for Steven Spielberg's famous film about the Nazi Holocaust, *Schindler's List* (1993).

Did you know?

Tennessee Williams considered *Cat on a Hot Tin Roof* his best play, partly because of 'the kingly magnitude of Big Daddy. Yet I seem to contradict myself. I write so often of people with no magnitude, at least on the surface. I write of "little people". But are there "little people"? I sometimes think there are only little conceptions of people. Whatever is living and feeling with intensity is not little and, examined in depth, it would seem to me that most "little people" are living with that intensity that I can use as a writer.'

desecration of gravestones as symbolic of a broken and polarized society. The graffiti includes the word 'united', as in Leeds United, the local football team, and Harrison contrasts this 'unity' with the binary divisions summed up in the poem's title, which is short for the Latin 'versus' meaning 'against'. Harrison's poems are often inspired by his memories of growing up in a traditional working-class family, and reflect upon the personal and political tensions that came about as he and his postwar generation moved away from their cultural roots.

Poetry: *New Selected Poems 1966–1987* by Seamus Heaney (1990)

Seamus Heaney writes of family, identity and community, anchoring his poetry in the Irish landscape and the Irish past. In some ways his work seems timeless and almost mythic, yet the years in which many of these poems were written were urgent and turbulent ones spanning the height of the sectarian 'Troubles' in Northern Ireland. The selection reflects the ways in which Heaney engaged with the world about him, and many of these poems chart his responses to contemporary society, culture and politics.

Further reading

Dennis O'Driscoll's *Stepping Stones: Interviews with Seamus Heaney* (Faber, 2009) is a fascinating series of interviews shedding light on Heaney's work and life through the poet's stories, opinions and memories.

Prose: *Birthday Letters* by Ted Hughes (1998)

Released only months before his death, this collection of 88 poems is Ted Hughes's attempt to tell his side of the story of his troubled marriage to the poet Sylvia Plath. From her tragic suicide in 1963 until the publication of these poems 35 years later, Hughes kept silent about his life with Plath to protect the privacy of their two children, but in the absence of accurate information, speculation over 'the real story' of these two iconic poets was relentless. This poetic epitaph has, therefore, been interpreted as Hughes's apparent wish to have the final say in his last, most autobiographical, collection of poems.

Poetry: *Ariel* by Sylvia Plath (1965)

The *Ariel* collection was originally published in 1965, two years after Sylvia Plath's suicide, and deals unflinchingly with the raw material of the poet's own tragic personal history, troubled relationships and yearning to be a poet. Plath's widower, Ted Hughes, edited the collection, dropping some poems Plath had wanted to include in favour of others he preferred and rearranging their order. In so doing he fulfilled her burning wish to leave behind a genuine poetic legacy, but set up decades of controversy about the extent to which this collection is Sylvia Plath's *Ariel* or that of Ted Hughes.

Extension activity

Having read the text summaries above, choose *one* extra poetry, prose or drama text from within the shared context to read for pleasure. If your fellow class members select from the full range of texts on offer, you can produce a really useful set of PowerPoint slides or printed guides to inform each other about the ways in which each text reflects the time period in which it was produced.

Did you know?

When Channel 4 broadcast a film of Tony Harrison reading 'v' in 1987, many newspapers expressed outrage at the poem's extensive use of strong taboo language and it was discussed in Parliament during a debate on obscenity.

Did you know?

'The Troubles' is the common name for the bitter conflict in Northern Ireland that began in the late 1960s and is usually taken to have ended with the signing of an agreement between the British and Irish governments 30 years later. Communities were divided along political and religious lines, with the mainly Protestant unionists and loyalists who wanted Northern Ireland to stay part of the UK totally opposed to the mainly Catholic nationalists and republicans who wanted to form part of a united Ireland. More than 3500 people were killed during the violence. You can find out more about this dark period in modern Irish history on the BBC History website: http://www.bbc.co.uk/history/troubles.

Did you know?

The fact that Ted Hughes had been unfaithful to Sylvia Plath and had destroyed some of her poems after her death led some feminist critics to characterize him as her evil persecutor. One extreme Hughes-hater went so far as to chip his name off her tombstone so that it read 'Sylvia Plath' as opposed to 'Sylvia Plath Hughes'.

This chapter will:

- identify some relevant social, historical, political and cultural contexts which can be applied to the 'Modern times' set texts
- identify some of the methods used by writers to shape meanings.

This chapter contains extracts from seven of the 21 set texts, which are linked to the seven key issues listed on page 145. Each extract is accompanied by a commentary, an interesting comment from the writer to provide useful background information, and an activity to get you thinking about how your three chosen texts might tap into specific aspects of the overarching context.

To get the most out of this option, you need to think laterally. Obviously, not every theme and context is relevant to every text; *Translations* (set in 1833) and *Our Country's Good* (set in 1798) can hardly reflect directly on the impact of World War II, for example, any more than *All My Sons* (written in 1947) can predict the changing roles of women or the Civil Rights movement. But what all these texts can (and do) explore are some of the pre-eminent literary issues of the postwar context: conflict, power and justice.

The overarching concerns within these texts – what they are really all about, in other words – are essentially the same as those explored by poets, writers and dramatists of all eras and cultures: everything that contributes to our experience of what it means to be human. Love and hate, war and peace, greed and betrayal, loneliness and death were as important to the audiences who first watched the ancient Greek plays as to contemporary *Game of Thrones* fanatics. Your three texts will contain narrators, speakers and characters all trying to answer the eternal questions that once tortured Oedipus and now obsess the Starks and the Lanisters: Who am I? How did I get here? Where have I come from? What am I here for? Where am I going? How do I know if I am loved?

Within this exam component, however, you need to think specifically about the ways in which these perennial themes have been dealt with in literature produced between 1945 and the present day. By filtering your three texts through the lens of the 'Modern times' context and considering the impact of the social, cultural, historical, political, economic and literary circumstances within which they were originally produced, you will reach a richer and more rewarding understanding of them.

All of the 'Modern times' set texts present ideas about individuals coming into conflict with the society in which they live – be they young or old, rich or poor, male or female, black or white, gay or straight, liberal or conservative, religious or atheist. Like them, we all sometimes feel lonely, misunderstood, isolated or out of step, and this theme unifies and underpins all of the texts grouped together within this context. They were all produced within a time period marked by uncertainty, instability and massive social, cultural and political change; it makes no difference whether these key concerns emerge via a play about a motley crew of prisoners exiled to Australia, a novel about a lesbian schoolgirl in a grim northern mill town, or a collection of poems probing the writer's own terrible emotional wounds. As you work through this option, therefore, you need to think first about the big themes embedded within this specific context, and then about how the 'Modern times' framework could have affected the ways in which these themes have been represented.

1 Wars and the legacy of wars

Sample text: 'Lady Lazarus' from *Ariel* by Sylvia Plath

Written in October 1962, just three months before she committed suicide at the age of thirty, 'Lady Lazarus' (below) is one of Sylvia Plath's most famous poems. The blending of the notorious real-life horrors of the Nazi Holocaust and Plath's own personal psychological trauma is simultaneously appalling and unforgettable, as her female speaker (named after the New Testament character raised from the dead by Jesus) describes her strange recurring pattern of last-minute resurrections.

Activity

Plath's decision to use the most appalling historical event of the 20th century to explore her own feelings has caused controversy; some readers might find her approach daring and innovative, while others could see it as disrespectful and self-indulgent. How do you respond to the methods the poet has used below to convey her ideas and attitudes?

Did you know?

Sylvia Plath's semi-autobiographical novel *The Bell Jar* is an iconic feminist text often interpreted as a fictionalized version of the writer's own struggle with mental illness. It tells the story of high-achieving American college student Esther Greenwood's fight to forge her own identity rather than conform to the ideas of others. Originally published under the pen-name Victoria Lucas, it finally came out under Plath's own name four years after her suicide.

I have done it again.
One year in every ten
I manage it –

A sort of walking miracle, my skin
Bright as a Nazi lampshade,
My right foot

A paperweight,
My face a featureless, fine
Jew linen.

Peel off the napkin
O my enemy.
Do I terrify? –

The nose, the eye pits, the full set of teeth?
The sour breath
Will vanish in a day.

Soon, soon the flesh
The grave cave ate will be
At home on me

And I a smiling woman.
I am only thirty.
And like the cat I have nine times to die.

This is Number Three.
What a trash
To annihilate each decade.

What a million filaments.
The peanut-crunching crowd
Shoves in to see

Them unwrap me hand and foot –
The big strip tease.
Gentlemen, ladies

These are my hands
My knees.
I may be skin and bone,

Nevertheless, I am the same, identical woman.
The first time it happened I was ten.
It was an accident.

The second time I meant
To last it out and not come back at all.
I rocked shut

As a seashell.
They had to call and call
And pick the worms off me like sticky pearls.

Dying
Is an art, like everything else.
I do it exceptionally well.

I do it so it feels like hell.
I do it so it feels real.
I guess you could say I've a call.

It's easy enough to do it in a cell.
It's easy enough to do it and stay put.
It's the theatrical

Comeback in broad day
To the same place, the same face, the same brute
Amused shout:

'A miracle!'
That knocks me out.
There is a charge

For the eyeing of my scars, there is a charge
For the hearing of my heart –
It really goes.

And there is a charge, a very large charge
For a word or a touch
Or a bit of blood

Or a piece of my hair or my clothes.
So, so, Herr Doktor.
So, Herr Enemy.

I am your opus,
I am your valuable,
The pure gold baby

That melts to a shriek.
I turn and burn.
Do not think I underestimate your great concern.

Ash, ash –
You poke and stir.
Flesh, bone, there is nothing there –

A cake of soap,
A wedding ring,
A gold filling.

Herr God, Herr Lucifer
Beware
Beware.

Out of the ash
I rise with my red hair
And I eat men like air.

Did you know?

Valuable archive recordings of Plath discussing and reading her poems have been released on CD. *Sylvia Plath: The Spoken Word* (British Library Audio CD, 2010) includes a BBC interview with Plath and Ted Hughes in which they discuss their marriage and their work.

Activity

Assess the ways in which the poet's decision to use major world events to express her personal pain helps to place 'Lady Lazarus' within the 'Modern times' context.

Commentary

Plath's speaker likens herself to the Biblical figure raised from the dead by Jesus, although of course she outdoes the original Lazarus in resurrection terms, since she has pulled off the trick three times and he managed it only once. One of a group of American poets active in the 1950s and 1960s whose work is described as **confessional**, Plath's raw material is highly personal, autobiographical and often controversial, and 'Lady Lazarus' is a prime example of the writer exploiting her own individual pain to express a more broadly applicable truth. Just as the Nazi death camps were filled with disjointed body parts – 'skin', a 'foot', 'flesh', 'bone' and even a 'gold filling' – so the speaker's own sense of self has fragmented. The blending of private pain and historical horror expressed in this poem depends upon the reader accepting that one woman's suicide attempts can be legitimately compared with the atrocities of Auschwitz. As the speaker equates her own mental anguish with the suffering of the Jews, the ghoulish creepiness of the 'peanut-crunching crowd' goggling at her return from the dead raises uncomfortable questions about the reactions of those closest to her when they witness the extent of her despair.

'Kindness', one of the last poems that Plath wrote before she died, contains the ominous line: 'The blood jet is poetry, / There is no stopping it.' Yet the very controlled technical structure of elegant **tercets** in 'Lady Lazarus' gives the lie to the idea that all the poet had to do was open a vein and let her personal pain pour out; one of the most striking things about the text is the glaring disconnect between the speaker's mocking, flippant, jaunty tone and the ultimate horror of suicide. Using the rhythms of everyday colloquial speech, Plath parodies the voice of a control freak, a performer, a showgirl, a striptease artist or an

Sylvia Plath and Ted Hughes

escapologist bragging about how she has cheated death. Among the speaker's many roles are the cat with nine lives, the washed-up showbiz act pulling off a last-minute comeback, the iconic medieval martyr and the avenging devil-woman. Yet the crowd's cheer is 'brute' and her rescuers are enemies as deadly as the Nazi doctors who performed hideous experiments on live human beings in the death camps: 'Herr Doktor' is 'Herr Enemy'. Defying those who regard bringing her back from the dead as their 'opus' or great work, the speaker ends by claiming the right to recreate herself. The ultimate paradox at the heart of 'Lady Lazarus' is that even as the speaker reassures her audience that she is 'the same, identical woman' after her resurrection, she is revealing that she has been unwillingly dragged back into the very life that made her to want to commit suicide in the first place. Surely, therefore, in the end, what she is really promising the crowd is to 'do it again'.

What does the writer say?

In a reading prepared for BBC radio, Sylvia Plath introduced 'Lady Lazarus' like this: 'The speaker is a woman who has the great and terrible gift of being reborn. The only trouble is, she has to die first. She is the Phoenix, the libertarian spirit, what you will. She is also just a good, plain, very resourceful woman.'

Activity

Discuss with the rest of your class how the three writers you are studying represent the weight of the past, both personally and in terms of politics and history. What methods do they use to convey their ideas and attitudes?

2 Personal and social identity

Sample text: *The Handmaid's Tale* by Margaret Atwood

In the Christian fundamentalist Republic of Gilead, the role of the handmaid, Offred, is to bear a child for the Commander and his wife, Serena Joy. Following the delivery of a healthy baby and the successful completion of her assignment, Offred will then leave the Commander's household. Before the all-important Ceremony, which is designed to ensure Offred gets pregnant, the husband, wife and handmaid take part in a religious service in which the Commander asks for 'a moment of silent prayer' and 'a blessing, and for success in all our ventures'. Ominously, however, while Serena Joy is crying, as she always does on the night of the Ceremony, Offred's secret prayer is '*Nolite te bastardes carborundorum*' – 'don't let the bastards grind you down.' In the extract below, Offred describes the Ceremony – a fertility ritual – itself.

> Above me, towards the head of the bed, Serena Joy is arranged, outspread. Her legs are apart, I lie between them, my head on her stomach, her pubic bone under the base of my skull, her thighs on either side of me. She too is fully clothed.
>
> My arms are raised; she holds my hands, each of mine in each of hers. This is supposed to signify that we are one flesh, one being. What it really means is that she is in control, of the process and thus of the product. If any. The rings of her left hand cut into my fingers. It may or may not be revenge.
>
> My red skirt is hitched up to my waist, though no higher. Below it the Commander is fucking. What he is fucking is the lower part of my body. I do not say making love, because this is not what he's doing. Copulating too would be inaccurate, because it would imply two people and only one is involved. Nor does rape cover it: nothing is going on here that I haven't signed up for. There wasn't a lot of choice but there was some, and this is what I chose.
>
> Therefore I lie still and picture the unseen canopy over my head. I remember Queen Victoria's advice to her daughter. *Close your eyes and think of England.* But this is not England. I wish he would hurry up.
>
> Maybe I'm crazy and this is some new kind of therapy.
>
> I wish it were true; then I could get better and this would go away.
>
> Serena Joy grips my hands as if it is she, not I, who's being fucked, as if she finds it either pleasurable or painful, and the Commander fucks, with a regular two-four marching stroke, on and on like a tap dripping. He is preoccupied, like a man humming to himself in the shower without knowing he's humming; like a man who has other things on his mind.

Activity

There are hints that the narrator of *The Handmaid's Tale* is really named June; she is known as Offred only because the Commander is called Fred (that is, she is a possession 'of Fred'). Today, many women choose not to take their husband's surname when they marry – yet Shakespeare's Juliet once asked, 'What's in a name? that which we call a rose / By any other name would smell as sweet'. Think about the symbolic importance of names as markers of one's personal and social identity in the texts you are studying.

Commentary

Atwood uses the Ceremony to encapsulate one of the great themes of *The Handmaid's Tale* – the exploitation of women's bodies as part of their social and political subjugation. The declining birth rate has caused the Republic of Gilead to assume full control of the reproductive process, and woman are banned from reading, voting, working or any other actions that could allow them to challenge the power of the **patriarchal** state. In the Old Testament book of Genesis, sisters Leah and Rachel use their handmaids to bear their husband Jacob's sons, and here Offred must perform a similar function for the Commander and Serena Joy. Atwood makes this episode simultaneously appalling and blackly comic; after all the solemn religious fuss in the previous chapter, sex in the context of the Ceremony is as impersonal and mechanical as artificial insemination performed in a laboratory.

Offred calls what the Commander is doing 'fucking' and the importance she attaches to the accuracy and precision of her word choice here is striking. She categorizes this taboo expletive as suitable in the absence of any other option in a world where language has become a tool of repression. **Dystopian** texts often explore the ways in which totalitarian regimes manipulate language, and Gilead's classification of women is a classic example of this technique. While men like the Commander are accorded the respect of their military rank, women are defined and divided by their specific roles as Wives, Handmaids, Aunts (who train the Handmaids), Marthas (older, infertile female servants), Jezebels (prostitutes) and Unwomen (widows, nuns, lesbians, feminists and other 'difficult' types), and thus encouraged to dislike and fear each other. Atwood's representation of an extreme anti-feminist backlash is another aspect of *The Handmaid's Tale* that situates the novel firmly within the 'Modern times' context.

The psychological distance that Atwood creates between the three characters is shocking. While the Commander has sex as if he is performing the dullest parts of his military role, pointlessly marching and drilling, Offred disappears inside her own head. Elsewhere in the novel, she lies in the bath and remembers the days when her body brought pleasure to her and allowed her to fulfil her own desires; as a Handmaid, however, she is no more than a walking womb. Interestingly, it is only the jealous Serena Joy who displays any genuine human emotion during the Ceremony. As a former religious television presenter, Serena Joy helped to market the theocratic dictatorship that now oppresses her. Stigmatized as sterile (since in Gilead infertility is always taken to be the Wife's fault), she loathes the monthly Ceremony which degrades her; at the end of the chapter, Offred describes Serena Joy 'lying on the bed, gazing up at the canopy above her, stiff and straight as an effigy' and asks 'Which of us is it worse for, her or me?'

Did you know?

A really useful online audio resource is BBC Radio 4's World Book Club. Podcasts are available to download of broadcaster Harriett Gilbert interviewing the author of a major text in the presence of a live audience. Currently available are Margaret Atwood on *The Handmaid's Tale*, Arundhati Roy on *The God of Small Things*, Alice Walker on *The Color Purple* and Jeanette Winterson on *Oranges are not the Only Fruit*. They can be accessed at: http://www.bbc.co.uk/podcasts/series/wbc/all

What does the writer say?

'As soon as you have a language that has a past tense and a future tense you're going to say, "Where did we come from, what happens next?" The ability to remember the past helps us plan the future.' Defining her work as 'speculative' as opposed to 'science' fiction, Atwood says, 'The divide is "couldn't happen". Some people get very prickly about it because they think you're dissing science fiction. That's not what I'm doing, I'm simply pointing out I cannot write those books. Much as I'm a devotee of *Star Trek*, I'm not good at writing them.' She goes on: 'I grew up in the golden age of Flash Gordon and sci-fi. Ray Bradbury was publishing his classic works right then and there. I mean, you were reading them hot off the press.'

Activity

Discuss how the three writers you are studying present the struggle to maintain a personal sense of self in challenging circumstances. What methods do they use to convey their ideas and attitudes?

3 Changing morality and social structures

Sample text: 'Work' from *Feminine Gospels* by Carol Ann Duffy

In this poem a Mother Earth figure is represented, with her life describing the inexorable march of 'progress' and the relentless movement of women into the workplace over the past half-century.

To feed one, she worked from home,
took in washing, ironing, sewing.
One small mouth, a soup-filled spoon,
life was a dream.

    To feed two,
she worked outside, sewed seeds, watered,
threshed, scythed, gathered barley, wheat, corn.
Twins were born. To feed four,

    she grafted harder, second job in the alehouse,
food in the larder, food on the table,
she was game, able. Feeding ten
was a different kettle,

    was factory gates
at first light, oil, metal, noise, machines.
To feed fifty, she toiled, sweated, went
on the night shift, schlepped, lifted.

    For a thousand more, she built streets,
for double that, high-rise flats. Cities grew,
her brood doubled, peopled skyscrapers,
trebled. To feed more, more,

    she dug underground, tunnelled,
laid down track, drove trains. Quadruple came,
multiplied, she built planes, outflew sound.
Mother to millions now,

    she flogged TVs,
designed PCs, ripped CDs, burned DVDs.
There was no stopping her. She slogged
night and day at Internet shopping.

    A billion named,
she trawled the seas, hoovered fish, felled trees,
grazed beef, sold cheap fast food, put in
a 90-hour week. Her offspring swelled. She fed

the world, wept rain, scattered the teeth in her head
for grain, swam her tongue in the river to spawn,
sickened, died, lay in a grave, worked, to the bone,
her fingers twenty-four seven.

Activity

Assess the ways in which the ecological message embedded in Duffy's poem can be seen as a contemporary aspect of the 'Modern times' context.

Commentary

This poem seems to extrapolate the perennial fate of the single mother working to feed her children across the centuries from pre-industrial times to the age of the Internet. From simple everyday beginnings, however, the working mother's problem expands horrifically and absurdly until she is left trying to feed a global family – or indeed the entire planet. Perhaps, therefore, Duffy wants us to see this struggling single mum as Mother Earth herself – forced to do whatever she can to feed her growing family, resorting to prostitution if need be and resigned to working 'the night shift'. The contemporary resonance of the 'green' message embedded within the poem situates the text firmly within the latter stages of the 'Modern times' context.

Advertisers have always tried to sell us the myth that the latest labour-saving device will transform the drudgery of housework into a relaxing pleasure – only for the stakes to be continually raised and increasingly impossible high standards expected. Here, too, the whole conception of 'progress' is challenged in a global and environmental context as well as a personal and feminist one. The violent verbs ironically collocated with aspects of progress and technology tell their own story as TVs, CDs and DVDs are 'flogged', 'ripped' and 'burned'. As her children multiply, she plunders the planet to feed them. Duffy lists the constant plundering of the earth's finite resources as she 'trawled the seas, hoovered fish, felled trees, / grazed beef, sold cheap fast food'; it is with a sudden shock that we realize Mother Earth's attempts to feed her children will end by killing both them and herself.

What does the writer say?

Speaking in 2011, Carol Ann Duffy responded to questions about the future of poetry in the modern age: 'We've got to realise that the Facebook generation is the future – and, oddly enough, poetry is the perfect form for them. […] I think increasingly in this century poetry is probably the literary form that will last the most.

Poems are the original text messages in that they use language in a very concise way and I think they will become more relevant in this century than in the last century.

We are reading less now than we did and a lot of young people spend a lot of time in front of a computer on Facebook or tweeting.

So the poem is the literary form that is the most accessible simply because of its brevity […] It's a kind of time capsule – it allows feelings and ideas to travel big distances in a very condensed form. […] If you look at forms like rap, they are skilfully using language, rhyme, and rhythm. Rap is a form of poetry. So the word is very important to young people.'

Activity

Discuss how the three writers you are studying present changing attitudes towards the way in which people choose to live their lives and their responses to changes in society as a whole. What methods do the writers use to convey their ideas and attitudes towards this theme?

4 Gender, class, race and ethnicity

Sample text: *The Color Purple* by Alice Walker

Celie, a black woman living in rural Georgia in the early years of the 20th century, has lived a life of cruel oppression in which her only outlet has been writing secret letters to God. Over time, however, Celie has begun to see life differently – influenced by her feisty daughter-in-law Sofia and the glamorous blues singer Shug Avery. Towards the end of the novel, Celie discovers that for years her abusive husband, Mr. _____, has been hiding the letters Celie's beloved sister Nettie had written to her. Celie has now read them all and come to embrace Shug's **pantheistic** religious ideas, which involve rejecting the notion of God as an 'old white man' and 'conjur[ing] up flowers, wind, water, a big rock' instead. In the extract below from one of Celie's first letters to Nettie, whom for years she had thought was dead, Celie describes Mr. _____'s reaction to the news that she plans to move to Memphis with Shug, who has been both Mr. _____'s and Celie's lover.

> **Key term**
>
> **Pantheistic / Pantheism.** The belief in many gods.

Activity

One of the most famous aspects of *The Color Purple* is the distinctive narrative voice which Alice Walker constructs for Celie. Discuss with your class how Walker's methods of telling the story here help to anchor the novel within the 'Modern times' context.

Mr._____ try to act like he don't care I'm going.

You'll be back, he say. Nothing up North for nobody like you. Shug got talent, he say. She can sing. She got spunk, he say. She can talk to anybody. Shug got looks, he say. She can stand up and be notice. But what you got? You ugly. You skinny. You shape funny. You too scared to open your mouth to people. All you fit to do in Memphis is be Shug's maid. Take out her slop-jar and maybe cook her food. You not that good a cook either. And this house ain't been clean good since my first wife died. And nobody crazy or backward enough to want to marry you, neither. What you gon do? Hire yourself out to farm? He laugh. Maybe somebody let you work on they railroad.

Any more letters come? I ast.

He say, What?

You heard me, I say. Any more letters from Nettie come?

If they did, he say, I wouldn't give 'em to you. You two of a kind, he say. A man try to be nice to you, you fly in his face.

I curse you, I say.

What that mean? he say.

I say, Until you do right by me, everything you touch will crumble.

He laugh. Who you think you is? he say. You can't curse nobody. Look at you. You black, you pore, you ugly, you a woman. Goddam, he say, you nothing at all.

Until you do right by me, I say, everything you even dream about will fail. I give it to him straight, just like it come to me. And it seem to come to me from the trees.

Whoever heard of such a thing, say Mr. _____. I probably didn't whup your ass enough.

Every lick you hit me you will suffer twice, I say. Then I say, You better stop talking because all I'm telling you ain't coming just from me. Look like when I open my mouth the air rush in and shape words.

Shit, he say. I should have you lock up. Just let you out to work.

The jail you plan for me is the one in which you will rot, I say.

Shug come over to where us talking. She take one look at my face and say Celie! Then she turn to Mr. _____. Stop Albert, she say. Don't say no more. You just going to make it harder on yourself.

I'll fix her wagon! say Mr. _____, and spring toward me.

A dust devil flew up on the porch between us, fill my mouth with dirt. The dirt say, Anything you do to me, already done to you.

Then I feel Shug shake me. Celie, she say. And I come to myself.

I'm pore, I'm black, I may be ugly and can't cook, a voice say to everything listening. But I'm here.

Amen, say Shug. Amen, amen.

Commentary

The epistolary form of *The Color Purple* allows the letter writer to reveal her most intimate thoughts and feelings; the impression of being allowed a privileged insight into someone else's life creates a very powerful bond between the character and the reader. In this late letter addressed to her sister Nettie, Celie's climactic cursing of Mr.___ is enough to make us stand up and cheer, as Walker shows the power of narrative and speech in shaping one's personal identity.

The representation of the rich, **demotic** Georgia **dialect** in Celie's letters to God earlier in the novel emphasizes her inability to speak out and resist those who abuse her; the written word is the only way she has of expressing her feelings of loss, oppression and loneliness. As time passes, however, through her relationships with Shug and Sofia, Celie gradually finds her own voice. Her personal religious beliefs have led her to accept white male power without question; her very traditional conception of an elderly white male God who doesn't listen to poor black women has convinced Celie that her voice will never be heard. Only when she embraces Shug's pantheism, a form of worship in which everyone finds God for themselves, does Celie realize that she can also challenge other forms of male dominance. This epiphany signals the end of Mr. ___'s control over her, and the incantatory power of her curse provides a stunning contrast with the previous years of silence that shocks her husband to the core.

'You too scared to open your mouth to people,' Mr. _____ jeers at first, before Celie takes control of their conversation and utterly confounds him. At first he is lulled into a false sense of security as Celie lets him hold the floor with a typical barrage of demeaning insults culminating in 'You black, you pore, you ugly, you a woman. Goddam… you nothing at all'. Then, however, he is blindsided by a simple question that reveals she knows he has been treacherously intercepting

Key terms

Demotic. This refers to ordinary people.

Dialect. As used here, it refers to the speech of a particular area.

Nettie's correspondence; 'Any more letters come? I ast'. Mr. _____ grows increasingly desperate as Celie's characteristic Georgian dialect is temporarily superseded by a voice of eerie prophetic authority, as she channels the voice of female power through the 'trees' the 'air' and even the 'dust devil' like a medium or shaman. Mr. _____ tries to counter this by stripping Celie of her sense of self, as he has throughout the novel, making a final bid to deny her personal truth by questioning her sanity; 'Shit, he say. I should have you lock up'. But the weapons he has used to oppress her for years are now misfiring as she replies, 'The jail you plan for me is the one in which you will rot.' The final reversal of power comes when Celie throws Mr. _____'s insults back in his face by giving them an entirely new positive message; 'I'm pore, I'm black, I may be ugly and can't cook... But I'm here.'

This extract encapsulates all the great 'Modern times' themes of the novel: race, power, gender, sexuality, the power of female friendship and the nature of God. At one point in the text, Celie and Sofia make up after a quarrel by sewing a patchwork quilt together, and in time the women create an equally rich oral narrative of stories that challenge oppression and celebrate survival. Walker's quilting motif serves to place Celie at the heart of her patchwork family.

▌ What does the writer say?

Speaking in 2007, 25 years after the publication of *The Color Purple*, Alice Walker commented: 'I do like the way that I have been well taken care of by this particular story. It means that I can write any other story that I want to write, do whatever I want to, pretty much. And I tell you how I really see it – I see it as the people in the book actually doing that, for me. And through them I see that this is my ancestors, especially my parents, making sure that I don't suffer unnecessarily from a lack of material things, like housing, or good food, medical care. So it feels to me like I was in service to create this vision, to create this story that was inspired by their lives and after I did that then they turned around and said: "You've taken really good care of us, we'll take really good care of you."'

▌ Activity

Discuss how the three writers you are studying present prejudice and discrimination. What methods do they use to convey their ideas and attitudes?

5 Political upheaval and change

Sample text: *Waterland* by Graham Swift

Tom Crick, whose childless wife has had a mental breakdown after kidnapping a baby, is just about to lose his job as a history teacher. Previously, when challenged by a bright 17-year-old student, Price, about the value of his subject, Crick had jettisoned the official syllabus and begun to tell his class about different kinds of 'history'. In the following extract, taken from a chapter called 'A Teacher's Testament', Crick bumps into Price, who has been to a meeting of the Holocaust Club, a group of students increasingly worried about the threat of nuclear war. Teacher and student go to the pub together.

'You know where we got the idea from, sir?'

'No.'

'No? Not really? That lesson. You remember. When we all told our dreams…'

'Ah yes.' (So my classes have taught something: how to be afraid.) 'That lesson.'

He looks at me.

'Look, I'm sorry I messed up your classes, sir. I'm sorry I cocked things up for you.'

But that's what education's about, Price. (And don't look so sheepish. What's happened to the revolutionary fire? Or doesn't it work any more when the tyrant's taken a different sort of tumble? When he turns out, after all, to be a bit of a sad case.)

It's not about empty minds waiting to be filled, not about flatulent teachers discharging hot air. It's about the opposition of teacher and student. It's about what gets rubbed off between the persistence of the one and the resistance of the other. A long, hard struggle against a natural resistance. Needs a lot of phlegm. I don't believe in quick results, in wand-waving and wonder-working. I don't believe, as Lewis [the headmaster] would have it, in equipping for today's real world. But I do believe in education.

Sacked school teacher, husband of baby-snatcher, says: 'I believe in education …'

Do you know why I became a teacher? OK – because I had this thing about history. My pet hobby-horse. But do you know what prompted me to *teach*? It was when I was in Germany in 1946. All that rubble. Tons of it. You see, it didn't take much. Just a few flattened cities. No special lessons. No tours of the death-camps. Let's just say I made the discovery that this thing called civilization, this thing we've been working at for three thousand years, so that now and then we get bored with it and even poke fun at it, like children in school (sometimes it takes the form of a pompous headmaster), is precious. An artifice – so easily knocked down – but precious.

That was thirty-four years ago. I don't know if things are better or worse than they were then. I don't know if things were better or worse than they were in the year nought. There are myths of progress, myths of decline. And dreams of revolution… I don't know if my thirty-two years as a teacher have made any difference. But I do know that things looked dark then and they do now. In 1946 I had a vision of the world in ruins. (And my wife-to-be, for all I knew, was having visions, too – but let's not go into that.) And now here you are, Price, in 1980, with your skull-face and your Holocaust Club, saying the world may not have much longer – and you're not much younger than I was then.

Dresden after Allied bombing in February 1945

Commentary

The year 1980 is as remote from you today as World War II was for Price back then; the passage of time since *Waterland* was first published means that the rebellious teenager in this extract would be Tom Crick's age (in his early fifties) now. Graham Swift's narrative method, with its cross-cuts between the conversation in the pub (reported in direct speech) and Crick's memories of bombed-out Germany at the end of the war, is **mimetic** of the ebb and flow of history itself. Crick is fascinated by the meaning of history – how we understand it, what we do with it and what stories we tell ourselves to make sense of it. The nature and value of history is of paramount importance to Crick, but his own fractured past prevents him from believing that studying the mistakes of the past

Key term

Mimetic. A copy or imitation of something.

stops us repeating them. His bleak view encompasses 'myths of progress' and 'myths of decline'. In terms of the 'Modern times' context, Tom Crick seems to feel that, despite the enormous political upheaval and change that have taken place since 1945, paradoxically nothing much has altered for ordinary people; 'things looked dark then and they do now.' He tells Price that in the same way as he 'had a vision of the world in ruins' in 1946, so his student, in 1980, feels the 'world may not have much longer'. The cosy idea of continual human progress is a bad joke, and yet somehow Crick cannot give it up entirely. Civilization, 'this thing we've been working at for three thousand years, so that now and then we get bored with it and even poke fun at it' is, he declares, 'precious'. This extract captures the great themes of *Waterland*, as Crick's alternative histories form the bulk of the novel, which straddles two time frames: 1980 and 1943, when Crick was a 15-year-old schoolboy.

Earlier in the novel, in one of his off-beat lessons, Crick had offered his class a definition of man as 'the story-telling animal'. His own gothic personal history of abortion, incest, murder and madness, with its elements of **magic realism**, unfolds against the background of seismic world events such as the great wars of the 20th century, but he finds time to tell them about the life cycle of the eel and the unique topography of the Fens. As well as a narrative that sometimes mimics the flow of the river itself, Swift's integration of non-narrative, non-fictional material is strikingly **postmodern**.

The events of those long-ago Fenland days shape the rest of Crick's life, and Graham Swift's frequent narrative time shifts evoke the thin line between past and present. Whether our lives play out against the horrors of Hitler's Holocaust (like Crick) or the threat of all-out nuclear Armageddon (like Price), change is presented as constant and life as a mystery we are prepared for. The personal and historical past haunts the narrator, just as it haunts the narrative, pushing its way into the present and forcing onwards into the future.

Key terms

Magic realism. A genre of writing where magic or unreal events impinge upon the representation of an otherwise realistic world.

Postmodern / Postmodernism. This very complex term can have many definitions, but when used with regard to literature it involves notions of self-conscious playfulness resulting from the understanding that nothing, at least when represented, can be 'real'. The pleasure of reading texts comes from the reader's recognition of the way in which the texts are constructed, rather than what they definitively mean.

Link

See pages 173–175, where postmodernism is discussed.

What does the writer say?

Of the novel's origins, Graham Swift has said: 'I think I started with [....] a picture in my head of the corpse in the river, the floating corpse, and then certain things started to emerge around that, to do with location, setting, other characters, time. So it began as a kind of detective thing, classic case of a dead body and whodunit? [.... I] felt for some reason that this was back in the 40s, in wartime. But I wanted it to be seen and told from a much later perspective, the 1980s. So the question is, naturally, what becomes of this boy Tom in later life? Then, when I made him a history teacher, there was a little – not so little – there was an explosion of ideas.'

Further reading

Patrick McGrath's 1986 interview with Graham Swift offers a very interesting and helpful insight into the writing of *Waterland*, and can be accessed at http://bombmagazine.org/article/769/.

> ## Activity
>
> Discuss how the writers you are studying present the ways in which living in a time of conflict, upheaval and change can affect the lives of ordinary people. What methods do they use to convey their ideas and attitudes?

6 Resistance and rebellion

Sample text: *One Flew Over the Cuckoo's Nest* by Ken Kesey

> ## Activity
>
> The cuckoo lays its single egg in the nest of another bird, and, when the cuckoo chick hatches, it tosses all of the other birds' eggs out of the nest. The tyrannical unwelcome 'lunatic' takes over the 'asylum', in a sense. Discuss the ways in which Ken Kesey's choice of title might be related to the 'Modern times' context.

Nurse Ratched ('The Big Nurse') has been waiting to take her revenge on the tragic inmates of the ward she runs in a mental institution – the Chronics, who have no hope of a cure, and the Acutes, whose 'madness' is felt to be temporary. The arrival of a new patient, the free-spirited trickster Randle Patrick McMurphy, has galvanized the Acutes into beginning to resist Big Nurse's authority. McMurphy has bet the others that he can disturb Big Nurse's famously calm exterior and one of his most successful attempts to undermine her has resulted in the patients setting up a poker school. In the extract below, after biding her time for several weeks, Big Nurse has banned the card game. The episode is seen through the eyes of Chief Bromden, a Native American patient who pretends to be deaf and dumb in order to survive the Ratched regime.

> Her head didn't move. She didn't look. But one by one everybody else looked at him sitting there in his corner. Even the old Chronics, wondering why everybody had turned to look in one direction, stretched out their scrawny necks like birds and turned to look at McMurphy – faces turned to him, full of a naked, scared hope.
>
> That single thin note in my head was like tires speeding down a pavement.
>
> He was sitting straight up in his chair, one big red finger scratching lazily at the stitchmarks run across his nose. He grinned at everybody looking at him and took his cap by the brim and tipped it politely, then looked back at the nurse.
>
> 'So, if there is no discussion on this ruling, I think the hour is almost over…'
>
> She paused again, took a look at him herself. He shrugged his shoulders and with a loud sigh slapped both hands down on his knees and pushed himself standing out of the chair. He stretched and yawned and scratched the nose again and started strolling across the day-room floor to where she sat by the Nurses' Station, heisting his pants with his thumbs as he walked. I could see that it was too late to keep him from doing whatever fool thing he had in mind, and I just watched, like everybody else. He walked with long steps, too long, and he had his thumbs hooked in his pockets again. The iron in his boot heels cracked lightning out of the tile. He was the logger again, the

swaggering gambler, the big redheaded brawling Irishman, the cowboy out of the TV set walking down the middle of the street to meet a dare.

The Big Nurse's eyes swelled out white as he got close. She hadn't reckoned on him doing anything. This was supposed to be her final victory over him, supposed to establish her rule once and for all. But here he comes and he's big as a house!

She started popping her mouth and looking for her black boys, scared to death, but he stopped before he got to her. He stopped in front of her window and he said in his slowest, deepest drawl how he figured he could use one of the smokes he bought this mornin', then ran his hand through the glass.

The glass came apart like water splashing, and the nurse threw her hands to her ears. He got one of the cartons of cigarettes with his name on it and took out a pack, then put it back and turned to where the Big Nurse was sitting like a chalk statue and very tenderly went to brushing the slivers of glass off her hat and shoulders.

'I'm sure *sorry*, ma'am,' he said, 'Gawd but I am. That window glass was so spick and span I com-*pletely* forgot it was there.'

It took just a couple of seconds. He turned and left her sitting there with her face shifting and jerking and walked back across the day room to his chair, lighting up a cigarette.

The ringing that was in my head had stopped.

Commentary

Ken Kesey was a 24-year-old recent graduate of the University of Oregon when he took part in a unique series of drug experiments sponsored by the US government, and his experience of the drug trials, plus the time he spent working in a mental hospital, saturates *One Flew Over the Cuckoo's Nest*. In terms of the 'Modern times' context, this extract captures the way in which Kesey uses Ratched's iron control over the mental ward as a metaphor for the institutionalized conformity and confinement of postwar America.

The central, terrible dilemma at the heart of the novel is that the only way to escape Nurse Ratched is to conform absolutely to her regime; if anyone resists, things only get worse.

The drugs she administers are not meant to cure but to control, as Harding, another of the Acutes, sees only too clearly towards the end of the novel: 'We shall be all of us shot at dawn. One hundred cc's apiece. Miss Ratched shall line us all against the wall, where we'll face the terrible maw of a muzzle-loading shotgun which she had loaded with Miltowns! Thorazines! Libriums! Stelazines! And with a wave of her sword, *blooie!* Tranquilize all of us completely out of existence.' With McMurphy stirring them up, the patients awaken from their suspended animation to realize that they have voluntarily allowed 'The Combine' to control them. The fine line between madness and sanity is mirrored by the division between freedom and captivity, and as McMurphy declares war on the bafflingly pointless boredom and relentlessly petty rules imposed by Big Nurse, Kesey dramatizes the wider attempts of conformist conservative America to stigmatize and criminalize any difficult or rebellious elements of society. As a famously **counter-cultural** figure, happiest when hovering on the outer limits of respectable society and taking pot-shots at mainstream conventional morality, Kesey can be seen to embody the rebellious attitudes of the 1960s.

Did you know?

The 'Swinging Sixties' is a term often used to sum up the radical and often subversive social, cultural and political movements of a decade that saw massive changes in attitudes towards everything from 'free love' to capital punishment. With hindsight, some see the 1960s as an era of drug-fuelled hippy self-indulgence, while for others those years ushered in a brave new 'live-and-let-live' world with no time for sexism, racism or uptight puritanism.

Key term

Counter-cultural. A counter culture is one whose beliefs and behaviour differ considerably from the mainstream views held at the time.

Earlier in the novel, Chief Bromden begins by asserting 'But it's the truth even if it didn't happen.' In fooling everyone around him into thinking he is a deaf-mute, the Chief realizes that paradoxically he 'has to be deaf to hear'. What he hears is the relentless onward march of the 'Combine', of which Big Nurse is only a minor representative. She is chillingly professional, and her dispassionate ruthlessness is all the more fearsome for being cloaked in the rhetoric of puritanical morality. Kesey structures the novel around the classic protagonist–antagonist personal conflict of Greek tragedy: McMurphy, the ex-soldier who won a Distinguished Service Cross in the Korean War for escaping from a Communist prison camp, takes on the ex-army nurse. In this episode, the Native American Chief Bromden watches McMurphy swagger through a variety of different popular culture stereotypes, from 'the logger again, the swaggering gambler, the big redheaded brawling Irishman' to the clichéd 'cowboy out of the TV' who has presumably come to town to depose the corrupt local sheriff in some corny old Western. For Big Nurse, McMurphy's role-playing and rebellion only goes to prove his madness, and in the end she engineers a lobotomy to silence him forever.

What does the writer say?

Speaking about his participation in the government-sponsored drug trials, Ken Kesey has said this of the hospital ward where the experiments took place: 'All the other people in it were nuts. I went out and looked through the window, a little, tiny window, and the door there with a heavy, heavy screen between two panes of glass. There was no way to break out. You could barely see out through it. I'd look out there and see these people moving around, and I could understand them a whole lot better than I could understand the doctors and the nurses, or the interns – and they knew this. They would come in and look at me in there, and I'd look at them through this little window. It was a regular ward, and there were about a hundred people on the ward.'

Activity

Discuss how the writers you are studying present the ways in which people can hold firm to what they believe in despite extreme pressure. What methods do they use to convey ideas and attitudes?

7 Imperialism, post-imperialism and nationalism

Sample text: *Translations* by Brian Friel

In the following extract, set in 1833, the young English soldier George Yolland – who has come to rural Ireland to translate the Gaelic place-names into English as part of the Ordnance Survey's mapping expedition – is finally alone with Maire, the local girl with whom he is falling in love. Their growing attraction to each other is complicated by the fact that Yolland speaks no Irish and Maire speaks no English.

Maire	George –
Yolland	That's beautiful – oh that's really beautiful.
Maire	George –

Yolland	Say it again – say it again –
Maire	Shhh. (*She holds her hand up for silence – she is trying to remember her one line of English. Now she remembers it and she delivers the line as if English were her language – easily, fluidly, conversationally.*) George, in Norfolk we besport ourselves around the maypoll.
Yolland	Good God, do you? That's where my mother comes from – Norfolk. Norwich actually. Not exactly Norwich town but a small village called Little Walsingham close beside it. But in our own village of Winfarthing we have a maypole too and every year on the first of May –
	He stops abruptly, only now realising. He stares at her. She in turn misunderstands his excitement.
Maire	(*to herself*) Mother of God, my Aunt Mary wouldn't have taught me something dirty, would she?
	Pause.
	Yolland extends his hand to Maire. She turns away from him and moves slowly across the stage.
Yolland	Maire.
	She still moves away.
	Maire Chatach.
	She still moves away.
	Bun na hAbhann? (*He says the name softly, almost privately, very tentatively, as if he were searching for a sound she might respond to. He tries again.*) Druim Dubh?
	Maire stops. She is listening. Yolland is encouraged.
	Poll na gCaorach. Lis Maol.
	Maire turns towards him.
	Lis na nGall.
Maire	Lis na nGradh.
	They are now facing each other and begin moving – almost imperceptibly – towards one another.
	Carraig an Phoill.
Yolland	Carraig na Ri. Loch na nEan.
Maire	Loch an Iubhair. Machaire Buidhe.
Yolland	Machaire Mor. Cnoc na Mona.
Maire	Cnoc na nGabhar.
Yolland	Mullach.
Maire	Port.
Yolland	Tor.
Maire	Lag.
	She holds out her hands to Yolland. He takes them. Each now speaks almost to himself/herself.
Yolland	I wish to God you could understand me.
Maire	Soft hands; a gentleman's hands.
Yolland	Because if you could understand me I could tell you how I spend my days either thinking of you or gazing up at your house in the hope that you'll appear even for a second.
Maire	Every evening you walk by yourself along the Tra Bhan and every morning you wash yourself in front of your tent.
Yolland	I would tell you how beautiful you are, curly-headed Maire. I would so like to tell you how beautiful you are.

Maire	Your arms are long and thin and the skin on your shoulders is very white.
Yolland	I would tell you…
Maire	Don't stop – I know what you're saying.
Yolland	I would tell you how I want to be here – to live here – always – with you – always, always.
Maire	'Always'? What is that word – 'always'?
Yolland	Yes – yes; always.
Maire	You're trembling.
Yolland	Yes, I'm trembling because of you.
Maire	I'm trembling, too. (*She holds his face in her hand.*)
Yolland	I've made up my mind…
Maire	Shhhh.
Yolland	I'm not going to leave here…
Maire	Shhh – listen to me. I want you, too, soldier.
Yolland	Don't stop – I know what you're saying.
Maire	I want to live with you – anywhere – anywhere at all – always – always.
Yolland	'Always'? What is that word – 'always'?
Maire	Take me away with you, George.

Activity

This extract contains elements of both comedy and romance seemingly at odds with the troubled history of Anglo-Irish relationships. Think about the dramatic methods that Brian Friel uses to show the difficulties the characters face in trying to cross the linguistic and cultural divide between them.

Commentary

Translations is concerned with the power of language, the uneasy history of the English in Ireland and the nature of cultural imperialism, and this tender, tragi-comic love scene – the central turning point of the play – encapsulates all these important 'Modern times' issues and ideas. As Yolland and Maire struggle to communicate their growing love for one another, Maire's comically random single line of rote-learned English and her panic about what filthy phrase Aunt Mary may have taught her create a vein of comedy which only accentuates the difficulties they face in trying to cross the barriers of language and culture. Through the use of proxemics (how the characters are positioned on stage and manage their personal space) Friel reveals the gulf between them visually as well as metaphorically, as Maire firstly *turns away from him and moves slowly across the stage* before *turn[ing] towards him* and finally *hold[ing] his face in her hand*. Only when Yolland wistfully and hesitantly begins to recite his list of the Irish place-names he is there to wipe out does he finally reach her, both physically and emotionally. In a sense, of course, in coming between Maire and her Irish boyfriend, the English soldier Yolland is 'colonizing' her just as the British army is colonizing the whole country. The moonlight kiss is a romantic cliché that might encourage a sentimental audience to hope against hope that the coming together of this pair in fact symbolizes a new stage in the troubled history of the English in Ireland. Yet Friel's dialogue reveals the essential paradox that makes a real thaw in Anglo-Irish relations unlikely. The ultimate irony is that while Yolland sees Maire as an emblem of the beautiful and romantic Irish language and culture he has come to love, declaring 'I want to be here – to live here – always – with you', Maire is in love with the idea of getting out of Ireland altogether and sees him as her means of escape – 'Take me away with you, George.'

Friel captures this moving moment poised in time in a technically complex and unusual way. While the audience knows that the divided lovers (like all the other characters in the play) are meant to be speaking their own languages, the dialogue is mostly English to make the drama more widely accessible. The audience willingly accepts that Yolland's precious hoard of Gaelic words consists only of the place-names he has been translating for the Ordnance Survey, and that Maire's dialogue, while rendered in English, is actually spoken in her own language. This is how Friel ensures that while the onlookers can understand both characters, they also know that Yolland and Maire cannot comprehend each other. This ingenious method allows the playwright to dramatize the unbridgeable gulf between the English and the Irish as here, for the first and only time, the doomed lovers manage to cross the divide. Tragically, the bridge they build to do so is perilously fragile and liable to collapse at any moment.

What does the writer say?

On the website 'Gate Friel', Brian Friel notes that:

'The tools that are available to the playwright to tell his story are few enough – words, action, silence. In the theatre that has engaged me, words are at the very core of it all. The same words that are available to the novelist, to the poet; and used with the same precision and with the same scrupulous attention not only to the exact kernel meaning but to all those allusive meanings that every word hoards. But there is a difference. The playwright's words aren't written for solitary engagement – they are written for public utterance. They are used as the story-teller uses them, to hold an audience in his embrace and within that vocal sound. So, unlike the words of the novelist or poet, the playwright's words are scored for a very different context.'

Activity

Discuss how the writers you are studying present a sense of community – based on nationality, race, class or gender – or conversely a sense of isolation. What methods do they use to convey their ideas and attitudes?

This chapter will:

- explore the literary background to the set texts within this shared context
- introduce some ways of making meaning which you can apply to the set texts available for study.

Overview: literature before 1945

In order to get a clear sense of what is most noticeable and distinctive about the postwar literary context, you need some sort of yardstick to measure it against. Knowing something of what came just before the time period you are studying can give you a useful contextual reference point.

Extension activity

As you work through the first part of this chapter, think about how to create a visual representation of the literary background to the 'Modern times' context. Working with other students, you could design a timeline of the literary periods discussed – signposting the 21 set texts within this option and specifically highlighting your own poetry, prose and drama choices. A wall display that illustrates the key literary movements of the century, set against its historical, political, social and cultural contexts, could be a useful resource.

The major literary movement of the first half of the 20th century has become known as **modernism**. The keystone of modernist literature is its deliberate rejection of traditional forms of discourse in poetry, prose and drama. One way of visualizing this break with the past is to look at the two iconic Spanish paintings below: *Las Meninas* (*The Maids of Honour*) by the court artist Diego Velázquez (1656) and one of Pablo Picasso's famous 1957 reinterpretations.

Las Meninas by Velázquez, 1656

A 1957 reinterpretation of *Las Meninas* by Pablo Picasso. Picasso painted this scene 58 times, using different reinterpretations (see page 173).

Three centuries after Velázquez painted his masterpiece, the dominant Spanish artist of the 20th century (Picasso) dissected, reimagined and reconfigured it within a very different context. Fascinated by Velázquez's unusual fusion of two genres – the traditional royal commission and the self-portrait of the artist at work – Picasso deliberately both reflects and distorts aspects of his predecessor's composition in a way that seems to reflect the very different social, cultural and historical environment within which he was working. When Velázquez painted his *Las Meninas*, the Spanish monarchy had grown fabulously rich on the gold and silver plundered from their territories in South America. By the time Picasso painted his version, however, the royal family had been forced into exile and Spain was ruled by the oppressive military dictator General Franco. In this chapter, these paintings are used as visual indexes for several of the important literary ideas discussed below.

Firstly, Picasso's decision to subvert conventional artistic modes of representation mirrors the experimental literature produced by the likes of James Joyce and Virginia Woolf, after the impact of World War 1 and the rise of new ways of thinking about what it meant to be human – such as the work of Sigmund Freud – smashed the comfortable social and cultural status quo which existed before 1914. Disillusioned and often cynical, responding to and also reflecting their shifting and unstable times, the modernists chose to write complex, fragmented, distorted and unreliable narratives that exposed the senseless and dangerous irrationality of the world in which they lived, as opposed to comfortable representations of mainstream culture.

Overview: postmodernist literature

The dominant literary movement of the latter half of the 20th century, especially the period 1960–1990, was **postmodernism**. Looking at that prefix 'post' might make you think that postmodernism is simply a chronological descriptor that identifies *what came after* **modernism**. In a sense, however, the term 'antimodernism' might be more accurate, since it foregrounds the fact that many postwar writers were *reacting against* modernism and consciously opposing the technically ambitious and extensively crafted literature of the writers who dominated the first half of the century.

After World War II, new ways of thinking about the nature of the text challenged the authority of the author. Perhaps you can imagine Picasso's radical reinvention of *Las Meninas* as posing an artistic challenge to Velázquez's authority; in choosing to reinterpret the scene in 58 different ways, he may be seen as denying the old master the last word on the subject. Once Picasso contests Velázquez's ownership of the essential 'meaning' of *Las Meninas* by painting multiple competing versions of it, the 1656 original may be seen to lose its status as the only source of narrative 'truth'. And just as we might see Picasso's many fragmented, jarring re-creations as reflecting the disorientating times in which they were produced, so much of the literature of the later 20th century also seems to mirror the uncertainties and ambiguities of the nuclear age.

> **Did you know?**
>
> Much 'psychoanalytic' literary criticism (see pages 181–182) is based on the theories of the Austrian neurologist Sigmund Freud (1856–1939) and seeks to analyse fantasies, unconscious desires and aspects of sexuality. Freudian interpretations attach great significance to the underlying hidden meanings of words and actions, and see these behaviours as revealing the essential truth about someone's state of mind. The famous 'Freudian slip' is a mistake (often a speech error or 'slip of the tongue') that can be interpreted as revealing a conflict between expected 'correct' patterns of behaviour and the hidden desires of the individual.

Features of postmodernist literature: intertextuality

The links between the two versions of *Las Meninas* are so obvious and arresting that if they were books we would be talking in terms of **intertextuality**. Despite being painted 300 years apart, the connections between the texts are so powerfully striking that we arguably gain a richer appreciation of both by reviewing them together.

Comparing literary texts can make you more aware of how you read. In 1966, the French literary theorist Julia Kristeva coined the term 'intertextuality' to describe the complex network of links that exist between texts. Were you to study Picasso's *Las Meninas* without knowing anything about his artistic debt to Velázquez, you would no doubt produce an interesting and creative response – but if you were then made aware of the Velázquez original, you might well modify your views about both paintings. They illuminate one another; they become more than the sum of their parts. Readers pick up on patterns and interconnections in literature too. The title of Seth Grahame-Smith's 2009 novel *Pride and Prejudice and Zombies* demands attention because of the reader's intertextual knowledge of what promises to be a really offbeat genre mash-up: the subtitle *The Classic Regency Romance – now with Ultraviolent Zombie Mayhem!* says it all.

Features of postmodernist literature: metafiction

Look again at the two images of *Las Meninas*. The fact that both Velázquez and Picasso insert images of themselves as artists at work within their paintings – did you spot them? – can be seen as a visual equivalent of the literary device of metafiction. Metafiction highlights the processes by which texts are made and the ways in which they work, and in drawing attention to their roles as working artists and makers of meaning, Velázquez and Picasso do the same thing. In the very act of doing this, of course, they remind us that each picture is 'only' one man's view and can 'only' capture a partial view of things. All in all, Picasso's reimagining of Velázquez can be seen as characteristically postmodernist; just as the writers of the latter half of the 20th century scrapbooked multiple literary styles and elements to form **pastiches** that mirror the impossibility of pinning down one immutable 'truth' about the modern world, so this visual artist does a very similar thing in a different medium.

The photograph opposite of the Pompidou Centre in Paris (opened in 1977) offers another visual way of thinking about postmodern texts. The skeleton of the building is outside, with essential elements such as ducts, pipes, air vents and electric cables encased in eye-catching, brightly coloured external tubes. By showcasing these core functional components of the structure, rather than hiding them away, the architects draw attention to their modern methods of construction and the high-tech raw materials they have used. Postmodern metafictions, like the Pompidou Centre, don't conceal the way they work.

This technique is not wholly new. Jane Austen draws attention to the part the writer plays in the fictional process when she begins the final chapter of *Mansfield Park* (1814) by breaking into the narrative to state her aims: 'Let other pens dwell on guilt and misery. I quit such odious subjects as soon as I can, impatient to restore everybody not greatly in fault themselves to tolerable comfort, and to have done with all the rest.' Again, in his comic masterpiece *Vanity Fair* (1848), William Makepeace Thackeray introduces himself as 'the Manager of the Performance' and stresses that the reader may choose to 'step in for half an hour' to view the 'appropriate scenery [...] brilliantly illuminated

> **Key term**
>
> **Pastiche.** A work which deliberately copies the style of another.

◄ **The Pompidou Centre in Paris**

with the Author's own candles'. This deliberately stylized and self-conscious preamble concludes with a flourish as 'the Manager retires, and the curtain rises'. Thackeray sustains this artful distancing technique right up until the last lines of the novel, when he seems to gently patronize a reader who has come to believe too fully in the characters he has created: 'come, children, let us shut up the box and the puppets, for our play is played out'.

Yet there is a clear difference between these witty 19th-century authorial interpolations and the decision of many 20th-century postmodernist writers to directly challenge the whole notion that literature is best when it is 'realistic'. Far from setting out to imitate real life, postmodern narratives are often complex, fragmented and non-linear. They frequently make use of disorientating time slips, bizarre dreamscapes and fantastic rewritings of other text types (such as myths and fairy tales) as they reflect on the nature of storytelling itself and think about its possibilities and limitations. Again, it seems, we come full circle, back to Picasso and his reworking of *Las Meninas*.

Overview: contemporary literature

From roughly 1990 to the present day, we are in the realm of contemporary literature. During this time, perhaps the most interesting development has been the much more inclusive and open-minded attitude towards **genre fiction** of all types, with texts originally labelled as 'historical', 'teenage', 'detective' and many others selling millions of copies and also receiving detailed and respectful critical attention.

> **Key term**
>
> **Genre fiction.** Fiction written to fit into a known genre, which will appeal to fans of that genre. Examples are Crime Fiction, Chick Lit, etc.

**A greeting card based on a 1960s
'Ladybird' illustration**

Contextual change over time

When thinking about the three texts you are studying within the shared context, remember that at least one of them will have been published since 2000 and will be an example of contemporary literature. Given the immediacy of this **context of production**, it is almost inevitable that some of the ideas you will want to explore and express about this text may not be equally relevant to, say, *One Flew Over the Cuckoo's Nest*, which was written in 1962, let alone *A Streetcar Named Desire*, which was first performed in 1947. Remember that the shared context in which you are working – 1945 to the present day – means thinking about change over time, or history within history, if you like. When you look at the picture on this page, remember that although it was first printed well within the 'Modern times' era, those young children would be of a similar age to your grandparents now.

Activity

Look at the illustration on the left and discuss the following contextual questions with your fellow students.

● What aspects of two different 'Modern times' time periods can you find in this text?

● How are young children represented within the contexts of each time period?

● How do the contexts of each time period help to create humour when set against each other?

Did you know?

In their 1960s and 1970s heyday, almost all British children either owned a set of Ladybird books or read them at school. As times and attitudes have changed, however, a half-admiring and half-ironic minor cult has emerged in which the iconic Ladybird with its comically outmoded gender stereotypes is simultaneously worshipped and mocked in a way that possibly parallels the contemporary popularity of the designer Cath Kidston's vintage kitsch.

Commentary

The two time periods referenced in the greeting card are the original context of production (the 1960s) and today's 21st-century **context of reception**. The humour is totally dependent on the disparity between the representation of the boy and girl then and now, and thus reveals the extent of social, cultural and historical change over time within the 'Modern times' context.

This illustration is taken from a classic pocket-sized hardback Ladybird book. These texts were famous for their beautifully painted, full-colour pictures, worthy educational values and reassuring evocations of an idyllically safe and happy childhood. The famous *Key Words Reading Scheme* (the 'Peter and Jane' books) describes the soft-focus, sunshiny everyday lives of a pair of affluent, white, middle-class children, using simple declarative sentences such as 'Here is Peter' and 'I like Jane'. Although the series began in the mid-1960s, the lovingly detailed illustrations seem to reflect the social context of an earlier and more innocent age; there is no sense of the 'Swinging Sixties' encroaching on the lives of Peter (usually to be found helping Daddy mend the car) or Jane (who can only be parted from her dolly to help Mummy in the kitchen).

The card reproduced here is from a range of tongue-in-cheek greeting cards in which the original Ladybird images are paired with jarringly satirical new captions. The text relies heavily on the reader's previous intertextual and contextual knowledge by playing with the traditional parameters of the original Ladybird genre. The humour lies in the knowing mismatch between the imagined innocence of the original caption to this picture – it's possible to envisage something along the lines of 'See Peter and Jane play let's pretend' – and the arch new version, in which an annoyingly precocious modern six-year-old orders a more than usually pretentious designer coffee.

The context of critical reception in contemporary fiction

In this section, you will explore the different critical receptions given to two of the texts available for study within the shared context of 'Modern times', both of which can be categorized as examples of contemporary fiction: *The God of Small Things* and *The Help*. Both are the first (and, to date, only) published novels by young women writers who have set their powerful and moving narratives against particularly resonant 1960s social, cultural, political and historical backdrops. Reviewing the critical receptions afforded to each of these texts when they were first published is a potentially eye-opening experience that may help you to evaluate the available secondary sources and interpretations of the contemporary set text(s) you study.

Activity

Compare the following reviews of *The God of Small Things* and *The Help*. What are the similarities and differences between the ways in which each text is discussed and analysed? How is each text being represented in literary terms?

Publishers Weekly on *The God of Small Things* (1997)

With sensuous prose, a dreamlike style infused with breathtakingly beautiful images and keen insight into human nature, Roy's debut novel charts fresh territory in the genre of magical, prismatic literature. Set in Kerala, India, during the late 1960s when Communism rattled the age-old caste system, the story begins with the funeral of young Sophie Mol, the cousin of the novel's protagonists, Rahel and her fraternal twin brother, Estha. In a circuitous and suspenseful narrative, Roy reveals the family tensions that led to the twins' behaviour on the fateful night that Sophie drowned. Beneath the drama of a family tragedy lies a background of local politics, social taboos and the tide of history – all of which come together in a slip of fate, after which a family is irreparably shattered. Roy captures the children's candid observations but clouded understanding of adults' complex emotional lives. Rahel notices that 'at times like these, only the Small Things are ever said. The Big Things lurk unsaid inside.' Plangent with a sad wisdom, the children's view is never oversimplified, and the adult characters reveal their frailties – and in one case, a repulsively evil power – in subtle and complex ways. While Roy's powers of description are formidable, she sometimes succumbs to overwriting, forcing every minute detail to symbolize something bigger, and the pace of the story slows. But these lapses are few, and her powers coalesce magnificently in the book's second half. Roy's clarity of vision is remarkable, her voice original, her story beautifully constructed and masterfully told.

Toby Clements of *The Daily Telegraph* on *The Help* (2009)

> Set in Jackson, Mississippi, in 1962, Kathryn Stockett's first novel is narrated by three women: Aibileen and Minny are both black maids working for ladies from the cream of white society, while Miss Skeeter is the 23-year-old daughter of one of those pillars of the community. Aibileen has raised 17 white children, but her own son has been recently killed in an accident at a lumber yard; Minny is forever losing jobs because she talks back to her employers; and Miss Skeeter, so called because she looked like a mosquito when she was born, is ungainly and unmarried and seemingly the only one of her class able to see there might be something unjust about their society.
>
> While Aibileen and Minny are just trying to get by, working all the hours God sends them and then, in the case of Minny, putting up with a drunk, wife-beating husband, Skeeter is in the enviable position of being able to try to make something of her life. She wants to be a writer. Her first efforts are wonderfully wrong-headed, but inspired by thoughts of the woman who brought her up – Constantine, who has vanished in mysterious circumstances – she hits on the idea of collating the stories of the domestic maids, voices never before heard in print. In 1962 this is not only a radical project, since if any of the white ladies found out their help had been talking in public they would have fired them on the spot, but also illegal in Mississippi, since it contravenes the notorious Jim Crow segregation laws.
>
> The fruition of this project gives the book its narrative arc, but elsewhere the novel is a complex, immaculately structured but tremendously convincing nest built from secrets and lies. At some stages it resembles a Feydeau farce, with maids and mistresses popping up one after the other hoping they won't be seen, or the lies they have told won't get out, but there are also moments of real emotional heft, too.
>
> Each of the many relationships between the large cast of characters is perfectly captured, and there is layer after layer of irony to excavate when Stockett describes the lives of the society women of Jackson. But most impressive – and attractive – is the blend of rage and humour with which she writes and that is what makes this novel at once so horrifying yet so savagely funny.

Critiquing contemporary criticism

Although *The Help* is a rather complex metafiction – a book about the process of writing a book that deftly weaves together three different voices – it is noticeable that Kathryn Stockett's narrative methods are not reviewed with the same level of critical attention as Arundhati Roy's. The review of *The God of Small Things* draws attention to the ways in which the novel's patchwork narrative, comprised of non-linear flashbacks and digressions, allows Roy to explore postcolonial India by interweaving the big themes of past and present, culture and caste, as Rahel and Estha work though their tortured personal and political legacy to find their own space in the modern world; Roy's 'dreamlike style infused with breathtakingly beautiful images' is placed within 'the genre of magical, prismatic literature'. Toby Clements, contrastingly, sums up *The Help*'s 'most impressive – and attractive' stylistic feature as 'the blend of rage and humour' that makes the novel 'at once so horrifying yet so savagely funny'. These reviews seem to encapsulate the view that *The God of Small Things* is a denser, richer and basically more 'credible' example of contemporary fiction than *The Help*. It is, it seems, being declared more 'literary'.

The Help is usually classified as **popular fiction** or even **women's fiction**; unsurprisingly, it has proved a firm favourite among book clubs and reading groups. But what is the significance of labelling a text in this way? Interestingly, while most of the time describing something or someone as 'popular' is considered positive and flattering, when it comes to art, music and literature, this is not always the case. Indeed some especially elitist readers might dismiss a text precisely *because* it is popular. In this instance, labelling a text 'popular' may be seen as synonymous with calling it simple, straightforward, accessible and/or unthreatening. The critical divide between literary and popular fiction – for which we could almost substitute the loaded terms 'classics' and 'trash' – calls into question the ways in which texts get pigeonholed in the first place.

Further reading

Penguin Books has produced a reading group guide for *The Help* that contains an interesting interview with Kathryn Stockett on her writing methods. You can access this at:

http://www.penguin.com/static/packages/us/thehelp/index.php

While some writers accrue both critical acclaim and bestseller status – the Victorian novelist Charles Dickens being a prime example – during the 20th century, balancing plaudits and sales got a lot trickier. Whereas, for instance, in the 1860s both literary critic and general reader alike would have appreciated Dickens's *Great Expectations*, half a century later while the literary critic was puzzling over Virginia Woolf's *Mrs Dalloway*, the general reader was probably enjoying Agatha Christie's *The Murder of Roger Ackroyd*. As time passes, however, literary reputations rise and fall; once Agatha Christie was categorized (and arguably patronized) as 'The Queen of Crime', but today her radical decision to challenge the classical rules of detective fiction is interpreted as a genuine generic paradigm-shift, and increasing critical attention is paid to her work.

Traditionally, texts have been categorized by influential journalists, critics and academics; university courses are often structured around the study of a specific genre, sub-genre or text type as defined by elite literary experts. Yet while this endorsement of certain texts as worthy of academic study can be a good thing (and has certainly been taken into account when choosing the texts you can study at A-level), ring-fencing certain texts as the preserve of a small in-group may be seen as tending to aggravate an 'us and them' split between popular (working-class) culture and high (middle- and upper-class) culture. If you think about the notion of **cultural capital** – your personal stake in society or the extent to which you think you fit in – it seems likely that some readers are exposed to subtle but powerful messages telling them that while they might enjoy Kathryn Stockett's novel, they won't enjoy Arundhati Roy's. Ironically, while the enthusiastic labelling of *The God of Small Things* as literary fiction might have put off ordinary readers and limited its audience, calling *The Help* 'popular fiction' probably boosted its sales and helped to generate the 2011 Hollywood film adaptation. It may be that the original critical reception of these two contemporary fictions has had a significant impact upon the ways in which they have been read and received ever since.

Key terms

Cultural capital. A term coined by the French sociologist Pierre Bourdieu, which describes your social assets, your personal stake in society other than your finances.

Popular fiction. A genre of fiction that has wide readership and, by implication, is plot driven. It is often compared to literary fiction, which is seen as more subtle.

Women's fiction. A genre fiction aimed specifically at women and dealing with issues said to be of interest to women in particular.

Activity

Try to find early reviews of the texts you are studying, and see to what extent they contribute to your understanding of the texts as a reader now.

Working with critical contexts

In this section you are going to look at different ways of making meanings within texts – which is, at its most basic, what 'doing English Literature' is all about. However, thinking critically about language and literature is not only always relevant to your English studies, but specifically highly relevant to the time period in which you are working, because at around the same time as postmodern literature began to gain widespread attention, literary theorists were beginning to interrogate the very nature of the relationships that exist between readers, writers and texts. In 1967, the French critic Roland Barthes' influential essay *The Death of the Author* argued that the very idea of an 'author' or 'authority' led people to mistakenly believe that the essential 'meaning' of a text was knowable. For the Marxist Barthes, the multiple ways of making meaning in language, and the sheer impossibility of knowing any author's state of mind, pretty much exploded this idea; indeed he saw the whole concept of the 'author' as a way of transforming texts into the disposable consumer products typical of a bourgeois capitalist culture.

In one way, of course, Barthes' 'death of the author' heralded the 'birth of the reader'. The reader-response approach to literature suggests that writers and readers collaborate to make meanings, and that our responses will depend upon our own experiences, ideas and values. Because it does not privilege the author, content or form of the text, reader-response theory recognizes the role of the active reader in creating meaning. If you remember this, you may well feel more confident when weighing up the critical views and interpretations of others. By challenging the notion of fixed meanings, you liberate the shifting and unstable nature of the text and its critical contexts. Working with different critical methodologies may draw your attention to specific aspects of each text, or help you to see how the same episode can be interpreted very differently. So remember that while you will explore several methods and approaches that can open up new ways of looking at texts in this chapter, as a critical reader you are fully capable of making your own meanings. Whether your awareness of multiple readings stems from reading the views of named critics, trying to apply specific critical perspectives, or through a lively discussion in class with other students and your teacher, what really matters is that you make up your own mind about your literary texts by engaging with ideas that challenge your own.

Marxist and New Historicist criticism

In *The Communist Manifesto* (1848) German philosopher and political thinker Karl Marx (1818–1883) stated: 'The history of all hitherto existing society is the history of class struggles.' Marx saw capitalism as a system in which most people work to produce goods and services but do not share equally in the benefits of their labour, because the ruling class owns the means of production. Hence, Marxist critics see literature as inevitably bound up with the economic and political forces of the times in which they were written. Meanwhile New Historicists link texts to their cultural contexts, using history to explore and explain literature. Both Marxist and New Historicist methodologies are political. They characterize literary texts as material products that are part of – and that can help to illuminate – the processes of history by revealing contemporary preoccupations and anxieties.

All of the set texts listed for study within the shared context of 'Modern times' can be looked at through this critical lens, but *The Handmaid's Tale, A Streetcar*

Study tip

As you work with different possible critical readings of your texts, keep a reading diary. Periodically reviewing your interpretations and those of others can help you chart developments, refinements and changes in your ideas over time.

Named Desire, *Top Girls*, *Cat on a Hot Tin Roof*, Tony Harrison's *Selected Poems*, Seamus Heaney's *New Selected Poems*, *Revolutionary Road* and *One Flew Over the Cuckoo's Nest* lend themselves especially well to being explored in this way.

Activity

Discuss and apply some of the following questions to your three set texts, or to the extract from *One Flew Over the Cuckoo's Nest* on pages 166–167 of this book. You could share out this task among the students in your class.

- Look at the ways in which characters interact. Is there inequality, injustice or oppression between different characters or groups of characters within the story?

- How far are the decisions of the characters presented as being driven by the social and economic conditions in which they live? What jobs or roles do the characters perform? How rich or poor are they? How hard do they have to work?

- Is a real or imagined system of government represented? If so, what are its characteristics? Does it aim to establish or suppress equality and fairness among the people it rules? Are its dominant ideas and values supported or challenged?

- How are other important aspects of the state, such as the law, religion and education, represented and debated within the text?

- To what extent can some voices be seen as having been 'silenced' in this text? Which characters have the power to get their stories heard?

Further reading

Anthony Clavane has written interestingly about Harrison's poem 'v' as 'a timeless portrayal of working-class aspiration'. You can access his article at: http://www.theguardian.com/books/2013/feb/18/tony-harrisons-poem-v-working-class

Psychoanalytic criticism

Psychoanalytic critics see literature as like dreams – fictional inventions of the mind that, while based on reality, are obviously not literally true. Often they are less interested in what the writer 'meant' to say than in what he or she meant to cover up; like practising psychoanalysts, these critics want to uncover the ways in which hidden thoughts have been censored, warped, concealed or distorted by the conscious mind. When exploring representations of character, psychoanalytic critics often interpret the text as providing evidence of the writer's own mental state. It is worth thinking about the extent to which, when you 'psychoanalyse' a fictional character, you are in fact examining a coded version of the writer's own personal thoughts and feelings. Much psychoanalytic criticism is based on the theories of Sigmund Freud, and analyses fantasies, unconscious desires and aspects of sexuality. Freudian interpretations attach great significance to the underlying hidden meanings of words and actions, and see these behaviours as revealing the essential truth about someone's state of mind.

'Modern times' texts that you might find it useful to think about from this critical standpoint include *The Handmaid's Tale*, *Waterland*, *A Streetcar Named Desire*, *Top Girls*, *Spies*, *Cat on a Hot Tin Roof*, *Oranges are not the Only Fruit*, *One Flew Over the Cuckoo's Nest*, *The Color Purple*, *Birthday Letters* and *Ariel*.

Activity

Discuss and apply some of the following questions to your three set texts, or to the poem 'Lady Lazarus' from *Ariel* on pages 153–155 of this book. You could share out this task among the students in your class.

- Do the events of a character's childhood cause him or her to behave in a particular way?
- Does the text feature dream sequences or fantasy worlds? Are symbols used to represent things too frightening to be looked at directly?
- Do the characters seem to be burdened with or fixated upon guilty or ambivalent feelings – and, if so, do you find out what they feel so bad about?
- Are there any ways in which aspects of the writer's own life – childhood traumas, family relationships or issues with sexuality, for example – can be traced within the text?
- Can you see ways in which the behaviour of characters can be interpreted as disguised or encoded representations of anxiety, guilt or fear?

Feminist criticism

Feminist critics are interested in how women are represented in literature – challenging dominant traditional attitudes and ideas about how female characters (who are often seen through the eyes of male writers) feel, act and think. Feminist criticism challenges patriarchal assumptions by unpicking the gender stereotyping embodied in a text and exploring how such stereotypes can be undermined and resisted.

'Modern times' texts that you might find it useful to think about in this way include *The Handmaid's Tale*, *Feminine Gospels*, *A Streetcar Named Desire*, *Top Girls*, *Cat on a Hot Tin Roof*, *Oranges are not the Only Fruit*, *Revolutionary Road*, *One Flew Over the Cuckoo's Nest*, *The Color Purple*, *The Help* and *Ariel*.

Activity

Discuss and apply some of the following questions to your three set texts, or to the extract from *The Handmaid's Tale* on page 157 of this book. You could share out this task among the students in your class.

- To what extent do the female characters drive the narrative? Do they play major or supporting roles in the text? Are they presented as equal to men?
- Are issues associated with traditional male and female gender roles – such as childcare, homemaking, education, work and civil rights – discussed or debated within the text?
- How are relationships between female characters represented?
- How are male–female relationships represented?
- Are there aspects of the ways in which female characters are represented that you see as dated or stereotyped now? If so, would they have seemed so at the time the text was originally written?

Queer theory

Queer theory is grounded in a debate about whether a person's sexuality is part of his or her essential self or socially constructed, questioning the default representation of heterosexuality as 'normal' and exploring 'non-heteronormative' sexual behaviour.

'Modern times' texts that you might find it useful to think about in this critical context include *A Streetcar Named Desire*, *Cat on a Hot Tin Roof*, *Oranges are not the Only Fruit* and *The Color Purple*.

Activity

Discuss and apply some of the following questions to your three set texts, or to the extract from *The Color Purple* on pages 161–162 of this book. You could share out this task among the students in your class.

- To what extent does the text question the idea of heterosexuality as everyone's default status? Does anyone query the idea that heterosexuality is 'normal' and homosexuality 'abnormal'?
- Do homosexual characters drive the narrative? Do they play major or supporting roles in the text?
- How are homosexual and/or heterosexual relationships represented?
- Are there aspects of the ways in which homosexual characters are represented that you see as dated or stereotyped now? If so, would they have seemed so at the time the text was originally written?

Theatre and performance criticism

Because drama is the only type of literary text that involves being filtered through the lens of a theatrical performance, performance critics often examine plays by setting them against what is known of their original staging and the ways in which they have been reinterpreted since. By exploring key elements of setting and staging, performance critics challenge the notion of a definitive version of a dramatic text, given that theatrical productions are collective, collaborative and temporary (unless and until they are captured on film).

This critical lens is obviously most useful when applied to your drama set text.

Activity

As a class, collect different published reviews of a wide variety of film and stage productions of your drama set text. Then apply as many of the questions below as you think are relevant to *either* the reviews you have collected *or* to those film or stage interpretations you have seen of your drama set text, *or* (of course) to both.

- What balance of fact and opinion do you think a performance review should contain? Which review do you find most helpful and illuminating – and why?

- How do you see the role of the drama critic? Is it acceptable to be a provocative or amusing mischief-maker, even when negative reviews can hasten the closure of a production?

- Would you respond in the same way to the views of an amateur critic using social media – for example an anonymous blogger – as to a professional critic? Does it matter that whereas amateur critics are unpaid (and probably bought their own theatre tickets) professionals are paid (and attend free press previews)?

- What aspects of the drama text are emphasized, critiqued and analysed within different modalities of theatre criticism? An academic approach by a university professor is likely to differ from that of a newspaper, magazine, radio, television or online arts journalist – but how and why might this be?

- To what extent (if at all) was the playwright involved with any of the stage or film production(s) of their work that you have seen? Is there any record of whether they approved or disapproved of the ways in which their work has been performed and presented?

- Has one production of a text come to be seen as definitive? Has one performance in a leading role been left unchallenged as effectively unsurpassable – the last word on the subject?

Further reading

Reading a playwright's own ideas about the ways in which their texts have been dramatized can be very illuminating. Arthur Miller's *Timebends: A Life* (1987) is funny, wise and moving; Tennessee Williams's *Memoirs* (1975) and *Notebooks* (2006, edited by Margaret Bradham Thornton) are equally thought provoking.

The contextual linking question

So far the chapters in this option have introduced you to the set texts available for study within the shared context of 'Modern times', and have looked at some of the ways in which you might explore them. Now you will extend the literary and contextual knowledge and understanding you have built up so far to enable you to apply your skills in the examination to a prose extract you have never seen before.

The wording for this task on the examination paper has a very clear framework:

> **'By exploring the methods [WRITER X] uses, write about the significance of [THEME Y] in this extract.'**

Following on from this test of your close-reading skills is a linked task which tests your wider reading by asking you to explore the same theme as it is represented in two of your 'Modern times' texts:

> **'By exploring the methods used, compare the significance of [THEME Y] in two other texts you have studied.'**

The fact that the given theme appears in both questions is important. Because everyone answers the same contextual linking questions, the tasks must be accessible to all, regardless of which texts you have studied. Knowing that the given theme has to be broad enough to work with every possible grouping of three texts makes it quite possible to design questions of your own. Thinking like an examiner can help you to work on the close-reading skills you need in order to respond with confidence to unseen prose in your exam. In this chapter you will explore some ways of responding to both prose fiction and prose non-fiction that you have not read before.

Analysing unseen prose fiction: *The Bell Jar* by Sylvia Plath (1963)

Read the following extract carefully. It is the opening section of *The Bell Jar*, a semi-autobiographical novel written by Sylvia Plath in 1963. The narrator, college student Esther Greenwood, is one of the 12 winners of a prestigious writing competition; her prize is a month's work experience with a New York fashion magazine. Esther's arrival in the city in the summer of 1953 coincides with the execution of a married Jewish couple, Julius and Ethel Rosenberg, for passing information about the USA's atomic bomb technology to the Russians. This real-life event, one of the most controversial of the Cold War period, made headlines around the world.

> **Activity**
>
> Working either on your own or with other students, plan a response to this typical AQA-style sample question: 'By exploring the methods Sylvia Plath uses, write about the significance of isolation in this extract.'

It was a queer, sultry summer, the summer they electrocuted the Rosenbergs, and I didn't know what I was doing in New York. I'm stupid about executions. The idea of being electrocuted makes me sick, and that's all there was to

> This chapter will:
>
> - introduce the idea of contextual linking
> - investigate ways of responding to an unseen prose extract
> - look at ways of comparing two texts from different genres
> - help you start your further research into your chosen texts and contexts.

read about in the papers – goggle-eyed headlines staring up at me on every street corner and at the fusty, peanut-smelling mouth of every subway. It had nothing to do with me, but I couldn't help wondering what it would be like, being burned alive all along your nerves.

I thought it must be the worst thing in the world.

New York was bad enough. By nine in the morning the fake, country-wet freshness that somehow seeped in overnight evaporated like the tail end of a sweet dream. Mirage-grey at the bottom of their granite canyons, the hot streets wavered in the sun, the car tops sizzled and glittered, and the dry, cindery dust blew into my eyes and down my throat.

I kept hearing about the Rosenbergs over the radio and at the office till I couldn't get them out of my mind. It was like the first time I saw a cadaver. For weeks afterwards, the cadaver's head – or what there was left of it – floated up behind my eggs and bacon at breakfast and behind the face of Buddy Willard, who was responsible for my seeing it in the first place, and pretty soon I felt as though I were carrying that cadaver's head around with me on a string, like some black, noseless balloon stinking of vinegar.

I knew something was wrong with me that summer, because all I could think about was the Rosenbergs and how stupid I'd been to buy all those uncomfortable, expensive clothes, hanging limp as fish in my closet, and how all the little successes I'd totted up so happily at college fizzled to nothing outside the slick marble and plate-glass fronts along Madison Avenue.

I was supposed to be having the time of my life.

I was supposed to be the envy of thousands of other college girls just like me all over America who wanted nothing more than to be tripping about in those same size seven patent leather shoes I'd bought in Bloomingdale's one lunch hour with a black patent leather belt and black patent leather pocket-book to match. And when my picture came out in the magazine the twelve of us were working on – drinking martinis in a skimpy, imitation silver-lamé bodice stuck on to a big, fat cloud of white tulle, on some Starlight Roof, in the company of several anonymous young men with all-American bone structures hired or loaned for the occasion – everybody would think I must be having a real whirl.

Look what can happen in this country, they'd say. A girl lives in some out-of-the-way town for nineteen years, so poor she can't afford a magazine, and then she gets a scholarship to college and wins a prize here and a prize there and ends up steering New York like her own private car.

Only I wasn't steering anything, not even myself. I just bumped from my hotel to work and to parties and from parties to my hotel and back to work like a numb trolley-bus. I guess I should have been excited the way most of the other girls were, but I couldn't get myself to react. I felt very still and very empty, the way the eye of a tornado must feel, moving dully along in the middle of the surrounding hullabaloo.

Commentary

In terms of the 'Modern times' context, this extract captures perfectly the institutionalized conformity of postwar America. The central paradox for Esther is that, in escaping her humdrum small-town existence and coming to New York, she has merely swapped a minor prison for a bigger one. Her isolation within the big city as it attempts to swallow her up dramatizes the wider attempts of conventional conservative society to stigmatize and criminalize any difficult or rebellious elements of society. Esther's self-identification with the Rosenbergs

– also doomed outsiders – embodies her feelings of not belonging and the appalling loneliness of being alone in the greatest city on earth.

Plath's methods involve the **pathetic fallacy**, with the harsh, stultifying weather almost suffocating Esther. The authentically 1950s touches – Bloomingdale's, the patent leather accessories, the full-skirted tulle ball gown, the Starlight Roof – evoke the glamour of the specific social and cultural context while serving to emphasize the extent to which, whatever uniform Esther adopts to blend in, she still feels like a fake. The clothes can't disguise who and what she really is. With its 'goggle-eyed headlines' and the 'fusty, peanut-smelling mouth of every subway', the modern city is presented as a hideous, unfeeling monster waiting to swallow her up. You might detect an echo of the 'peanut-crunching crowd' which featured in Plath's poem 'Lady Lazarus' here. Plath uses heavy irony to underline the gulf between appearance and reality, as Esther's personal sense of disconnection frames a wider condemnation of the shallowness of contemporary culture and clearly critiques the American Dream: 'Look what can happen in this country, they'd say. A girl lives in some out-of-the-way town for nineteen years […] and ends up steering New York like her own private car. Only I wasn't steering anything, not even myself.' Even though the 'other girls' – her fellow prize-winners – are always with her, Esther wanders the streets of New York as if in a bubble, as sealed off as the Rosenbergs awaiting electrocution in Sing Sing prison.

Activity

In the previous activity, you worked through a sample contextual linking question. Now you are going to design your own. Read the extract from Don Mullan's article below and explore with the other students in your class the 'Modern times' themes you feel he deals with. Then, to create your question, drop the name 'Don Mullan' into the standard question template as WRITER X and any one of the big issues you have identified as THEME Y.

Read the following extract carefully. It is taken from an article published in *The Independent* newspaper in June 2010. The writer, Don Mullan, was 15 years old in 1972, when he witnessed the events in Northern Ireland that came to be known as 'Bloody Sunday'.

It was the first civil rights demonstration I had ever taken part in. As I left my home that sunny Sunday afternoon, little did I realise that I would find myself in the vortex of a military operation which would leave 13 civilians dead, 14 wounded and a nation in turmoil.

I was at the corner of Glenfada Park and the rubble barricade on Rossville Street when the 1st Battalion Paratroop Regiment advanced. I have very clear memories of the paras fanning out across the waste ground to the north of the Rossville flats complex. I can still vividly recall one para, about 20 metres away, firing a rubber bullet which bounced off the barricade.

Another took up a firing position at the corner of the first block of flats diagonally across the road. Behind him I could see three paratroopers viciously raining the butts of their rifles down upon a young man they had caught.

Then the unmistakable cracks of high-velocity SLR (self-loading rifle) shooting started. I distinctly remember a youth clutching his stomach a short distance away, his cry filling the air with despair and disbelief. For a moment we were stunned. People ran to his aid while others, including myself, sheltered behind the barricade.

Suddenly the air was filled with what seemed like a thunderstorm of bullets. The barricade began to spit dust and it seemed to come from every direction. The wall above me burst. That's how it appeared as bits of mortar and red brick showered around us.

Our nervous systems reacted simultaneously, as though a high-voltage electric shock had been unleashed. Absolute panic ensued as we turned and ran. Doors and alleyways choked as waves of terrified adults and children tried to reach safety. 'Jesus, they're trying to kill us!' 'Jesus, let me through!' 'Get out of the way!' 'Ah Jesus, they're after shooting a wee boy!'

I escaped through Glenfada Park but there are several minutes of that afternoon of which I have absolutely no memory. Five young men died at the barricade and four between Glenfada Park and Abbey Park. As many again were wounded in those locations. What I know is somewhere hidden in my subconscious. […]

The entire west bank of Derry was deeply traumatised by the attack. It must be something akin to the aftermath of an earthquake. I shall never forget the silence that descended upon my native town. […]

There was something surreal about watching television coverage of a bloodbath I had just escaped, at the bottom of the local hill. This was something that happened in Sharpeville or Soweto, but not in Derry. Certainly not to neighbours and friends.

Sleep did not come easy that night. We knew that the angel of death had entered many homes in our estate and throughout Derry. Tomorrow, 13 homes would have a brown box delivered, containing the packaged remains of loved ones with whom, just 24 hours before, they had sat down to their Sunday dinners.

We were stunned and grieving. The next three days would be not just a time of community mourning, but a national wake.

Commentary

The fact that you may never have heard of the specific political event that prompted Don Mullan's article is, of course, completely irrelevant in terms of the 'Modern times' context: this exam is testing your knowledge and understanding of English literature, not sociology, politics or history. In this extract it is the overarching and widely applicable contextual issues of injustice, oppression, rebellion and resistance which should concern you, not the precise geopolitics of the Irish 'Troubles'. Mullan himself reminds us that such tragic events take place all over the world in many different contexts, when he likens 'Bloody Sunday' to the notorious Sharpeville and Soweto massacres in apartheid South Africa.

What you should notice is the extent to which injustice and oppression, as represented here, are both intensely personal and highly political; Don Mullan voices both his own individual struggle to make sense of what happened that day in 1972 and his consciousness of speaking as an eyewitness to history nearly 40 years after the event. His article encompasses a rhetorical condemnation of the bloodshed – 'We knew that the angel of death had entered many homes' – with an emotive and authoritative plea for understanding – 'The entire west bank of Derry was deeply traumatised by the attack. It must be something akin to the aftermath of an earthquake.' His words are simultaneously ferociously condemnatory – 'I could see three paratroopers viciously raining the butts of their rifles down upon a young man they had caught' – and powerfully immediate, with the use of direct speech adding a sense of urgency and panic: 'Jesus, they're trying to kill us!' 'Jesus, let me through!' 'Get out of the way!' 'Ah Jesus, they're after shooting a wee boy!' The piece ends with a **valedictory** invocation of history as both private and public; 'a time of community mourning' but also 'a national wake'.

> **Key term**
> **Valedictory.** Saying farewell.

Comparing writers' ideas and attitudes to a given theme

This section focuses on comparing texts within the shared context of 'Modern times'. In your examination, you must explore the same theme represented within two texts from different genres. In order to do this, you need to think about what reasons a writer might have for choosing to express ideas in the form of poetry, prose or drama.

Just to remind you, the key issues that underpin the set texts within this shared context are:

1. Wars and the legacy of wars
2. Personal and social identity
3. Changing morality and social structures
4. Gender, class, race and ethnicity
5. Political upheaval and change
6. Resistance and rebellion
7. Imperialism, post-imperialism and nationalism

When comparing the ways in which different writers have approached these key issues, you need to think about why the ways in which they have dealt with them are so different. The most important variables here are:

- Context
- Genre
- Gender
- Purpose
- Writers' lives

Comparing in terms of context: time flies

Contextual factors can profoundly affect the ways in which writers approach any given topic. Comparing the specific time periods (how early or late within the 'Modern times' period the text was produced) can illuminate the differences between a text that reflects with urgency and immediacy on an aspect of contemporary culture, society or politics, and one that has the benefit of hindsight. You will also see that time is an important comparative factor when you consider the gap between the context of production (when the text was written or produced) and the context of reception (when it is read or received).

Comparing in terms of genre: form is meaning

Thinking about writers' methods is a little like noticing how a good craftsman always has the right tools for the job in hand: electricians don't wire plugs with hammers, plumbers don't cut pipes with brushes, and decorators don't paste wallpaper with screwdrivers. While there's nothing wrong with any of these tools in themselves, of course, in the wrong context they're all totally useless. If you think of writers as builders of meaning, you might see that one genre (or sub-genre) might be a much better fit than another when it comes to conveying that chosen meaning in the most expressive and memorable way.

Imagine for a moment having to advertise the different literary genres of poetry, prose and drama to a group of sceptical writers. One of your first tasks would be to explain the 'USP' of each text type to your audience – USP is marketing jargon, standing for 'Unique Selling Proposition'. This term is used to illustrate those highly specific qualities, features or aspects that set a product apart from everything else. Hence, if Writer A – let's call her Sylvia Plath – wanted to capture her own troubled personal history in an extremely direct, condensed and technically rigorous way, you could suggest poetry – specifically a dramatic monologue; if Writer B – say, Tennessee Williams – wanted to challenge and debate conventional views about homosexuality, alcoholism and mental illness, you might suggest drama – specifically an expressionist memory play.

Activity

Review the three texts you are studying as a group. What is it about the genre of each one that allows the writers to express their ideas and attitudes most fully? What would be gained and lost by altering the genre? One way to visualize this is to watch a film or television adaptation of your set prose text and discuss the changes that take place in the transition from page to screen. It is equally useful to consider how your drama text may be altered in a move from stage to screen. Think, too, about the reasons why it is almost impossible to adapt a poetry collection in this way. The list of film and television adaptations below provides a starting point for this activity.

Film and television productions

- *The Handmaid's Tale* (1990). Directed by Volker Schlöndorff. Starring Natasha Richardson and Robert Duvall. A handsomely filmed adaptation with some powerful individual performances.

- *Waterland* (1992). Directed by Stephen Gyllenhaal. Starring Jeremy Irons and Ethan Hawke, this interesting film relocates the novel's present-day action to the USA.

- *Oranges are not the Only Fruit* (1990). Directed by Beeban Kidron. An excellent BBC series starring Charlotte Coleman and Geraldine McEwan; the screenplay was written by Jeanette Winterson herself.

- *A Streetcar Named Desire* (1951). Directed by Elia Kazan and starring Marlon Brando and Vivien Leigh, nothing can top this iconic version – with which Tennessee Williams himself was closely associated.

- *Cat on a Hot Tin Roof* (1958). Directed by Richard Brooks. Starring Paul Newman, Elizabeth Taylor and Burl Ives. Despite the excellent performances,

Tennessee Williams loathed this version. Still well worth watching despite (or even because of) the great liberties it takes with the text.

- *One Flew Over the Cuckoo's Nest* (1975). Directed by Milos Forman and starring Jack Nicholson and Louise Fletcher, this iconic film swept the board at the Academy Awards, winning Best Film, Actor, Actress, Director and Screenplay.
- *The Color Purple* (1985). Directed by Steven Spielberg, with Whoopi Goldberg as Celie and Oprah Winfrey as Sofia, this is a moving and sensitive interpretation of the text.
- *Ariel / Birthday Letters: Sylvia* (2003). Directed by Christine Jeffs, *Sylvia* is a respectful biopic with Gwyneth Paltrow as Sylvia Plath and a pre-James Bond Daniel Craig as Ted Hughes. A moving portrayal which suffers from being unable to quote from any of Plath's poetry.
- *Seamus Heaney: Out of the Marvellous (Celebrating Heaney at 70)* (2009). Made with Heaney's cooperation by Charlie McCarthy, this RTE documentary (now on DVD) is a very interesting portrait of the poet.
- *Revolutionary Road* (2008). Directed by Sam Mendes and starring Leonardo DiCaprio and Kate Winslet, this is a beautiful and bleak adaptation of the text.
- *The Help* (2011). Directed by Tate Taylor, this successful adaptation stars Emma Stone as Skeeter Phelan. Octavia Spencer won an Academy Award as Best Supporting Actress for her role as Minny.

Further reading

The *New York Sun* published a very useful article about the cult status of *Revolutionary Road* to coincide with the release of the 2008 Sam Mendes film version. It can be accessed at: http://www.nysun.com/arts/reconsiderations-richard-yatess-revolutionary-road/81093/

Comparing in terms of gender: sugar and spice?

French feminist critic Hélène Cixous coined the term écriture féminine in 1975 when she articulated what she saw as the challenge women writers face to find a way of expressing female difference in texts. Her standpoint is that language is not neutral, but forces women writers to communicate in a 'male' voice that encapsulates patriarchal oppression; écriture féminine theoretically offers a way for women writers to escape this trap. Within your class you may well find your fellow students have equally strong feelings for and against the idea that male writers are incapable of presenting convincing female characters.

Activity

Carol Ann Duffy's poem 'White Writing', which features in the *Feminine Gospels* collection, can be seen to reflect on the notion of 'women's writing'. Whether or not this collection is one of your three set texts, read the poem and discuss the ideas it raises about women's writing with the rest of your class.

Link

See page 182 for a discussion of feminist criticism.

Comparing in terms of purpose: the message

Sometimes the imprint of the precise circumstances in which a text was produced is so strong that it becomes impossible to disentangle the literature from its context of production. One example of such a text within the 'Modern times' context is *Top Girls*, which was originally produced when the Conservative politician Margaret Thatcher (1925–2013) was in her first term of office as the UK's first female Prime Minister. This groundbreaking political context, of which contemporary audiences could not help but be powerfully aware, is now part of the historical past, given that it is a quarter of a century since Thatcher ceased governing the country. But 30-odd years ago, a leftwing feminist playwright like Caryl Churchill had a particularly compelling reason to debate the role of women, given that for the first (and so far only) time in UK history, there really *was* a 'top girl' running the show.

This example illustrates the fact that as time passes, therefore, new generations of readers often need to excavate these embedded meanings as they lose their immediate importance. This is often especially true of texts that can be seen as strongly didactic or politically committed, as the specifics of the writer's intended message fade over time. Thus while a general sense of protest may remain, the precise circumstances within which the text was originally generated become less urgently and immediately relevant to a modern audience.

Further reading

'Material Girls', a sharp and thought-provoking review of a 2002 London stage production of *Top Girls* by theatre critic Lyn Gardner, can be accessed at: http://www.theguardian.com/culture/2002/jan/02/artsfeatures

Activity

Review the three texts you are studying as a group. Discuss the extent to which you think specific contextual aspects seem to 'date' each text, and the ways in which this factor affects your interpretations.

Comparing in terms of the writers' lives: the personal is political

Sometimes a writer's biography seems impossible to separate from the text he or she has produced; as a reader you may come to the conclusion that because of the unique perspective of the writer, no one else could have written about that subject in quite the same way. Within the 'Modern times' context, there are several writers whose personal lives, experiences and personalities seem ingrained within the literature they have produced. One of those writers, Ted Hughes, once said, 'Every work of art stems from a wound in the soul of the artist [...] Art is a psychological component of the auto-immune system that gives expression to the healing process. That is why great works of art make us feel good.' While it is a mistake to assume that literature is just a simplistic reworking of the writer's own personal experience, it is at least worth discussing how far some aspects of your three texts may be seen to reflect aspects of the writers' lives. It can be fascinating and rewarding to explore the interplay between life and art, personal truth and imagined world.

Further reading

Erica Wagner's *Ariel's Gift: Ted Hughes, Sylvia Plath and the Story of Birthday Letters* (2000) offers an illuminating commentary that sets the poems within the context of the Hughes–Plath marriage, while Anne Stevenson's biography *Bitter Fame: A Life of Sylvia Plath* (1989) was updated in the light of the publication of Ted Hughes's *Birthday Letters*.

Activity

Find out as much as possible about the lives and work of the three writers you have chosen to study for this option. Your class could share out the workload and present the findings to each other. Discuss the extent to which you think specific aspects of each writer's life and experience may be seen to have had a direct impact upon the text they have produced, and the ways in which this affects your critical response.

Connecting texts

Activity

Explore any important links you can find between the writers in terms of shared thoughts and feelings, ideas, values and interests relevant to the 'Modern times' context. Are there any connections between the three texts you are studying in terms of significant themes or focus? The following pairings of texts from different genres are worth considering to get you started, although the nature of the link(s) has been left for you to think about:

- *Our Country's Good* and *The God of Small Things*
- Tony Harrison's *Selected Poems* and *Top Girls*
- *The Handmaid's Tale* and *Ariel*
- *Spies* and *All My Sons*
- *Ariel* and *One Flew Over the Cuckoo's Nest*
- *Revolutionary Road* and *One Flew Over the Cuckoo's Nest*
- *Birthday Letters* and *Spies*
- *Translations* and *Skirrid Hill*
- *The God of Small Things* and *Translations*
- *A Streetcar Named Desire* and *Revolutionary Road*
- *The Help* and Seamus Heaney's *Selected Poems*
- *The Color Purple* and *Feminine Gospels*
- *Oranges are not the Only Fruit* and *Cat on a Hot Tin Roof*

Here are some useful comparative questions to get you started:

1. Has a specific historical, social, political or cultural event sparked off an artistic chain reaction?

2. Are there references to contemporary events, similar subject matter or common political concerns?

3. Do the texts have similar themes and focus, despite being relatively widely separated within the time period of 1945 to the present day?

Further reading

- Bill Greenwell's article 'Editing with a Purpose: *Our Country's Good*' in *English Review* 23:4 pages 28–31 (April 2013) is a very interesting exploration of the play's rewriting of history, fiction and drama.

- Owen Sheers' own website www.owensheers.co.uk/ is an excellent resource which covers not only his poetry, but also his diverse career as a novelist, essayist, journalist, television and radio presenter, and official Writer in Residence for the Welsh Rugby Union. Meanwhile the Poetry Archive website www.poetryarchive.org/ section on Owen Sheers contains some excellent resources, including readings from *Skirrid Hill* by the poet himself.

- Stewart O'Nan's article 'The Lost World of Richard Yates' comprehensively reviews the writer's life and work. It can be accessed at: http://bostonreview.net/stewart-onan-the-lost-world-of-richard-yates. Also very useful is an excellent *New York Times* article that gives an elegant and detailed overview of Yates's literary achievement. This can be accessed at: http://www.nytimes.com/2000/04/09/books/essay-american-beauty-circa-1955.html

Extension activity

Find out about any important links between the writers in terms of significant personal relationships, professional partnerships or critical clustering. The following pairings are worth considering as starting points:

- Arthur Miller and Tennessee Williams, as friends and fellow playwrights
- Sylvia Plath and Ted Hughes as poets married to each other
- Ted Hughes and Seamus Heaney as co-editors and colleagues
- Margaret Atwood and Alice Walker as close contemporaries who came to prominence during the 1980s.

Further reading

Sean McEvoy's *Tragedy: A Student Handbook* (English and Media Centre, 2009) contains a brilliant section on 'Modern American Tragedy' invaluable for anyone studying Miller or Williams.

Component 3:
Independent critical study:
Texts across time

This chapter will:

- look at the challenges of the non-exam assessment component

- look at how you identify a topic or genre that connects your two chosen texts

- understand how a good essay title is constructed

- help you work effectively with critical views and interpretations

- review the stages of writing your essay – planning, structuring, redrafting, proof-reading and editing

- help you complete your non-exam assessment component by proofreading, presenting and referencing your work appropriately and producing an accurate bibliography.

Key term

Bibliography. The full list of books, articles, films and stage productions that you consulted during the writing of an essay.

The 'Independent critical study' component of AQA Specification A involves writing a 2,500-word essay connecting two texts of your own choice. Because this specification sets such a high value on the notion of autonomous personal reading, very few limitations are placed upon your freedom to choose your own texts. The only conditions that apply are that:

- at least one of your texts must have been written before 1900

- you cannot write about two texts by the same author

- you cannot write about any of the set texts listed for study in Component 1 or Component 2

- you must pay equal attention to both texts

- if you choose to write about poetry, you must choose a substantial whole collection (one that is clearly the equivalent of studying a full-length novel or play) and *not* merely a handful of short poems.

Your non-exam assessment component is designed to encourage you to read independently, follow your personal interests and develop your own ideas. Working with your teacher, you need to:

- choose two texts to read and connect around a shared theme, topic or genre

- create a carefully worded task that allows you to access all five Assessment Objectives and that can be completed within 2,500 words

- source relevant secondary research material (such as film and stage performances, books, articles and Internet sources relevant to your two primary texts)

- evaluate the most interesting alternative points of view you find and use them in your essay to scaffold meanings of your own

- plan, draft and complete a well-structured, interesting and independent essay with an original approach

- produce an accurate and appropriate academic **bibliography** and reference section.

The specification mentions the following possible themes and genres that you could trace across and within your chosen texts, but of course this list is offered just to get you started:

- The struggle for identity
- Crime and punishment
- Minds under stress
- Nostalgia and the past
- The gothic
- Satire and dystopia
- War and conflict
- Representations of race and ethnicity
- Representations of sexuality
- Representations of women
- Representations of men
- Representations of social class and culture

Activity

Discuss with your fellow students the alternative themes and genres that might be studied within the parameters of this unit, and see how many textual pairings you can suggest. Remember that at least one text must have been published before 1900.

Developing your research skills

Imagine that in ten years' time your employer wants you to analyse your firm's main business rivals. The chances of your boss deciding that you'll do your best work locked in an office for a couple of hours with no access to any external sources of information are virtually nil. In terms of the world of work, the tasks you complete in an exam context probably resemble a quick-fire discussion session rather than finishing a project. The independent learning skills you will hone during your non-exam assessment component, however, are likely to benefit you directly when you move on to higher education or the world of work.

This longer-term way of working poses a new set of challenges, very different from those you face in an examination. While you are free to set your own agenda, you also have to be very self-motivated, well organized and efficient at time management. Given that you can work onscreen, drafting, proofreading and editing your writing over a substantial length of time, it is much less forgivable if you include a botched misquote, wobbly spelling or mangled argument, which might be understandable in an examination context.

Working independently

Imagine that ten years from now you are working for a major clothing brand. If asked to report on the state of the competition, you would begin by making detailed notes about your rivals' product lines and marketing strategies; this primary research is the equivalent of the preliminary reading of your two chosen literary texts. Next you might focus on a particular area of interest that you have identified as characteristic of the competition's offering – their innovative sportswear, for example; this replicates your streamlining your topic focus to something manageable in 2,500 words. Once you've identified your area of special interest, you will use every source at your disposal, from experienced senior colleagues (your teachers) to co-workers busy with their own projects (the rest of your English Literature class). Before long you will begin your own independent research, utilizing all of your existing study skills and developing still more. You might investigate the expert opinions of a range of bloggers and trend-watchers (read some literary criticism, see live stage performances or watch film or television adaptations of your chosen texts). Both in the world of work and in terms of your A-level studies, the quality, depth and reliability of the work you do at every stage of the planning and research process will affect the ultimate success of your final written piece.

Your teachers will offer a different kind of support with your non-exam assessment component than they do when helping you to prepare for the two examined units, since here, above all, you must play an active role in the learning process. Specification A, with its emphasis on encouraging the autonomous

Did you know?

Because the study skills that you will build through your non-exam assessment component are highly valued, a discussion of your working methods could enhance your university application. Admissions tutors reading personal statements will be interested in how you selected your texts, decided on a personal research focus and sourced your own critical materials; while a positive, can-do approach to this component will give your school or college referee the chance to write something positive and concrete about your potential to succeed at undergraduate level.

Key term

Compare / Contrast. When we connect texts, the words 'compare' and 'contrast' often appear together, so it is important to remember that they have significantly different meanings. **Comparison**, as used here and more widely in academic contexts, involves finding aspects of *similarity* in texts. **Contrast**, on the other hand, involves finding aspects of *difference*.

critical reader, asks you to fully engage with your texts and tasks to produce a genuinely independent response. Because the non-exam assessment component is designed to get you working with texts in ways that differ from the preparation you do for written exams, the work submitted by your A-level class cannot and must not involve you all saying more or less the same things about the same two books. Having selected your texts with the guidance and support of your teachers, you can then work with them to negotiate your own individual topic and task. Don't expect your teachers to spoon-feed you by providing endless notes, hand-outs and essay plans; they are much more likely to engineer a flexible and exploratory way of working that involves one-to-one tutorials and supervisions as well as whole-class study sessions. The title of this component, 'Independent critical study', makes it clear that you must take responsibility for your own learning.

Connecting texts

In this component you need to connect (that is, **compare** and **contrast**) two texts of your choice. This sheds light on the reading process as a whole and is a reflection of what we all do as readers – that is, we read and process a new text by consciously or subconsciously relating it to all the other texts we have previously read and processed in our lives. You will explore the relationship that exists between your chosen texts. When you come across a new text, you apply your previous knowledge about how texts work to construct meanings as you read. Connecting two texts can cast fresh light upon them both and open up a range of new potentialities and interpretations.

Often students choose their two texts because of a broad topic area, common to both of them, that is of interest. Once you have brought your texts together, however, you then need to tease them apart; connecting texts via comparing and contrasting them might mean tracing patterns of similarity and difference in terms of, for example:

- form or genre (e.g. two novels; two plays; novel and play)
- content (e.g. crime fiction, science fiction, gothic fiction)
- narrative method (e.g. first person, unreliable narrative, multiple narrators)
- intended response (e.g. tragedy to make you think, comedy to make you laugh, satire to make you consider the world around you)
- critical response (e.g. the range of readings and interpretations that can be applied and debated)
- contexts (e.g. the contexts of production and reception).

To construct a strong premise for your investigation, you need to find a sensible baseline connection between your chosen texts; your starting point will usually be that they have something in common, being apparently 'about' the same thematic topic or able to be categorized within the same genre. Given the 2,500 word limit, having a defined connective focus is imperative, so once you have identified the link you want to explore, you need to work closely with your teacher to design a task that is sufficiently challenging to keep you interested, but sufficiently sharply focused to be manageable within the word count.

In summary, your core thematic link is the starting point that opens up your exploration of these 'literary' areas, rather than being the primary focus of your writing; it's all about the *how*, not the *what*. In Component 1, AQA has grouped the set texts diachronically under an overarching theme to help you make purposeful links between them; the very least the central topic of 'Love through the ages' tells you is that from William Shakespeare to Ian McEwan, all these writers thought that love was a subject worth discussing. In Component 3, however, *you* have to bridge the gap between your chosen texts. Investigating the methods used by your two chosen writers to deal with the same topic enables you to make suggestions about what that central idea may have meant to them – and, of course, what it means to you.

Analysing how effective tasks work

It is very important that, because all the Assessment Objectives are tested in this component, your task must include some key words designed to help you fulfil them.

Activity

Analyse the wording of the following non-exam assessment task carefully before referring to the commentary that goes with it.

The two texts to be compared are the quintessential example of 19th-century **sensation fiction**, Wilkie Collins's *The Woman in White* (1859–60), and a modern text that consciously and deliberately echoes it, Sarah Waters' **pastiche** *Fingersmith* (2002).

Discuss with your teacher and the rest of your class what this example may suggest about how to construct your own task in order to access all five Assessment Objectives:

'Sarah Waters has argued that the Victorian sensation novel genre 'was at its best when tugging at the seams of certainties and easy solutions.' Compare and contrast the presentation of Sue Trinder in Waters' *Fingersmith* and Marian Halcombe in Wilkie Collins's *The Woman in White* in the light of this view.'

Commentary

This task's focus is firmly on genre and **intertextuality**, filtered through the theme of the role of women. The way in which readers receive and understand *Fingersmith* is shaped and controlled by their expectations of the generic practices and conventions of the classic Victorian sensation novel, as exemplified by *The Woman in White*. Collins's text provides the reader with a yardstick against which to measure his or her response to Waters' modern reboot; connecting the two provides a new way to think about both texts. The different contexts in which each of these 'Victorian' texts were written and produced will allow fascinating parallels to be drawn between the positions of two writers widely separated by time, and interesting reflections upon the changing ideas and values they express.

Sometimes the views expressed within a text will be consciously challenged or subverted by a self-conscious rewrite: when comparing them, a key focus must be to tease out why this might be. Writers (like Sarah Waters) and readers (like us) are both aware of generic conventions, and much of the interest that emerges as we puzzle out our own textual meanings can be found in the extent to which we are aware of the writer's ideas and intentions.

Did you know?

If you choose, say, two novels that examine the same theme, it is very helpful if they are separated by a significant period of time; the differing contexts of production can shed light upon key similarities and differences in both the writers' methods and perspectives. Because of this component's interest in texts across time, selecting two texts from within the same genre that were both written in 1899 is unlikely to lead to a very successful outcome.

Link

See page 200 for an explanation of the Assessment Objectives.

Key term

Sensation fiction. A term given to a genre from the 1860s onwards that tends to involve crime and passion. An often-quoted example is Wilkie Collins's *The Woman in White* (1859–60). Although the term sounds dismissive, such fiction has had a huge influence on all sorts of literature since the 1860s.

The title quotation, which is not from a critical source but a statement by one of the two novelists being studied, draws attention to Waters' thoughtful and sophisticated reinvention of Collins's literary landscape; including this viewpoint opens up both AO3 and AO5. In foregrounding the role of the heroine, the task provides a manageable focus clearly linked to the different time periods within which each novel was written (AO3). The crucial imperative verbs *compare* and *contrast* should draw your attention to AO4 and the need to connect your texts through similarity and difference, while the word *presentation* signals AO2 and the importance of writing about the authors' methods. The inclusion of Sarah Waters' personal critical standpoint, together with the phrase *in the light of this view,* accesses AO5 by reminding you of the need to debate the ways in which texts are received and understood. This neatly shaped task needs to be approached in clear, well-argued and accurate prose (AO1), and then the job is done.

The Assessment Objectives

As you read about the Assessment Objectives below, the key thing to remember is that they are all assessed in all questions, so although you need to understand what they are and what you are required to do about them, you do not need to worry about whether they operate in some questions and not in others.

Assessment Objective 1 (AO1)

Within AO1 you are required to *articulate informed, personal and creative responses to literary texts, using associated concepts and terminology, and coherent, accurate written expression*. This Assessment Objective describes, then, the need for good writing and a use of terminology appropriate to the task you are doing.

Assessment Objective 2 (AO2)

AO2 requires you to *analyse ways in which meanings are shaped in literary texts*. This Assessment Objective describes the need to analyse authorial methods of writing, with the shaping of meanings a key idea here, indicating that you should link an author's ways of writing with the meanings that arise from them.

Assessment Objective 3 (AO3)

AO3 requires you to *demonstrate understanding of the significance and influence of the contexts in which literary texts are written and received*. This specification is closely linked to historical contexts in particular.

Assessment Objective 4 (AO4)

AO4 requires you to *explore connections across literary texts*. There is a requirement here to show an understanding of the typical features of a genre, and/or a theme, and/or a historical period, and then you can show the extent to which your text has such typical features.

Assessment Objective 5 (AO5)

AO5 requires you to *explore literary texts informed by different interpretations*. It should be clear that if you are working with ideas of time, there cannot be a single fixed interpretation. If the question you are answering is framed as a debate, then you will need to consider different possible ways of interpreting your texts.

Activity

Review the suggested non-exam assessment activity below and discuss how it ensures a strong basis for connecting (by both *comparing* and *contrasting*) the chosen texts in order to access the Assessment Objectives. Look carefully at how the suggested link or given view helps to structure the connection.

If you don't know anything about the texts mentioned, do an Internet search and read a simple outline of each one before you begin (Wikipedia is fine for this purpose).

'Compare and contrast the presentation of women in Keats's narrative poems 'Lamia', 'Isabella' and 'The Eve of St Agnes', with that of Anne Brontë in her novel *The Tenant of Wildfell Hall*. In what ways do you think the gothic settings of these texts shape the writers' presentation of heroines in peril?'

Commentary

At first glance, the theme here looks very broad – the presentation of women – and there may seem to be too much ground to cover in just 2,500 words. Yet in fact the question refines this wide area in two ways. First, the fact that the texts are already connected within the framework of the gothic is underlined, which invites the student to look at how a poet and a novelist use very different methods within the parameters of their respective genres. Secondly, the idea of *heroines in peril* provides a more defined and specific area of focus within the overarching *presentation of women* topic.

Writing your essay

Beginning to write is perhaps the hardest thing to do, so the best advice is simply to get on with it. Aim to work effectively with your teachers by turning up well prepared and on time to all tutorials and lessons. Keep copies of all your drafts and back up your computer files. Make sure you have detailed notes of sources for your **bibliography**.

Once you put pen to paper, remember that your introduction needs to clarify your chosen topic, contextualize both texts, define the parameters of your debate and do something to indicate the likely shape of the argument to come. As you work on, your aim must be to connect your texts in terms of narrative structure, genre, critical debate and context. You will lose a lot of marks if you link your texts only tenuously, even if what you say about each one is very good, because you will not be shaping a sophisticated *connective* argument.

One of the most difficult things to do in a sustained piece of writing is to achieve good cohesion across paragraphs. Examiners and moderators often come across essays that contain worthy individual sections, but fall apart into disparate chunks rather than combining to create an overarching argument. Imagine slicing your essay up into its separate paragraphs with a guillotine, throwing them into the air and rearranging them in whatever random order they land. Would it really make any difference to your argument? Now imagine doing this with a historical timeline or the write-up of a scientific experiment: it would be completely impossible to rearrange their components without wrecking the integrity of each document.

To improve your work, treat both of your texts equally and interweave them using an appropriate discourse structure. The language of comparison and contrast can help to hold your texts together, with *similarly*, *likewise*, *correspondingly*, *in the same way* and *equally* suggesting similarity and *on the contrary*, *whereas*, *then again*, *on the other hand*, *in contrast*, *quite the reverse* and *contrastingly* denoting difference. Another useful way to shape your essay is to range around the texts and cluster your points, rather than adopting a chronological approach that reads like a list; since there is no way you can trace every link you find within the 2,500 word limit, you should always try to write 'a lot about a little' than 'a little about a lot'.

Considerable skill is involved in thoughtfully and precisely selecting the best points to support your argument. As you write, make sure you fully understand the literary-critical terminology you use, and never drop in a technical term without identifying its use and analysing its effects. When analysing the methods that writers use to make meaning, you must write about the genre, form and structure of your texts as well as their language. You are not meant to laboriously dissect tiny lexical items – single words, very short phrases or (worst of all) small elements of punctuation – extracted from a lengthy novel; this approach suggests that you cannot see the wood for the trees. You will do far better to write about the ways in which texts from different genres present similar themes or subjects, and how narratives can be organized. Analyse language closely by all means, but retain a sense of perspective about the bigger organizational features of your texts too.

Aim to finish your essay crisply by clinching your argument and leaving your reader thinking (and perhaps even smiling). Avoid ending with a bland claim to have proved the point you said you were going to prove. Instead conclude with a balanced overview that not only seals your argument but sheds light on what you have previously written. Remember that even though this is a non-exam assessment component, rather than an exam question, your essay must still relate very closely to the title you chose to put at the top. Your final mark will reflect the relevance of your approach, which shows the significance of getting that title right in the first place.

Working with critical views

Activity

Remind yourself of the major critical positions discussed on pages 180–184 and think about which of these ways of interpreting texts might be most relevant to the texts and topic you have chosen.

When it comes to working with the ideas of other readers, your aim should be to explore a range of alternative interpretations (be they books, articles, film versions or stage performances) and set these views alongside both the primary texts themselves and your own emerging ideas about them. Debating the opinions of other readers can take your understanding of a text to another

Did you know?

Teachers and examiners groan when they read comments along the lines of 'here is a metaphor'. This is known as 'feature-spotting' and the only possible reaction to such a point will be 'So what?' rather than 'Well argued'.

level, by allowing you to develop a more conceptualized 'big picture' overview. The importance of having a yardstick against which to measure your texts is hard to overemphasize. Working with a particular critical standpoint can help you to interrogate your texts more precisely and confidently, as seen in some of the Activities earlier in this chapter. Indeed, the notion of undertaking a literary debate about the ways in which your texts can be interpreted can often provide the central spine of your essay.

Of course, any debate that you engage in has to be real; you can't just name-check a couple of critics and say you agree with them. Rather, you should use an interesting secondary reading as a lens through which to refocus your attention on the primary text. So, for instance, if a film adaptation of your text cuts out a character, what is lost (or gained)? If an article presents a viewpoint you fundamentally applaud (or object to), apply it to an aspect of your text and evaluate the extent to which it helps you to refine, extend or reverse your previous ideas about the primary text.

> ### Did you know?
> A simple but effective way of sustaining the idea of a debate as you write is to use modal verb phrases, such as 'may be seen as', 'might be interpreted as' or 'could be represented as'. These suggest an awareness of the range of potential meanings encoded within literary texts.

Extension activity

If possible, try to compare different film, television and/or stage productions of your chosen texts – especially if you have chosen a play. Search, too, for online reviews of any dramatic interpretations. What are the similarities and differences between the ways in which the text has been represented, discussed and analysed?

Activity

Review the example provided below of a student's work, and discuss how this student has used another reader's ideas to connect the two texts and shape their own critical argument. If you don't know anything about the texts mentioned, do an Internet search and read a simple outline of each one before you begin (Wikipedia is fine for this purpose).

Chosen texts: Thomas Middleton and William Rowley's *The Changeling* (1622) and Mary Shelley's *Frankenstein* (1818)

The idea of a 'changeling' child suggests a warped and unnatural parent–child relationship. In *Frankenstein* Victor perverts nature by giving birth to the Creature without a mother and then abandoning him; the absence of a mother figure is one of the causes of the Creature's fall into sin, just as it is for Beatrice-Joanna in *The Changeling*. Shelley's presentation of women as a force for good challenges the traditional idea that Eve brought sin into the world and in the novel it is Victor who challenges the authority of God; 'how dangerous is the acquirement of knowledge'. Meanwhile feminist critic Ellen Moers sees *Frankenstein* as a classic 'birth myth' used by Shelley to overcome her pain at the death of her young children and the guilt she felt because her own mother Mary Wollstonecraft died giving birth to her. I do agree with Moers, but I would go further and argue that the way Shelley presents Victor's attitude towards the Creature as stereotypical masculine arrogance suggests that the novelist was also working through her poor relationship with her father, William Godwin, by imagining herself as the abused Creature.

As well as using your school or college resource centre, see if you can visit your nearest city or university library. Do some Internet research beforehand (opening times can vary and sometimes you can save time by checking the catalogues online before you visit.)

Commentary

This student handles debate very effectively when comparing the presentation of damaged parent–child relationships in a Jacobean revenge tragedy and the originator of all Gothic novels. He uses both feminist and psychological critical views to underpin his argument, but also goes on to employ the ideas of a named feminist critic, Ellen Moers, as a way of developing his own subtle and original argument.

Proofreading and presentation

Once you've done all the hard work and actually written your essay, don't fall at the last hurdle and throw marks away through careless presentation. Your teacher isn't allowed to proofread for you and if you fail to make certain key final checks, things can go badly wrong with little warning. Make everyone's life easier by avoiding unsuitable typefaces (use Times New Roman, Arial or Cambria instead), supersized or microscopic font sizes (11 or 12 point are acceptable), or any colour combination other than black print on white paper. Use 1.5 line spacing as opposed to single, as it is much easier to read. Number your pages. Identify titles in bold or italic: unless you do so, how will your reader know if you mean *Emma* (the novel) or Emma (the heroine of the book that bears her name)? Be consistent about single inverted commas; lay out paragraphs and paragraph breaks clearly; and staple your Candidate Record Form securely to your completed essay. It really is that easy.

Word count

The word count for this unit is 2,500 words and there is a space to declare your count exactly on the official Candidate Record Form. Never be tempted to write 'approximately 2,500'; since everyone produces their essay on a computer these days, there is no excuse whatsoever for not providing an accurate figure. Neither can you fudge the issue by including a word count 'excluding quotations'; there is no such thing. Whenever you include quotations to illustrate your points, advance your argument and/or strengthen your analysis of writers' methods, they always count towards your tally – so be selective. Copying out vast chunks of either your primary or secondary texts will eat up your 2,500 words at an alarming rate, whilst highlighting your inability to select the right quotation to clinch your argument. Instead, incorporate short, relevant quotations into your own sentences and adapt them to fit with your own syntax.

Be honest with yourself; if you have vastly exceeded the 2,500 word limit, are you sure there aren't any sections that should be slimmed down or just deleted? Narrative and description are unforgivable if you've gone over the limit. On the other hand, if your essay is significantly shorter than 2,500 words, can you expand upon some of your better points?

Bibliography and references

A bibliography is the full list of books, articles, films and stage productions you consulted during the writing of your essay; references (sometimes called citations) record the secondary sources you have quoted and allow your readers to trace them. When you quote or paraphrase (that is, closely reword) a critical view and use it to enhance your own argument, you must be honest and

The 2,500 word limit for the non-exam assessment component should prevent you from narrating and describing, but allow you to create, develop and illustrate your argument appropriately. Your bibliography and references do *not* count towards the total words used.

pay credit where it is due; providing full details of each source enhances your academic credibility and allows you to avoid accusations of plagiarism. By openly and transparently attributing your ideas, you enable your readers to check that your information is valid and provide them with a pathway into further research of their own if they choose to follow your lead.

By providing this rigorous academic supporting apparatus for your essay, you will be preparing yourself very well for further study within a higher education context, since all university departments have clear and highly specific methods of referencing, and can refuse to accept your work if you do not follow their rules to the letter. AQA does not insist on one particular form of referencing, however, so modelling your bibliography and references on the examples shown in this chapter will be fine.

There will certainly be times when you need to include the name of a critic within your essay and this can be done very simply, just by writing, for example, 'as Kate Millett has argued…'. This neat way of crediting a source is known as an in-text attribution, and to keep your essay uncluttered and clear, you do not need to include full details of the source you have used at this point. Instead, the simplest solution is to number it and either put the details into a footnote at the bottom of the same page or (even easier) include it in a consecutively numbered list attached to the end of your essay. Once in a while you may need to acknowledge a source that has added to your overall understanding but that you have not quoted directly; this kind of all-purpose reference should be included in your bibliography.

All sources listed within your bibliography should include the name of the author, the title of the text and any other available information such as the place of publication, relevant edition, volume, issue, page numbers, date, publisher, or URL in the case of an online source. You can use the following examples as style models.

- **How to cite a book:** Mullan, John. *How Novels Work*. Oxford: Oxford University Press (2006)
- **How to cite an article:** Forward, Stephanie. 'A New World for Women?' in *English Review* Vol. 19 Issue 4 pp25–27. (April 2009)
- **How to cite a website:** Mullan, John. *Guardian Book Club: Fingersmith by Sarah Waters*. (Accessed 29.7.14) http://www.theguardian.com/books/2006/jun/03/sarahwaters
- **How to cite a film/television production**: Thacker, David (director). *A Doll's House*. BBC television production (1992)
- **How to cite a stage performance:** Cracknell, Carrie (director). *A Doll's House*. Young Vic stage production (London 2013)

It simplifies things if you place your list of references directly after your bibliography. You can use the following example as a style model, remembering to number your sources consecutively as you go:

1. Forward, S. 'A New World for Women?' p25

2. Mullan, J. *How Novels Work* p194

3. Forward, S. 'A New World for Women?' p26

This section provides some useful hints to help you with your final preparations for your AS or A level English Literature examinations. Some of these hints apply equally well to all of your exams, whatever the subject. They are based on the assumption that you have worked hard up to this point and that you have read the texts and know them well.

The examination requirements

! EXAMINER'S TIP

Always make sure that your preparation and revision involve a specific task – with a specific amount of time allocated to it and a clear end result. Revision involves looking over something that you have done already, which is important, but it is equally important to do something new – to prepare some thoughts and ideas about topics that have not been covered so far.

One obvious way of preparing for your English Literature exams is to use this book. Take each of the chapters in turn and apply its focus to the actual set texts that you have studied. At this stage, make sure that you know what the precise requirements for your various exams are. What follows is a checklist of requirements.

AS level

Paper 1 (closed book – but working on given extracts and poems)	Paper 2 (open book for Section B)
Section A: You respond to a passage from a Shakespeare play and how it relates to the play as a whole.	**Section A:** You answer a question on an unseen prose extract.
Section B: You respond to a poem from your chosen anthology.	**Section B:** You answer an essay question comparing two prose texts.

A Level

(The requirements for the 'World War I and its aftermath' and 'Modern times: Literature from 1945 to the present day' options are the same in Paper 2.)

Paper 1 (open book for Section C)	Paper 2 (open book)
Section A: You respond to a passage from a Shakespeare play and how it relates to the play as a whole.	**Section A:** You answer an essay question on a core set text.
Section B: You answer a question on unseen poetry.	**Section B:** You answer a question on an unseen prose text, followed by a question comparing two set texts.
Section C: You answer an essay question comparing two set texts.	

The examinations themselves

The variety of questions

It should be obvious from the outlines of the examination requirements opposite, that this specification has different types of questions, including:

- questions with text
- essays on single texts
- essays comparing texts
- unseen material.

Each of these types of question requires subtly different approaches, as well as having common ground. The common ground is provided by the outline mark scheme, which requires you to debate meanings based on an application of all of the Assessment Objectives. The difference in question types is in part a matter of focus. It is vital that your revision includes practising for each of the different question types.

Open-book exams

One of the core requirements of these exams – in all but the unseen critical questions – is that you can demonstrate your detailed knowledge of the texts you have studied. It would be wrong to assume that an open-book exam replaces the need for a good knowledge of the text.

Open-book exams allow you to respond to questions by checking broad issues, such as the organization of scenes or chapters, or stanzas. Also, with a poetry text, you can fairly easily find and examine the detail of a specific poem that you may need for an answer. However, for novels and plays, the situation is very different – within the available time, you cannot afford to spend ages looking for a specific passage in a long novel or play. Therefore, it is vital that you come into the exam room mentally equipped with a good stock of quotations and references for all of your exams, so that you can quote and make references relevantly and quickly in your answers.

Providing evidence

Quotation

One form of textual evidence is direct quotation, and you are far more likely to use this with the poetry than the prose fiction. Quotation can involve quoting chunks of text, but it can also involve integrating words or phrases into your own syntax. So, while you could quote from Wilfred Owen's poem 'Strange Meeting' by writing:

> Owen begins the poem with the speaker describing the beginning of a dream:
>
> 'It seemed that out of battle I escaped
>
> Down some profound dull tunnel,'

You could also write:

> In the opening lines of the poem, Owen immediately identifies a dream world when the speaker says that 'It seemed' as though he 'escaped' from the immediacy of the battle.

The second method is often better, because it lets you get on with your argument while at the same time demonstrating that you know the text well. Practise this method of quoting and you will soon find that you become adept at it.

Reference

Equally effective, though, can be reference – especially when you are writing about a novel. Reference is when you show awareness of an event, a character, a place, etc., by referring to it with knowledge rather than using the exact words written by the author.

If we continue to use the lines above from 'Strange Meeting' as an example, if you were to refer to them you would write something like:

> Owen's use of the language of dreams immediately establishes that this is more than a realistic portrayal of battle.

Reference has particular value when you are dealing with novels, where direct quotation can be difficult, even in an open-book exam.

> To summarize, here is a list of points to bear in mind when you are using quotation and reference:
>
> - You should support your arguments with frequent and relevant textual evidence.
> - Quotations should be brief.
> - Quotations should be accurate.
> - The best quotations are embedded in your own sentences.
> - Reference to the text can also help to give evidence, and close references can often work better than quotations.
> - Quotations and references should never stand alone – they should be used to support particular points that you are want to make.

EXAMINER'S TIP

Always make sure that your focused stint of work leaves you **better informed** about the key topic than you were before you started. And also make sure that you have a **written record** of what you have prepared, so that you can glance over it in the final few days before the exam.

And finally...

It is common among students to talk about dreading exams, but this can sometimes be overplayed. Exams are a fact of the system we are all in, so we might as well make the most of them.

If you are well prepared, the exams should be seen – in part anyway – as a chance to show what you know. And the nature of English Literature as a subject also means that you should find some space in your head to think in the exam itself.

It is never really appropriate to say 'good luck' to someone before an exam, because exams are not about luck. They are about being well prepared in advance, and thoughtful on the day itself.

EXAMINER'S TIP

At some points in your preparation programme, actually write some sample exam answers and show them to your teacher for feedback and guidance.

Glossary

Agitprop. An art form with an explicitly political message.

Antagonist. The most notable character who opposes the **protagonist** (hero) of a narrative. Often the antagonist is the villain who wants to harm the hero/heroine or prevent him/her from achieving their goals.

Asyndetic listing. This involves omitting any conjunctions (such as 'and') from a list.

Ballad. A long poem that tells a story, and usually has a fast pace, with repetition a common feature

Ballade. A French form that was popular in the 14th and 15th centuries. It usually opens with an address to the poet's prince, and it uses eight-line **stanzas** (rhyming ababbcbc). The last line of the first stanza recurs as a refrain in the last line of the subsequent stanzas. A ballade ends with an envoi – a kind of postscript, which begins with an address to the poet's prince and is a **quatrain** (rhymed abab).

Bibliography. The full list of books, articles, films and stage productions that you consulted during the writing of an essay.

Bildungsroman. A novel that deals with one person's formative years and moral or spiritual development (a German critical term).

Blazon. A poetic listing of a loved one's beautiful qualities.

Byronic hero. An emotionally complex, mysterious and tormented male character, who is arrogant, cynical and contemptuous of normal society, but, despite such anti-heroic qualities, manages to be alluring to some of the other characters and many readers.

Caesura. A break within a line of verse, often indicated by a punctuation mark.

Compare / Contrast. When we connect texts, the words 'compare' and 'contrast' often appear together, so it is important to remember that they have significantly different meanings. **Comparison**, as used here and more widely in academic contexts, involves finding aspects of *similarity* in texts. **Contrast**, on the other hand, involves finding aspects of *difference*.

Conceit. An arresting or elaborate comparison that brings together two (typically dissimilar) elements in an unusual way. Such comparisons, while at first seemingly far-fetched, often prove to be apt.

Confessional. Confessional writing is deeply personal and intimate in its details.

Contexts of production and reception. Contexts are all of the various circumstances that can be taken into account when reading a text (*con* means with, *text* means something that has literally been woven together). **Contexts of production** are the various circumstances that can be considered as relevant at the time the text was written and first published / first performed. **Contexts of reception** are the various circumstances that can be considered as relevant at the time the text is being read or watched, which might be many years later (in the case of World War I, maybe a century later).

Counter-cultural. A counter culture is one whose beliefs and behaviour differ considerably from the mainstream views held at the time.

Couplet. Two lines with the same metre that also rhyme.

Cultural capital. A term coined by the French sociologist Pierre Bourdieu, which describes your social assets, your personal stake in society other than your finances.

Demotic. This refers to ordinary people.

Diachronic study. A study that considers texts through a wide time period.

Dialect. As used here, it refers to the speech of a particular area.

Dysphemism. The opposite of euphemism – where the grim reality is foregrounded, or exaggerated, rather than politely avoided. Heroic war literature and propaganda often use euphemism; writers try to shock readers about the brutal truth.

Dystopian. The opposite of Utopian – a (usually invented) society in which people are disjointed and unhappy.

End-stopped. When a line of verse ends with a punctuation mark.

Enjambment. Used in poetry to describe the continuation of a sentence or a clause beyond the end of a line and on to the next one.

Existentialism. A philosophy that stresses individual action and responsibility. This broad term emerged in the late 19th and early 20th centuries, and is often associated with feelings of disorientation and confusion in the face of a world that seems to be meaningless and absurd.

Extended metaphor. A metaphor which is carried beyond a single comparison of two elements and is developed further.

Free indirect speech. This refers to speech that is embedded in a narrative, so it is unattributed (free) and a report of the speech rather than the actual words (indirect).

Free indirect thought. This is a narrative technique where a character's thought processes form part of the narrative, but are not attributed to him or her.

Free verse. Poetry that conforms to no regular metre or rhyme scheme.

Genre. A way of categorizing texts. Genres can be arranged around ways of writing (such as poetry/drama/prose), around content (such as crime, politics) around purpose (such as satire) and so on. In a most general sense, genre involves grouping texts by type – and so connecting texts. There are many ways of grouping literary texts. They can be grouped in many ways through their connections with other texts, with which they have things in common. In most cases, generic groupings are not fixed, so thinking about genre involves connecting with other texts.

Genre fiction. Fiction written to fit into a known genre, which will appeal to fans of that genre. Examples are Crime Fiction, Chick Lit, etc.

Historicist / Historicism. Styles of criticism that highlight the importance of historical contexts in shaping the meaning of texts. For example, historicism recognizes how texts engage with historical events and ideas as well as with other texts; it also acknowledges that readers often interpret texts in ways that confirm their own experiences and ideas.

Image. This is quite a vague, but useful, term that is often used to denote the many types of language that conjure sensory perceptions in the mind of the reader. Other features – such as metaphor, simile, personification and symbol – are sometimes considered as sub-divisions within imagery.

Image patterns. Where an image or connected images are used more than once.

Imagism / Imagist. A type of poem which is concise and uses hard, clear and concentrated imagery as its main way of creating meaning and achieving effects.

Intentional fallacy. The error of basing an interpretation on assumptions about the author's intentions, rather than one's own response.

Intertextuality. This denotes the meanings that accrue when we explore the relationships between and across texts. This can be done explicitly, through direct reference, or implicitly through the use of similar content and/or techniques.

In-text attribution. This is when you include the name of a critic within your essay and this can be done very simply just by writing, for example, 'as Kate Millett has argued…'.

Magic realism. A genre of writing where magic or unreal events impinge upon the representation of an otherwise realistic world.

Metaphor / Metaphorical. A literary technique that involves the transfer of meaning, with one thing described as being another (e.g. education is a journey, as in the metaphor 'I'm stuck' or ' I am making good progress'). There are many types of metaphor, but in a broad sense metaphor involves the linking of something with something else that is otherwise not related to it.

Mimetic. A copy or imitation of something.

Modernist / Modernism. A trend in literature, the high point of which was from 1910-30. Modernist texts tend to be impressionistic and fragmentary, blurring genres and drawing attention to their own construction.

Motif. A recurring element that has symbolic significance in a text.

Octave. An eight-line verse.

Onomatopoeia. This is when the word chosen sounds like what it refers to. For example, the word plop is onomatopoeic in English.

Pantheistic / Pantheism. The belief in many gods.

Pastiche. A work which deliberately copies the style of another.

Pastoral. A mode of writing that typically presents rural people in an idealized way and uses natural imagery to create an impression of peace, innocence and contentment.

Pathetic fallacy. A form of personification, whereby things in the natural world are given human attributes. The term was coined by John Ruskin, with the 'fallacy' part suggesting that over-use of the device leads to poor writing.

Patriarchy / Patriarchal. A system of society or government controlled by men.

Personification. Something non-human is described as though it is human. This might be, for example, an object or an abstract idea.

Plot. The events as they are sequenced in the text (in comparison with story, which is all of the events as they happen naturally and chronologically).

Popular fiction. A genre of fiction that has wide readership and, by implication, is plot driven. It is often compared to literary fiction, which is seen as more subtle.

Postmodern / Postmodernism. This very complex term can have many definitions, but when used with regard to literature it involves notions of self-conscious playfulness resulting from the understanding that nothing, at least when represented, can be 'real'. The pleasure of reading texts comes from the reader's recognition of the way in which the texts are constructed, rather than what they definitively mean.

Pre-lapsarian. Before the loss of innocence.

Protagonist. The main character.

Quatrain. A four-line verse.

Satire. The mockery of various types of human behaviour, involving irony and exaggeration.

Scheme. Schemes are figures of speech, which deal with things like word order and sound, rather than the actual meanings of words.

Sensation fiction. A term given to a genre from the 1860s onwards that tends to involve crime and passion. An often-quoted example is Wilkie Collins's *The Woman in White* (1859–60). Although the term sounds dismissive, such fiction has had a huge influence on all sorts of literature since the 1860s.

Sestet. A six-line verse, often used to describe the second section of one form of sonnet.

Significant / Significance. This involves weighing up all of the potential contributions to how a text can be analysed (such as the way the text is constructed and written, contexts which can be applied, aspects of genre, possible theoretical approaches) and then finding potential meanings and interpretations.

Socratic dialogue. The form taken by many of Plato's philosophical works. Plato presents his teacher Socrates – a Greek philosopher of the fourth century BC – in dialogue with some apparently intelligent but naïve bystander. Socrates speaks as a simple man who confesses that he has little knowledge, but through the dialogue he shows the other person the way to real wisdom.

Speaker. The voice that speaks the poem. This is the default term to use when writing about the person speaking in a poem. It is helpful to reserve the term *persona* for a speaker who is a character who is clearly not the speaker; for example, Carol Ann Duffy adopts the persona of Shakespeare's wife in 'Anne Hathaway'.

Stanza. A stanza is a group of lines – a separate unit – that helps to break up and organize how the poem appears on the page; it is a place where the reader 'stands' and pauses.

Symbol. This stands for much more than its literal meaning. Unlike a metaphor (in which one thing is compared overtly to another), with a symbol the significance is left more open. For example, the flowers in Blake's 'The Garden of Love' might be taken to symbolize pleasure and fulfilled desires.

Synchronic study. A study that considers texts within a narrowly defined time period.

Synchronically. Looking at something within the concept of a particular time period.

Syntactic parallelism. This is where grammatical structures in one sentence are echoed in the next.

Tercet. A three-line stanza.

Totalitarian. A system of government which has complete State control and no democratic structures.

Triplet. A stanza of three lines in which every line rhymes.

Trope. A figure of speech which deals with meaning.

Valedictory. Saying farewell.

Verse paragraph. Stanzas of poetry without any patterns of rhyme or rhythm, usually separated by a blank line.

Voice. The characteristics of the speaker, or the narrative voice used; the perspective taken by the narrative.

Volta. A turning point, or shift in mood or argument, of a sonnet.

Women's fiction. A genre fiction aimed specifically at women and dealing with issues said to be of interest to women in particular.

Index